The Political Geography of the Oceans

J. R. V. PRESCOTT

The Political Geography of the Oceans

A Halsted Press Book

JOHN WILEY & SONS NEW YORK

*This book is dedicated to
Professor John Andrews
whose guidance and help
I will never be able to
repay*

Library of Congress Cataloging in Publication Data

Prescott, John Robert Victor.

  "A Halsted Press book."
  Bibliography: p.
  Includes index.
  1. Territorial waters. 2. Continental shelf.
3. Geography, Political. 1. Title.
JX4131.P73 1975   341.44'8   74–31813
ISBN 0470–69672–9

Published in the U.S.A.
by Halsted Press, a Division
of John Wiley & Sons, Inc.
New York
Printed in Great Britain

Contents

		Page
LIST OF FIGURES		7
LIST OF TABLES		9
PREFACE		11
1	Political Geography and the Oceans	13
2	The Concept and Measurement of the Territorial Sea	32
3	Claims to Territorial Seas	66
4	Fishing Zones	116
5	The Continental Shelves	142
6	Claims to Areas of the Continental Shelves	175
7	The High Seas	205
EPILOGUE: The Law of the Sea Conference, Caracas 1974		222
APPENDIX: National Maritime Claims		226
REFERENCES		229
INDEX		242

List of Figures

Page

1 Methods of defining bays — 52

2 Proposals for eliminating objectionable pockets of high seas — 56

3 Boundaries through territorial waters — 58

4 Rules for measuring the territorial sea — 63

5 Ireland's straight baselines — 84

6 Iceland's straight baselines — 86

7 Denmark's straight baselines — 88

8 Thailand's straight baselines — 91

9 Ecuador's straight baselines — 96

10 Boundaries between territorial waters off Cyprus — 102

11 Peter the Great Bay — 131

12 Optimum sustainable and economic yields — 139

13 Division of the continental shelf in the Bay of Fundy — 162

14 Division of the continental shelf between Cuba and Haiti — 164

15 Straight baselines and continental shelf boundaries — 165

Page

16   West Germany's shelf-locked position   167

17   The relationship between territorial water widths and
       continental shelf boundaries   171

18   Profile of an average continental margin   172

19   Boundaries in the Timor Sea   193

20   Continental shelf boundary between Saudi Arabia
       and Bahrain   200

21   Continental shelf boundary between the Soviet Union
       and Norway   202

List of Tables

		Page
1	Claims to territorial waters	67
2	The changing pattern of claims to territorial waters	68
3	Countries which have increased their territorial seas often, or by considerable distances	72
4	Proclaimed straight baselines, excluding archipelagos	80
5	Index to show the erosion of the high seas by selected straight baselines	82
6	Historic bays listed by various authorities named in the text	98
7	A suggested classification of archipelagos	105
8	International straits entirely occupied by territorial waters 12 nautical miles wide	108
9	Traffic on international canals	111
10	Countries claiming wider exclusive fishing zones than territorial seas	133
11	Selected figures to show changes in the Australian pearl-shell industry	148
12	Production of natural gas from the continental shelf	154

Page

13   Production of crude petroleum from the continental
      shelf   155

14   Index values representing number of square nautical
      miles per nautical mile of coast   178

15   Classification of states according to preferred seaward
      boundaries of the continental shelf   184

Preface

THE inspiration to write this book came primarily from two sources: one longstanding and the other more recent. For many years I have regretted that there was no general survey in political geography which would comprehend and relate the many excellent individual studies in the field of political geography and the oceans. Amongst those which I have found most stimulating are the papers on maritime boundaries by Boggs in the 1930s; the studies by East and Pounds on landlocked states; Minghi's investigation of salmon fishing policies in the north Pacific; and the symposia on the law of the sea edited for publication by Alexander.

The recent prompting has been provided by the studies on limits in the sea prepared since 1970 by the Geographer of the State Department of the United States of America. Political geographers owe a very great debt to Dr Hodgson, who has followed, with distinction, the eminent geographers who occupied that position. It is possible that scholars in the future will regard the contributions of Dr Hodgson's office to political geography as amongst the most important of the contemporary period.

Several persons have helped me at various times during the writing of this book. I particularly acknowledge my debt to the staff of the Reference Department of the Baillieu Library, in the University of Melbourne; to Dr E. C. F. Bird for informa-

11

tion and references on various aspects of the continental shelf; and to my wife for assistance in obtaining maps.

J. R. V. Prescott
University of Melbourne

CHAPTER ONE

Political Geography and the Oceans

WHETHER the roots of political geography are traced back centuries to the writings of Aristotle and Strabo, or only decades to the works of Ratzel, it is clear that there has been a continual interest in the political significance of the world's seas and oceans. The roles which the oceans played in influencing the rate and direction of exploration, the acquisition of colonies, the generation of commercial wealth, and the operation of naval strategies have all attracted attention at various times. This attention has focused on the waters nearest land because such areas are subject to precise claims by states, and because within them occurs the greatest harvest of ocean wealth, and through them passes the greatest density of commercial traffic. Political geographers interested in this subject have tended to concentrate on five principal aspects.

THE ROLE OF THE SEA IN INFLUENCING NATIONAL CHARACTERISTICS

First, some of the earliest studies investigated the influence which proximity to the sea, and the nature of the coastline, had

B   13

upon the national character of various peoples. Semple, following in the steps of Ratzel, has given most attention to this aspect, as the following quotations show.

> Inaccessibility from the land, a high degree of accessibility from the sea, and a paucity of local resources unite to thrust the inhabitants of such coasts (fjord) out upon the deep to make of them fishermen, seamen and ocean carriers.
> Here where a mild climate enables the boatman race to make a companion of the deep, where every landscape is a seascape, where every diplomatic visit or war campaign, every trading journey or search for a new coco-palm plantation means a voyage beyond the narrow confines of the home island, there dwells a race whose splendid chest and arm muscles were developed in the gymnasium of the sea. The coast is the natural habitat of the middleman.
> . . . it is the coast regions of the world that give rise to a lingua franca or lingua geral.[1]

The generalisations which Semple and other authors, such as Fairgrieve, made, always applied to early periods of history, when technical developments in respect of navigation, gunnery and fishing were limited.[2] Such studies today do not seem to attract any attention from geographers.

THE ROLE OF THE SEA IN DETERMINING NATIONAL POLICIES

More scholars were attracted by the second main aspect which dealt with the role of the sea in global and national strategies. A clear thread connects the studies of Mahan, Ratzel, Mackinder, Whittlesey, Spykman and Cohen. They were all concerned with the significance of factors of location and space in the perennial struggle for pre-eminence amongst the major powers. Mahan gave greater prominence to the importance of sea power than any of the other writers.[3] This emphasis may be attributed to his background and the time he wrote – at the end of the last century. He discerned six conditions which influenced the sea power of states. These were: the location of the state, the nature and length of its coastline, the size of the state's population, the national character and the quality of government. Certainly the first four points lend themselves to analysis by political geographers. The location of any state will determine the number of seas to which it has access, and influence the extent to which it can control strategic routes and important resources of the sea. The nature and length of the coastline will have important implications for policies connected with the defence of the state and the operation of an active merchant marine and navy. The size of the population and the relation of that population to the land resources will affect the extent to which the sea is deemed valuable as a source of food and raw materials and as a means of communication with other areas for commerce. Mahan did not openly advocate the acquisition of colonies, but his emphasis on the value which Britain derived from its string of overseas bases left his readers in no doubt that it was a sensible policy for major naval powers. Mahan must be given some of the credit for the policies which led to America securing bases in Hawaii, Guam, Puerto Rico, the Philippines, the Virgin Islands and Panama. Technical developments, which include atomic weapons, nuclear fuel for submarines and long-range aircraft, have destroyed the practical applications of Mahan's concepts and left them as a subject of historical interest.

Mackinder, in various studies, was concerned with the strength of land and sea powers and the possible conflict between them.[4] Pounds has pointed out that the dichotomy between land and sea powers is false; great powers had strong navies and armies and now, of course, they have powerful air forces. This basic weakness, and Mackinder's obsession with inner Asia as a heartland led him to make some simplistic judgements about the strength and limitations of sea power. He regarded the navigability of rivers from accessible oceans as being critical in determining the theatres within which maritime and land powers held sway, yet even in this crucial respect there were obvious inconsistencies. In 1904 he expressed the view that the Middle East lay open to the exercise of sea power because of its 'sea-gulfs and oceanic rivers'.[5] By 1919, he held that Arabia formed part of a broad region inaccessible to sea powers except by the Persian Gulf and Red Sea.[6] It is now a matter of history, that for thirty years after he changed his view the most influential major powers in the Middle East were so-called maritime states: Britain and France held a measure of political and strategic sway, while the United States was economically most important in terms of foreign investment. Mackinder's fascination with heartlands caused him to develop the concept of sub-Saharan Africa as a southern heartland; yet this area, despite its lack of rivers navigable from the coasts, was dominated by the maritime states Britain and France, even when he wrote his first essay on this theme.

Spykman inverted Mackinder's thesis, placed the United States of America at the centre of the map, and urged that his country should seek to avoid the unification of the opposing shores of the Atlantic and Pacific Oceans under one or two hostile powers.[7] For Spykman it was clear that American naval and general strategy required involvement in the rimland states which surround the Soviet Union, as well as the maintenance of strategic bases around the world's oceans. Finally in this section, reference must be made to the recent global view of Cohen.[8] This author presented 'a geographical view of contemporary international politics' by suggesting a division of the world into geo-strategic and geo-political regions and then describing the power cores of the world and the zones of contact between the major powers. The regional boundaries drawn by Cohen were extended across the oceans, although it was not clear on what basis these areas of water had been divided. The prime division between the trade-dependent maritime world and the Eurasian continental world owed something to the heartland concept of Mackinder, and throughout his book Cohen made frequent references to naval strategy.

What we cannot afford to do, however, is to take the American Mediterranean for granted.[9]
As long as its most important allies are so heavily dependent upon overseas trade the United States has to help them maintain their sea contacts.[10]

He refines Spykman's ideas by urging a selective involvement in the countries of the rimland.

It is regrettable that although global studies form only a small part of the total literature of the political geography of the oceans, it is the part which is best known by scholars in other disciplines. If political scientists mention any political geographers they are sure to be Mackinder and Spykman, and for most political scientists there is no difference between political geography and *Geopolitik*. Fortunately these strategic global studies now attract very little interest amongst political geographers for three reasons: they generally involve an oversimplification of real situations, they are unable to take account of important changes in technology which require the revaluation of geographical factors and if they have any validity, it will only be for a comparatively short time.

THE POLITICAL SIGNIFICANCE OF COASTAL FEATURES

The third aspect is concerned with the systematic study of the political significance of particular coastland situations. Early writers, such as Fairgrieve, and later contributors, such as Whittlesey and Fischer, examined the political significance of peninsulas, isthmuses, islands, fjords, deltas, lagoons and narrow straits.[11] Fairgrieve gave considerable weight to the importance of some of these features, in trying to explain the sequential development of empires but this aspect is now unfashionable in political geography. The very nature of the inquiry has connotations of determinism. It is now recognised that the significance of particular topographic circumstances will be conditioned by many variables, such as location, the political relations of the state with its neighbours, and the technical skills available to the government in control. It is simply not possible to make valid generalisations about the political significance of islands or deltas in different parts of the world. Each feature would have to be examined in the context of the region's political geography to reach any proper conclusion. This realisation should not prevent political geographers from making comparative studies. It would, for example, be interesting to investigate the political significance of the deltas of the Niger, Ganges, Nile and Mekong, but predictably, the scholar would learn more about the variable interaction of geography and politics than produce generalisations about the political relevance of deltas.

The other two aspects, which must now be considered, deal with more precise information than the three aspects already described, and they seem to offer better prospects for fruitful research.

LANDLOCKED STATES AND THEIR ACCESS TO THE SEA

The fourth aspect of the political geography of the oceans which has attracted attention, deals with landlocked states and the efforts which they make to gain access to the high seas. This obvious subject did not receive much attention until recently. Bowman referred to it when he considered the problems of Poland and Bolivia, but Whittlesey managed to discuss these countries without reference to this question.[12] Fischer examined the matter in more general terms, but it was left to Pounds and East, apparently working separately, to lay the foundation for the systematic study of this subject in 1959–60.[13]

Pounds, in a general work on political geography,[14] briefly refers to the concept of some American politicians, such as Secretary of State John Quincy Adams and President Grant, that all states had 'a natural right of communication with the oceans' and then examines three ways in which landlocked states had tried to overcome their handicap. The three methods are by using international rivers, by securing transit rights across a neighbouring coastal state, and by acquiring a corridor of territory to the sea. (The third method of course effectively ending the condition of being landlocked.) Pounds then examined some contemporary and historical cases of each solution. In the second edition of his book Pounds includes new material dealing with the African landlocked states which had become independent during the 1960s but omitted direct reference to the work of East who, in his presidential address to the Institute of British Geographers, examined the common characteristics of the fourteen independent landlocked states existing in 1959. East's analysis of their cultural and economic geographies appeared to show that these states had 'nothing in common save their aloofness from the sea'. So he then turned to the formation of these states, eleven of which could be considered as buffer states: Mongolia, Afghanistan and Nepal provided the best illustrations, while Bolivia seemed to be the hardest to assign to this category. The three independent landlocked states which did not fit this description were the Vatican, Liechtenstein and San Marino. The clue to East's penetrating analysis had been given by Fischer in 1957, who, in discussing the factor of location, noted that 'not all buffer states are land-locked'.[15]

Dale extended the work of East in a paper on the twelve landlocked African states which became independent after 1959,[16] but his slipshod paper sharply contrasts with its elegant predecessor.[17]

Glassner is concerned with access to the sea for developing landlocked states, and his book contains detailed studies of Bolivia, Uganda and Afghanistan, as well as more general introductory and concluding chapters.[18] Reviewing this book, Marshall-Cornwall wrote that the 'whole subject has been fully and cogently dealt with'.[19] Minghi, a specialist political geographer, takes a different position.

One looks in vain for some innovative Glassner classification or typology derived from the evidence of the case studies that would somehow shed more light on the complex relationships between internal economic development and the essential elements in the nature of land-lockedness.[20]

Minghi's view is undoubtedly valid: Glassner has not made any conceptual advance on the material presented by Pounds and East. There is insufficient attention to the processes which shaped the boundaries of the landlocked states. It is wrong to write in the following terms of Lesotho and Botswana.

Lesotho and Botswana in Africa, are refuges of harassed minorities escaping from the persecution, warfare and political persecution raging around them.[21]

Lesotho and Botswana fit the buffer state concept very well, because the British Government of the day used them to isolate the Boer Republics. Nor is it sufficient to write of the Durand Line in the following fashion, without any justification.

This border was completely illogical, having no basis in ethnology, geography or history.[22]

Such sweeping judgement should be based on a detailed analysis of the boundary's evolution, and such an analysis of the reports of the various demarcation commissions shows that although the line marked in the 1893 Agreement had some serious defects, many of these were corrected by authorised deviations of the line by the surveyors. When the boundary was drawn it certainly coincided with political realities. It is also important, as Minghi suggests, that some assessment should be made of the nature of the landlocked state's economy, so that its need for access to the sea can be measured, but Glassner is not alone in making this omission.

Regrettably, economic geographers do not appear to have paid much attention to the economic problems of landlocked states. Most writers, after reasonably assuming that landlocked states pay higher transfer costs than their coastal neighbours who allow them access to the sea, do not distinguish the degree of disadvantage of different landlocked states. For example, it would be very interesting to compare the unit transport costs of Mali and Malawi, since both countries conduct most of their trade with Europe. It is also possible that the closure of the Suez Canal imposes greater economic hardship on Kenya than the condition of being landlocked does on Upper Volta. Most economic geographers, such as Whittington, Grüll, Doganis and Perry, who have written on this subject recently, have confined their attention to the prospects and effects of railway construction involving landlocked African states.[23] Hilling alone published a useful regional account of the landlocked states of French West Africa.[24] He provides a detailed account of the policies employed by these states to overcome their economic problems, with special reference to the volume of traffic involved and the various routes available.

THE LAW OF THE SEA

The fifth aspect concerns the law of the sea, in which political geographers have expressed two clear interests. First, they have been concerned with the delimitation of maritime boundaries, and this study made its greatest single advance at the time of the Hague conference on the law of the sea, in 1930.[25] Boggs, then the Geographer to the United States' State Department, was a technical adviser to the American delegation, and he made a detailed study of this question. Most of his views on maritime boundaries were published in four useful papers, which dealt with the problems of defining boundaries in water and the particular problems of delimiting the territorial sea.[26] Boggs's work in this area was undoubtedly his main contribution to the field of political geography, and subsequent writers, such as Jones and Moodie, have tended to follow him.[27] The crucial technical problems of defining maritime boundaries have been solved, the remaining difficulties are of a political and legal nature. The work, initiated so well by Boggs, has been effectively continued in more recent times by his successors to the office of Geographer of the State Department. Pearcy wrote an illuminating paper after the 1958 conference on the law of the sea, detailing the decisions reached and examining their geographical significance.[28] Hodgson initiated a series of specific studies of limits in the seas, and these have an importance unmatched by any other contribution in this field.[29] Each study consists of the relevant sections of the acts fixing the maritime boundaries of particular states, together with a clear map and a brief comment on any points of special interest. They provide valuable sources of information for those political geographers wishing to make comparative studies, or wishing to test the application of various regulations for drawing maritime boundaries in different coastal situations.

The second interest relates to the laws of the sea which govern the exploitation of economic resources such as fish, or mineral deposits on the continental shelf, and the passage of commercial traffic through international straits. This interest came sharply into focus after 1945, when first the United States, and then other countries, began to lay claim to exclusive rights on the continental shelf, and when South American countries began to claim wide areas of the oceans as exclusive fishing zones. More geographers have written about fishing grounds and national policies connected with them – Black, Helin, Villanow, Logan, Minghi and Alexander have all published useful papers on this subject[30] – than about the mineral resources of the continental shelf. The papers by Alexander, Minghi and Logan probably have the greatest interest for political geographers. Alexander examined the relationships between offshore claims and fisheries in northwest Europe, while Minghi analysed the conflict of policies regarding salmon fishing in the North Pacific, paying particular attention to the policies of Japan and the United States. Logan analysed the Noyes Island salmon fishing dispute between Canada and the United States between 1957 and 1967. The best paper on boundaries and the continental shelf is not by a geographer, but an oceanographer,

Emery, who prepared a very useful account of the possible features of the shelf which could be selected to mark limits of sovereignty and the problems associated with each of them.[31] Mero has prepared the best account of the mineral resources of the sea and the continental shelf.[32] Melamid is one of the few geographers to have examined the question of passage through an international strait, in this case the Gulf of Aqaba, but the increasing attention which this subject is commanding suggests that his example will be followed by others.[33]

In both of these principal interests in the law of the sea the political and economic geographer is working alongside other scholars. International lawyers form the largest group of workers, and a number have made systematic studies of particular aspects. For example, Bruel has examined the legal question of international straits, while Bouchez and Strohl have done the same thing for bays, and Sorensen has examined the question of the territorial seas of archipelagos.[34] Shalowitz has written the most complete legal account dealing with the delimitation of maritime boundaries.[35] In addition, lawyers have published several papers considering specific legal cases relating to disputes over fishing grounds and passage through international straits. Other workers, including geologists, mining engineers, economists and political scientists, have also made contributions to this inter-disciplinary issue.

The work done by political geographers on this aspect has been much more precise and certain than most of their efforts into the fields described earlier. There have been additional benefits in that the relevance of their work has been obvious, and the combined interest of political, economic and physical geographers has underlined the unity of the subject. The geographer who has played the most important role in developing this subject along inter-disciplinary lines is Alexander who, in addition to writing on individual topics himself, has edited a volume of papers prepared for a symposium at the Law of the Sea Institute, Rhode Island, in 1965, and has published the best review article of the relevant geographical and legal literature.[36]

THE SCOPE OF THE STUDY

This review of the more important contributions to the study of the political geography of the oceans has provided a basis on which a statement of the content of that subject can be constructed. Political geographers are interested in the oceans because states claim sovereignty over part of them, because states use portions of the oceans during their commercial and strategic activities, and because these claims and activities involve states in some measure of conflict and co-operation. There are two main aspects of such study which concern political geographers.

First, it is evident that states differ from each other in their need and capacity to use the oceans, and that regions of the oceans vary in their usefulness for different purposes. Political geographers therefore have to examine the extent to which these variations in the characteristics of states and the nature of the oceanic regions interact to influence the use which is made of the seas by different states. Consideration of this aspect will require the investigation of many variables of which the following are the most important.

The delimitation and description of land regions has long been part of geography, but the regional geography of the oceans has not received the same attention. It would, however, be possible to construct maps which would show the regions of the oceans based on criteria influencing navigation and the success of fishing and mining enterprises. These criteria would include frequency of storms and fogs, incidence of icebergs, presence of plankton and fish breeding grounds, presence of shoals and islands, the nature of the sea floor and its depth, and the region's location relative to adjacent continents. It would be most instructive to compare regions determined by an inventory of the variables mentioned above with regions based on the degree of use by the world's merchant, naval and fishing fleets.

The nature of a state's coastline might be considered to have some influence on the use which it makes of adjoining waters.

The availability of good harbour sites, deep water offshore and an absence of reefs and shoals make it easier to develop maritime activities than along coasts devoid of sheltered inlets, with shallow, rocky conditions offshore. Such factors will not be decisive, but they may be significant. Other circumstances such as the level of technology available to the state and the nature of the coastal hinterland will also have to be taken into account. As techniques change so the value of any part of the ocean must be re-assessed. The capacity to build giant tankers, the increasing effectiveness of ice-breakers, and the ability to reclaim land from the sea, or construct artificial harbours and deep water drilling vessels, have all allowed some new or increased use of parts of the oceans by certain states. It follows that the more direct influences of the physical nature of the coast will be evident in earlier historical periods. The nature of the coastal hinterland and the relationship between resources and population will also have some bearing on this question. The lack of any significant sea-faring traditions in West Africa before colonial times may be partially explained by the regular nature of the coast, with the considerable surf, the supply of fish available in sheltered lagoons, the ease with which crops could be cultivated in the hinterland, and the ability to make a handsome living from trading in slaves. Although Semple was overstating the case when she wrote that inhabitants of fjord coasts were thrust out upon the deep by the paucity of local resources, this must have been a very important factor.

One of the critical factors which influences the use of the sea is the commercial, military and technological strength of the state. During Elizabethan times the relative strengths of the navies of Great Britain and Spain determined in large parts the routes to which merchantmen had access and the banks where fishermen could operate without hindrance. Today it is the fishing fleets of the Soviet Union, Japan, the United States and Britain which operate at considerable distances from their shores in the vicinity of other countries. The arguments of the Chinese government seem reasonable to developing countries when it is alleged that the United States and the Soviet Union wish to restrict the width of the territorial seas because they have the vessels to exploit the resources of the high seas. It should also be mentioned that the explanation of Japan's major long-distance fishing fleet must be partly found in the high demand for fish from the densely settled population, which cannot be met from the coastal waters of the comparatively short coast of the Japanese islands, which in the west have to be shared with Korea and the Soviet Union. It is also worth remarking that much of the Soviet coast is icebound for part of the year reducing opportunities for fishing.

The second main aspect which concerns political geographers studying the world's oceans involves an examination of the geographical consequences which follow from the varied use of the sea by states. Perhaps the most important consequence is that from earliest times states have claimed the exclusive use of certain areas and drawn boundaries around these preserves. There is now a plethora of boundaries marked on charts of the sea. They mark the limit of internal waters, territorial waters, exclusive fishing zones, areas of pollution control, the exploitable continental shelf and regions of conservation. The most apparent trends in recent years have been for the number of boundaries drawn for a single purpose to increase and for claims to exclusive use to stretch further and further from the shores of states, reducing the remaining area of high seas. For example, in 1965 seven countries claimed exclusive fishing zones of at least 100 nautical miles; by the end of 1972 that number had increased to thirteen. Another example is that before 1969 ten countries had enacted legislation imposing penalties for polluting adjacent seas; between 1969 and 1972 another seven countries enacted similar legislation.

This multitude of specific claims to areas of the oceans has created situations where states have developed a conflict of interest with each other. Some of these disputes concern claims to the continental shelf, such as that between West Germany and the Netherlands in the North Sea. Claims to exclusive fishing zones by countries such as Iceland and Peru have led to difficulties with fishermen of British and American nationalities respectively. Concern with the risks of pollution on the part of the Canadian government has caused a difference of opinion with the government of the United States over the right of tankers to use the northwest passage between Canadian islands. However, the problems associated with such disputes have also encouraged states to co-operate in finding a solution and, in addition to the principles agreed at international conferences on the law of the sea, countries have also concluded bilateral treaties on territorial waters and continental shelves.

Improved techniques for catching fish and whales have raised fears that stocks of these resources may be severely damaged. Suggestions were made at an international conference in 1973 that the catching of certain kinds of whales should be banned for ten years, and some governments have laid down strict conditions about the kind of equipment which should be used and closed fishing seasons in waters which they control. It is precisely this concern over the threatened depletion of fishing grounds which has led some countries to claim territorial waters 200 nautical miles wide.

Allied with this concern for the conservation of resources, there are fears of the dangers associated with pollution of coastal waters, either by the discharge of toxic wastes from land or the discharge of petroleum products from tankers or ruptured pipelines. As noted above, a growing number of countries are enacting legislation to control this potential problem. One of the obvious effects of this concern has been the insistence by some countries on the re-routing of large tankers. The Malaysian and Indonesian governments, whose territorial waters occupy all the Malacca Strait, stipulated in 1972 that tankers in excess of 200,000 dead weight tons may not pass fully laden through the strait and ships in excess of 500,000 dead weight tons may not pass through the strait under any circumstances. In July 1973 the South African government and the Inter-Governmental Maritime Consultative Organisation announced a new rule which requires all laden tankers to travel around the Cape of Good Hope outside a limit of 12 nautical miles, measured from the salient points of the coastline. As mining on the sea floor becomes more common, governments will have to ensure that these activities do not damage fishing grounds unnecessarily and that they do not create new, possibly destructive, patterns of coastal erosion.

Another important consequence of the increasing use of the sea to transport large quantities of crude petroleum in giant tankers has been the growth of deep-water terminal points in the Persian Gulf, where the tankers can be loaded, and in Europe and Japan, where the cargo can be discharged. President Nixon's major speech on energy policies on 18 April 1973 specifically referred to the need for the United States to construct deep-water oil terminals to allow the import of petroleum as cheaply as possible with the lowest risks to the environment.

Since political geographers have been much more concerned with the study of continents rather than oceans, it seems worthwhile to detail the relevant differences and similarities between them in terms of political geography. First, apart from the Caspian Sea and the Sea of Aral, the oceanic surface is continuous. Although the entrances to some seas such as the Black and Baltic Seas are narrow, it is possible to travel from any port to another without traversing land. This situation gives a strategic and commercial advantage to those states with strong naval and merchant fleets. The strategic advantage was evident in the early months of 1973 when the United States navy and air force, operating from the South China Sea, played such an important role in the fighting in Vietnam. A major power such as the Soviet Union still deems it worthwhile to have a strong navy and to sail that navy in seas remote from Russian shores.

Second, the regional variation which is found on the oceans is not as obvious as the regional variation on land. In one sense this simplifies the drawing of boundaries because there is no significant debate about 'natural boundaries', although President Jefferson once suggested that the Gulf Stream was the natural boundary of the United States. Boundaries are generally fixed at uniform distances from the coast or some selected baseline. It is also important to note that maritime boundaries are not demarcated; they are marked on charts, and it is the responsibility of the navigator to ensure that they are not violated. Unfortunately the oceans, unlike the land surface, are not thoroughly explored, and therefore the drawing of some boundaries is attended by the difficulty that the quality of the ocean and ocean floor, just inside and outside the selected line, may not be known. It is also possible that new volcanic islands will be created in the sea and then claimed by states because of the valuable fishing rights which attach to such islands. Another interesting difference is that the larger part of the oceans is not claimed by individual states, unlike the land, which is entirely parcelled out amongst states. This means that states can actively compete with each other for the resources of the high seas without the involvement of any overriding authority, which is always present on land. This has led to strenuous effort on the part of many countries to formulate a code of international law to govern states' activities on the high seas.

The world's oceans and coastal seas are not permanently occupied as are land areas, and parts of the sea may have a greater variety of use than an equivalent area of land. Mining on the sea floor, commercial fishing, recreational boating and the transport of cargoes are all activities which may occur in the same region of the sea at different but closely related times. States generally find that it is harder to enforce prescribed regulations concerning the activities of individuals in territorial waters than it is on land.

An important characteristic of the oceans' major resources is that they are more mobile than the corresponding resources on land. Fish form the most important resource and their mobility, sometimes of a regular and sometimes of an irregular nature, is renowned. But it is also true that the most valuable minerals taken from the sea floor are petroleum and natural gas. These

c

are also mobile resources in the sense that where a field straddles an international boundary the reserves may be almost completely extracted from the other side of the line. For this reason most bilateral agreements on continental shelf boundaries now either prohibit drilling for oil within a specified distance of the line, or agree that revenue derived from reserves exploited within that specified distance will be shared between the two states concerned.

Even between the land areas of a state and its territorial waters, which are generally considered to be an extension of the state's area, there is one important difference. Alien vessels have the right of innocent passage through territorial waters and this right is not matched on land.

Lastly it must be noted that while all states possess territory, some of them do not possess a coastline giving direct access to the continuous seas. In examining the political geography of the oceans it is necessary to keep the special problems of such states in mind.

However, these important differences do not mean that political geographers have to develop a new set of techniques to deal with the oceans, because there are vital similarities. States seek to use the oceans for precisely the same reasons as they use their territory: to provide security and the opportunity for development, which gives a rising standard of living to their citizens. Because there are marked regional variations throughout the oceans, states have particular interests in specific sections of water, in the same way that they perceived paramount interests in land areas during the formation of their boundaries. Finally, the ability of states to use particular areas of the oceans and therefore, to some extent, their interests in those areas, will be conditioned by the technical skills which are available for exploiting maritime resources.

The plan of this book is based on the political zones of the oceans. The second chapter examines the concept, width and measurement of the territorial sea in historical and modern times. This is then followed by a chapter considering the present state of national claims and international agreement regarding territorial waters, in addition to the vexed question of passage through international straits entirely occupied by territorial waters, and the status and importance of international canals. The fourth chapter is concerned with exclusive fishing and fisheries conservation zones. It is appreciated that there is a considerable overlap between territorial waters and these two zones, but the particular commercial importance of fishing seemed to make it worthwhile to treat this subject separately. The fifth chapter presents an account of the nature of the continental shelf, its resources and the difficulties which attend the determination of its boundaries. The present stage of claims and agreements regarding particular continental shelves is the subject of the sixth chapter. The seventh chapter relates to the high seas and examines the distinctive nature of the high seas, their use for navigation, fishing and security, and the attitude of groups of states to important topical questions.

CHAPTER TWO

The Concept and Measurement of the Territorial Sea

As long as there have been states with access to the sea, the governments of those states have had an important interest in the adjacent, coastal waters. Today the paramount interest of sovereign states in their coastal waters is recognised by the United Nations Convention on the Territorial Sea.

> The sovereignty of a state extends, beyond its land territory, and its inland waters, to a belt of sea adjacent to its coast, described as the territorial sea.[1]

The earliest political concern with coastal waters involved the distribution of favours by rulers.[2] These favours included exclusive rights to shallow fishing grounds, and to salt deposits in tidal marshes, exemption from port or harbour dues, unhindered transit through narrow straits, and the use of coastal features such as reefs to mark estate boundaries. Because it was also often easier to defeat enemies at sea rather than after they had landed, some states organised navies, which defended the state by actions in the coastal waters.

Since the development of this original interest, history records an increasing number of reasons why states have sought to establish their control over coastal waters. The growth of trade made it necessary to patrol coastal waters to prevent smuggling which would have deprived the state of revenue. These acts of supervision also made it possible to enforce regulations concerning health and immigration in respect of vessels approaching port. The increased demand for fish persuaded many coastal states to exclude aliens from certain nearby fishing grounds. The development of large navies, by countries such as France, Great Britain and Holland, and their frequent use as instruments of policy, caused many small states to seek for means of preserving their neutrality. This was achieved in some cases by proclaiming belts of neutral waters around their shores.[3] In modern times, concern with dangers of pollution through oil-spillage, fears for the safety of ships in view of the rising density of marine traffic, the need to prevent pirate broadcasting stations and floating casinos operating close to land, and the wish to avoid any interference with submarine cables, have confirmed the interest of coastal states in sovereignty over adjacent territorial waters. Now, with only one exception, a state's sovereignty on land and over the territorial waters are indistinguishable.

> . . . within three miles of the coast, a state may under international law, exercise any jurisdiction and do any act which it may lawfully do upon its own land territory. Exception must be made to this general statement only in favour of the servitude known as the right of innocent passage.[4]

It follows that the strategic and commercial relationships of any state with the adjacent seas and the high seas will be unique. Variable factors such as the location of the coast, the nature of the shore in plan and profile, the morphology of the adjacent sea floor, the presence or absence of mobile and sedentary fishing grounds, the characteristics of currents and tides, and the frequency of storms, will influence the use which the state's population makes of the coastal waters and the need of the state to control such areas. The following examples will illustrate this point. The existence of frozen seas along the northern coast of the Soviet Union for part of the year creates different problems of security to those faced by the People's Republic of China. The presence of rich fishing grounds close to Iceland has given that country a special interest in the width of exclusive fishing zones, which is not exactly shared by Nigeria. The fjord coast of Norway and the smooth shoreline of Belgium make it appropriate for these two countries to support different rules for the determination of baselines from which territorial seas are measured. Finally, the unique location of Israel gives it a particular concern with the question of innocent passage through international straits; such concern is not shared by the island state of Mauritius set in the Indian Ocean.

The development of territorial waters to their present status has involved the solution of three problems. First, it was necessary for the legal concept of states exercising jurisdiction over parts of the sea to be firmly established. This has now been successfully accomplished. Secondly, it was essential to establish the width of the territorial seas. This was a problem, which appeared to have been solved by the major maritime states in the nineteenth century, but about which there is serious dispute today. Thirdly, there was a need to establish accepted methods of delimiting the extent of the territorial seas. This problem has not been completely solved, although much progress has been made in this direction. It is now proposed to look at each of these problems in turn from the point of view of political and economic geography.

THE CONCEPT OF TERRITORIAL SEAS

Fenn, who identified the four main contributors to the establishment of the concept of the territorial seas as a doctrine of international law, has provided the most detailed analysis of this subject.[5] A careful reading of Fenn's arguments and examination of a large number of the multitude of ancient texts which he cites, do not reveal that geographical factors played a major role in the establishment of this concept. However, it is true that the most important contributions were made by Mediterranean lawyers and this may be a reflection of the important role which the sea played in the political and commercial life of that region. The claims of Venice to the waters between the islands owned by that state and to the deep bays of the northern Adriatic were often cited by jurists in favour of the concept of territorial seas. The possible relationship between the environment and legal systems was noted by Whittlesey.

> Legal systems are images of the regions in which they function, sometimes faithful and sometimes distorted. Individual laws mirror the society and the habitat by and in which they are created.[6]

The first important step in the evolution of this concept was taken by Roman glossators who determined that the emperor had the right to punish wrongdoers at sea in precisely the same way that he punished them on land. Azo, who lived in the twelfth century, then asserted with effect that the emperor had the right to limit the communal nature of the ocean. Azo stipulated that part of the sea could be appropriated through the grant of a privilege by the emperor or by long and uninterrupted use. Bartolus, a teacher of law at Pisa in the fourteenth century, held that the sovereign of any state owned adjacent islands within 100 miles of the coast and had authority in the intervening sea. Finally, Gentilis in the sixteenth century took the last decisive step. He was convinced, and his arguments persuaded others, that coastal waters are a continuation of the territory of the state whose shores they adjoin. It therefore followed that the territorial rights which the sovereign possessed on land extended over the coastal waters. Fenn has no doubt that 'after Gentilis, it is literally correct to speak of territorial waters in international law'.[7] Thus the controversy between Grotius and Selden over the concept of closed or open

seas began after the concept of territorial waters was firmly
established and has relevance only to the question of high seas.
Grotius admitted that states had the right to control waters in
bays;[8] and the concept of territorial waters underlay Selden's
claim to vast expanses of sea, which he made on behalf of
Great Britain.

As Fenn noted, the definitive judgement of Gentilis solved
the first problem and cleared the way for the attack on the
second which dealt with the width of the territorial sea.

> There remains a problem of placing a limit to these waters. The
> theory, however, is complete with Gentilis. The delimitation of
> the territorial waters is a mere matter of detail, and becomes a
> problem for state-craft and not for lawyers to settle.[9]

History may well judge that the detail was harder to settle than
the theory. Four centuries have elapsed since the theory was
completed, but the arguments over the width of the territorial
sea rage more furiously than ever before.

THE WIDTH OF THE TERRITORIAL SEA

The earliest published claim to specific widths was by
Bartolus in the fourteenth century who asserted that 100 miles
was the correct distance. His view was accepted by Gentilis at
the end of the sixteenth century; but, about the same time,
Plowden was insisting, in a British court, that Queen Elizabeth I
had territorial rights to the middle of seas between Great
Britain and foreign countries.[10] In 1576, Bodin, a French
lawyer, suggested that sovereigns could claim 60 miles of
territorial sea.[11] Less precise limits were also advanced, including the horizon seen from the shore. This was obviously a
distance which would vary according to the height of the shore,
the prevailing visibility and the keenness of the observer's
vision, and it was criticised by Bynkershoek on these grounds.
But this practice disappeared slowly; as late as 1740 Naples and

the Ottoman Empire signed an agreement that ships would be protected within sight of their shores. However, by the mid-nineteenth century the general rule, underwritten by the major naval powers, was that territorial seas only extended for 3 nautical miles.

The credit for unravelling the very complex origin of the territorial sea 3 nautical miles wide must be given to a group of lawyers and political scientists, of whom Walker, Kent and Baty are the most prominent.[12] This matter is of interest because claims to territorial waters of 3 nautical miles were general during the nineteenth century and the first quarter of the twentieth century, and because 3 nautical miles is the minimum modern claim to territorial waters. The earliest claim to a continuous belt of territorial waters measuring 3 nautical miles was made by Sweden on 9 October 1756, but the twin characteristics of this claim had earlier different origins. The concept of a continuous belt of territorial waters was born in Scandinavia; the specific distance stemmed from the range of a cannon rule, which was common in the Mediterranean and the southern reaches of the North Sea.

Following the rediscovery of Greenland in 1585, Denmark, which had acquired Iceland and Norway in 1381, completed its control over the shores of the northern Atlantic. On the grounds that it controlled the opposite shores, Denmark tried to assert a claim to sovereignty over the entire north Atlantic and the Skagerrak. Danish authorities issued licences freely to nationals of other countries to navigate and fish in these waters; however, these licences did not apply to a zone of coastal waters adjacent to Danish shores. For example in 1598 a Danish decree reserved a belt of waters 2 leagues wide around Iceland for the exclusive use of Danish fishermen. The Danish league measured 4 nautical miles. This decree sought to preserve the rich fishing grounds off the coasts of Iceland, from increasing depletion by foreign craft. During the reign of Christian IV (1588–1648), the exclusive limits claimed by Denmark varied from 2 to 8 leagues, and in his successor's reign were fixed at 4 leagues.[13] The practice of insisting on 4 leagues probably owed something to earlier claims to control adjacent seas which were in sight of land. Scottish fishermen were prohibited from fishing within sight of the Faeroe Islands by James I in 1618 after complaints by the Danish authorities.

Thus the first claims by Denmark were designed to restrict the opportunities for fishing and trade along Danish shores by aliens. However, the zone claimed had to take account of the strength of the country, whose citizens were seeking concessions. Holland, England, France and Russia at various times compelled the Danish sovereign to reduce the width of exclusive territorial waters. Aliens, in addition to seeking wealth through commerce and fishing, were concerned also with the capture of prizes during the frequent European wars, especially after the mid-seventeenth century. Denmark, anxious to preserve its neutrality and avoid involvement in the hostilities, was persuaded by Great Britain and Holland, in 1691, to guarantee the security of foreign ships against capture within sight of land.[14] By a decree of 26 June 1691, the Danish authorities defined the area within which ships were protected as lying east of a line linking Lindesnes, in southern Norway, to Ringkobing on the west coast of Denmark. Elsewhere along the Danish coast, ships would be protected within sight of land, which was defined as 'a distance of four or five leagues from the coastal islands'.[15] This new development put the French at a disadvantage since they had been more successful in capturing enemy prizes than their British and Dutch opponents. The French government protested and suggested that the range of a cannon was the limit of protection, but Denmark refused to alter the regulations and France was unable to insist.[16] This seems to be the first occasion in which the regional rules of the north Atlantic and the Mediterranean came into diplomatic contact; but there was no definite outcome. The second collision of this kind occurred in 1740 when six Dutch vessels were arrested for illegally trading with Iceland and two Dutch warships were sent to Icelandic waters to protect other Dutch vessels within cannon range of the shore. The intervention of other countries, including Britain, France and Sweden, prevented the outbreak of hostilities.

Three years later the Russians managed to force a significant reduction in Danish claims. Because the local authorities were afraid that Russia might close its land boundary with Norway to trade and the transhumance movements of Lapps, the Governor of Finnmark, in the extreme north of Norway, allowed Russian fishermen to have access to waters within 1 league of the coast.[17] The Danes charged the Russians a small fee so it could be argued that they had not abandoned their claim to the wider territorial seas; however, in 1745 the Danish government narrowed the zone within which foreign ships would be protected to 1 league or 4 nautical miles. Kent has suggested that this action was taken on economic grounds, since the smaller areas of sanctuary discouraged alien traders and the increased number of prizes captured were sold in Norwegian ports to the benefit of national revenue.[18]

Even this narrower limit did not save Denmark from diplomatic protest. In 1760 French ships captured two British prizes in the Kattegat. One was taken near Grenen, the other near Laeso island. Denmark had proclaimed the Kattegat, lying west of a line joining Grenen in northern Denmark, and Falsterbo in southern Sweden, as neutral. It was made clear by the French that they did not recognise such declarations; instead they would concede territorial waters measuring 'Three Miles, the Possible Reach of Cannon Shot from Land'.[19] This was the third recorded conflict between the Scandinavian and Mediterranean systems, and it will be noted that the gap between them had closed to 1 nautical mile. Before tracing their common history it is necessary to examine the development of the cannon shot rule.

The earliest traced reference to the cannon shot rule occurred in 1610, when it was used by Holland in a fishing dispute with Great Britain.[20] Therefore the earliest use of both regional systems referred to fishing limits, but it will become apparent that the cannon shot rule was subsequently concerned primarily with the definition of neutral zones in times of war.

Bynkershoek is credited with introducing the concept of territorial waters extending as far as a cannon's range into the literature of international law in 1703. However, Walker has shown conclusively that the rule had been applied by various countries including France and Holland throughout most of the seventeenth century.[21] Bynkershoek judged that states could possess the coastal seas which they could command from their shores.

> Therefore it evidently seems more just that the power of the land (over the sea) be extended to that point where missiles are exploded . . . the power of the land (over the sea) is bounded where the strength of arms is bounded; for this as we have said, guards possession.[22]

Bynkershoek was led to formulate this rule because he regarded claims to the sea within sight of land was being too imprecise. Unfortunately, his regulation is also open to conflicting interpretations. The cannon shot rule could apply only to the field of fire of actual pieces mounted on the shore. This would be precise in terms of location and width, although it is recognised that the width of waters claimed would vary with the type of cannon in place and the maximum charge which could be used. Under this interpretation if there were no cannon on the shore there was no claim to territorial waters and prizes could be taken up to shoal water. The second interpretation envisaged a continuous belt of territorial waters commanded by a line of imaginary guns mounted along the entire length of the coast. If this view prevailed, presumably the imaginary guns would be considered to be those which had the maximum range. There is, in the writing of Walker and Kent, evidence to show that both views were held. The specific view operated in favour of those countries which were strong and well armed, and which had a high density of ports along their coasts, such as France, Great Britain and Holland. The general rule made all states equal whatever the condition and number of their fortresses and whatever the nature of their coastline. It was probably this conclusion which led Galiani, in 1782, to propose that instead of waiting to see what guns a neutral state may mount at particular points along its coast, a belt of 3 nautical miles be fixed as the zone of territorial waters.[23] It is through Galiani that the concept of a continuous zone proposed by the Scandinavian system was finally united with a width of cannon shot used in the Mediterranean system. For Galiani, 3 nautical miles represented a convenient distance. He did not claim that cannon could fire that far, but this was a standard southern European league and a century before cannons had been able to fire nearly this distance. A French Great Culverin could fire 5,136 metres (16,850 feet), which is only 423 metres (1,390 feet) short of 1 league.[24] The British diplomatic correspondence of 1760 shows that the French authorities at that time considered 3 nautical miles to be the range of cannon. It is also widely assumed that the selection of territorial waters 3 nautical miles wide by Sweden in 1756 is attributable in large measure to the cordial relations between Sweden and France at that time.

Galiani's practical suggestion was quickly accepted by diplomats. When Britain and France engaged in war in 1793 President Washington of the United States of America declared that his country would insist on neutrality within 3 nautical miles of its coasts. The information was justified to the British authorities in the following terms, by Secretary of State Jefferson.

The greatest distance to which any respectable assent amongst nations has at any time been given is the extent of the human sight, estimated at upwards of twenty miles, and the smallest distance, I believe, claimed by any nation whatever, is the utmost range of a cannon ball, usually stated at one sea league.[25]

This showed a new development from the language of a treaty concerning neutral zones signed between the United States and Morocco in 1785. This treaty referred to 'the range of cannons in the castles', which was the most restrictive interpretation of the cannon shot rule. The French also accepted Galiani's suggestion quickly, because a treaty signed with Tunis on 25 May 1795 stipulated that the neutral zone was measured as the cannot shot, whether the guns were actually in position or not. Baty has given a very full list of instances where states accepted the 3 nautical mile rule in the first half of the nineteenth century.[26] Although Russian, Austrian, Prussian and Italian regulations referred to 'the range of guns' or 'the distance of a cannon shot from the shore', between 1848 and 1866, the practice was dying rapidly. It is impossible to disagree with the American Ambassador in Paris, who informed the French government in 1864 regarding a naval dispute that 'no other rule than the three-mile rule was known or recognised as a principle of international law'.[27] This generalisation was maintained by most unilateral declarations, bilateral agreements, and legal judgements until the 1920s. However, at the first attempt to establish the rule firmly in international law through a multilateral convention in 1930, it proved impossible to reach any agreement on the breadth of the territorial sea.[28] The conference at The Hague was attended by forty-seven states. Subsequent conferences held in 1958 and 1960, with eighty-six and eighty-seven participants respectively, also failed to reach any agreement on this question.

The long acceptance of territorial seas 3 nautical miles wide resulted from the firm policies of the major maritime powers of that period. The United Kingdom, the United States of America, Germany and Japan claimed only 3 nautical miles as their seaward territorial limits, and they refused to recognise greater distances for other states. These maritime powers were leaders in the field of merchant fleets, deep water trawlers, whaling fleets, and navies. It was plainly in their interests to keep the territorial seas as narrow as possible so that their commercial and naval vessels could operate freely over the high seas and through international straits. Even before the Hague conference various international lawyers such as Fulton, Hall and Westlake had warned that while 3 nautical miles represented the agreed minimum claim to territorial seas, there was no universal agreement about the maximum width which could be claimed.[29] The main opponents of the general rule were Italy, Russia, Portugal, Spain and Uruguay. Russia, Portugal and Spain claimed wider territorial seas in order to retain exclusive use of fishing zones. Russian authorities were particularly concerned to restrict seal hunting by foreigners, and issued various edicts setting limits between 10 and 100 nautical miles offshore. Spain had first claimed a territorial sea of 6 nautical miles in 1760 and continued to persist with this view, but without real success in the face of British and American protests.[30]

The task of securing general international agreement has been made more difficult by the increased number of independent states. The various claims by individual states to territorial seas is considered in the next chapter, but it will be useful at this point to indicate briefly the reasons for the differing views. The major, non-communist, maritime states, such as the United States of America, the United Kingdom, and Japan, are still in favour of narrow territorial waters for the identical reasons of the last century. The newly created states generally seek wider territorial seas and in this demand they are supported by the People's Republic of China and the Soviet Union, although the Soviet Union does not support claims in excess of 12 nautical miles. The newer states are mainly concerned with matters of fishing and defence, although their views are to some extent a reaction against the width of 3 nautical miles because of its colonial connotations. The Indian representative at the 1960 conference summarised these views very well.

It is not a mere accident that these newer and younger nations should be asking for a wider territorial sea; whereas the older maritime powers should be wanting a narrow territorial sea. Their past history, their sufferings, their economic under-development and, the most important thing, their passionate craving for a better life explain their eagerness to cling to and to appropriate to themselves for their exclusive use and occupation their adjacent seas as far as possible. For another, they feel rightly or wrongly, that a wider territorial sea would give them an insulated life, free from interference from the great Powers.[31]

THE DELIMITATION OF TERRITORIAL SEAS

There have always been two basic problems in delimiting the extent of territorial seas. First, it is necessary to select a baseline from which the width of the sea is measured. This is not a difficult problem when the coast is free from indentations, such as bays, estuaries and gulfs, and devoid of offshore islands and low-tide elevations. The Ninety-Mile Beach on the Gippsland coast of Australia provides the best example of this situation. In such cases the territorial sea can be measured from any one of the several tidal levels along the shore. It is usual to select the low-water mark, since this will push the outer limit of the territorial sea as far away from the coast as possible. Unfortunately many coasts are deeply indented and are fringed with islands and low-tide elevations. In these cases the selection of a baseline presents real difficulties. While coastal geomorphologists can classify coasts by many criteria such as process, stage, plan, profile and the arrangement of islands and low-tide elevations, no two sections of coast are identical. It is therefore necessary to devise a series of rules for drawing baselines, which would ensure that any two surveyors working independently would draw the same baseline for the same section of coast.

The second problem is to divide territorial waters between two or more states. This difficulty will arise when an international land boundary reaches the coast and has to be extended into the sea, and when the width of water between two opposite shores is less than double the breadth of territorial waters claimed. Both situations are common. For example, the extension of the boundary between Canada and the United States into the Pacific and Atlantic oceans, through the Strait of Juan de Fuca and Passamaquoddy Bay respectively, created problems for both administrations. Sweden and Denmark, Australia and Papua New Guinea, Indonesia and Malaysia, and Turkey and Greece, are just a few of the many pairs of countries which have to share territorial waters because the seas between them are too narrow to allow each to make full claims. Since the delimitations of such boundaries are exclusive matters for the states concerned it is not necessary to have a general rule which will apply in all cases. The states can voluntarily reach any agreement which is mutually acceptable. However, it would obviously be useful to have a general rule which would apply if states could not make a settlement of conflicting claims.

The present level of success in solving these problems has been reached through three stages. First, there was the period which lasted until 1930 when states made unilateral assertions about the baselines from which their territorial seas were measured, when pairs of states reached agreements about the extension of their land boundaries seawards, and when groups of states, such as those concerned with North Sea fishing grounds, agreed on general rules for the delimitation of territorial waters. The second stage occurred in 1930 when an international conference on the law of the sea was held at The Hague. It was attended by forty-seven countries. This conference brought forward many precise ideas about the delimitation of the territorial waters. Although they were never formally adopted by a vote, they undoubtedly eased the consummation of the third stage which occurred during the conference on the law of the sea called by the United Nations in Geneva in 1958. It is proposed now to trace the solution of each problem separately through each of the three stages: greatest emphasis will be given to the last two stages, which have been the most productive.

A survey of practices before 1930 reveals three main points. First, bays were considered as a special case of territorial waters from earliest times. It has already been noted that fishing grounds in bays were awarded to subjects by sovereigns even in Roman times. From the thirteenth century, Venice and Genoa

D

claimed control over adjacent bays and gulfs. During the reign of Edward II (1307–27) the English authorities claimed, as internal waters, all bays where the headlands could be seen from each other on a fair day. Three hundred years later, it was specified that British neutral waters were marked by straight lines linking twenty-seven headlands around the English coast from Holy Island, in the northeast, to the Isle of Man, in the west. These headlands were not selected to enclose the maximum area of water, but were those established by the tradition of sailing vessels navigating from headland to headland.[32] In 1804, President Jefferson of the United States invoked the same practice as the advisers of Edward II five hundred years earlier.

> The rule of common law is that wherever you can see from land to land all the waters within the line of sight is in the body of the adjacent country and within common law jurisdiction . . . The 3 miles of maritime jurisdiction is always to be counted from this line of sight.[33]

While it was considered that bays constituted special situations there was no general agreement about the maximum size of bays which could be claimed as internal waters. Lacking this agreement it is not surprising that there were fishing disputes between nationals of different countries. Scottish claims to the exclusive use of herring grounds in the Moray Firth between Duncansby Head and Kinncaird's Head led to disputes with England and Holland in the seventeenth century. In 1882 a conference on fishing in the North Sea produced a convention, which specified that bays could only be considered as internal waters when their mouths could be closed by a straight line not more than 10 miles wide.[34] If the mouth of the bay exceeded 10 miles in width, the line could be drawn between the points where the width first narrowed to that distance. The convention was signed by the United Kingdom, Germany, France, Belgium, Denmark and the Netherlands. This standard was adopted by a number of countries, including Denmark, Portugal, Spain and Italy. The United States agreed to a 10 mile closing line for bays in a treaty with the United Kingdom in 1912. According to Moor, the limit of 10 miles was based on practical considerations.

> The ten-mile line has been adopted in the cases referred to, as I understand them, as a practical rule. The transgression of an encroachment upon territorial waters by fishing vessels is generally a grave offence, involving in many instances a forfeiture of the offending vessel and it is obvious that the narrower the space in which it is permissible to fish the more likely the offence is to be committed. In order therefore that the fishing may be both practicable and safe and not constantly attended with the risk of violating territorial waters, it has been thought to be expedient not to allow it where the extent of free waters between the three-mile line drawn on each side of the bay is less than four miles. This is the reason of the ten-mile line.[35]

This general rule was not adopted by every country interested in this matter. Some insisted on closing bays where headlands could be seen from each other; some regarded any bay which could be swept by artillery from the headlands as belonging to the state, while others simply believed that the closing line must equal twice the width of territorial waters. Russia, in 1907, in a treaty with Japan, claimed exclusive rights in any bay where the length was at least three times the width of the mouth of the bay.[36]

The second main point, which the survey reveals, is that countries which possessed offshore islands measured their territorial waters from such points. On 18 June 1745 Denmark defined its territorial waters in the following terms.

> . . . no foreign privateers shall be permitted to capture any ship and vessel within one league of our coasts and the shoals and rocky islets which are situated there and are also included in that term.[37]

A declaration by the same country in 1812 measured the territorial sea from 'the outermost islands or islets which are not submersed by the sea'. Similar claims were made by Sweden in 1899 and by Russia in 1893. The Russian description mentioned the farthest islands, rocks, banks of stone or reefs showing above the sea.[38] By 1911 the Russian government claimed that the territorial waters were measured from 'the lowest ebb-tide, or from the extremity of the coastal standing ice'.[39]

This quotation leads directly to the third main conclusion which is that the low-water mark came to be accepted as the baseline from which territorial waters should be measured, in situations where straight lines did not close indentations. The Russian reference to 'lowest ebb-tide' and a Portuguese reference in 1909 to the line of 'extreme low water' were precise variations on this theme designed to secure the widest possible extent of territorial waters.

Thus it can be concluded that before 1930 there was general agreement that bays constituted special cases of internal or territorial waters, that islands possessed their own territorial waters, and that the low-water mark was the appropriate line from which to measure the width of the territorial waters, except where straight lines had been drawn across indentations. The Hague conference tried to make these general views sufficiently precise for use as part of international law.

A sub-committee of the conference considered the technical problems of determining the baseline from which the breadth of the territorial sea should be measured. This matter was considered under thirteen headings which can be grouped into five subjects. The first subject dealt with the baseline to be used on coasts with a simple plan and profile. There was general agreement that the low-water mark provided the best line in such situations, but it was felt necessary to define that line more closely. Two recommendations were made. First, that the low-water mark taken as the baseline should be that line marked on official charts used or issued by the coastal state. However, because the producers of charts are anxious that the users should not run aground, the low-water marks shown are often the lowest ever recorded. In areas where there is a large tidal range, and where the submarine gradient is slight, these exceptionally low tides may be several miles seaward of the mean low-water spring tides. The best examples of these conditions are found in the Bay of Fundy, in eastern Canada, and the Bay of St Michel in northwest France. Since the mean low-water spring tides are nearly constant they provide a more reliable datum. The height of the mean low-water spring tides is the height obtained by two successive low waters during those periods of twenty-four hours during the year when the maximum declination of the moon is 23° 30′. So the second condition was made that the low-water mark recorded on the charts of the coastal state must not 'depart appreciably' from the line of the mean low-water spring tide.[40]

The second subject concerned the delimitation of a baseline around ports, roadsteads and river mouths. There was complete agreement that the outermost permanent harbour structures should be considered as part of the land for purposes of drawing baselines. It was also unanimously decided that where rivers flowed directly into the sea, that the baseline would be drawn across the mouth of the river, whatever its width, so that all the river remained as internal waters of the state. If a river flowed into an estuary, it was recommended that the estuary be treated according to the rules laid down for bays. The conference did not attempt to distinguish between estuaries and rivers entering the sea directly: a serious problem when considering very large river mouths. Coastal geomorphologists agree that it is extremely difficult to define an estuary. Biological, chemical, physical and morphological criteria give differing areas, especially in the case of large estuaries. Pritchard provides the following definition.

> An estuary is a semi-enclosed coastal body of water which has a free connection with the open sea and within which sea water is measurably diluted with fresh water derived from land drainage.[41]

Now because of the general rise in sea-level in recent geological history, most rivers do enter the sea through estuaries, except in areas of local uplift, or via deltas under construction. The possibility of controversy can be illustrated by the claim of Argentina and Uruguay in 1961, that the Rio de la Plata flows directly into the sea, and that its mouth is legally closed by a straight baseline, 120 nautical miles long between Punta del Este in Uruguay and Cabo San Antonio in Argentina.[42] Other major rivers which could be the subject of controversy include the Orinoco and the Amazon.

The third subject included offshore islands and low-tide elevations. While it was easily agreed that each island possessed its own right to territorial waters, and that low-tide elevations which fell within territorial waters could be used as points from which the territorial sea was measured, there was no agreement regarding the arrangements for archipelagos. Some countries suggested that the arbitrary figure of 10 miles between islands should apply, while others recommended a distance equal to twice the breadth of the territorial sea. Still other delegates proposed that community of interest amongst the islands should determine whether the islands had a continuous area of territorial seas. There was also a disagreement about the nature of waters enclosed amongst the outer islands. The maritime powers were in favour of considering them as territorial seas, while the coastal states preferred that they should be classed as internal waters.

The fourth subject dealt with narrow straits. It was agreed that where the straits linked the high seas and internal waters the rules referring to bays applied. Where the opposite shores of straits linking two areas of the high seas were occupied by a single state, the territorial waters were measured in the normal way. If the strait was wider than twice the breadth of the territorial sea, a strip of high seas was left through the strait. If, however, the strait was narrower than this critical distance the entire waters of the strait were considered as territorial waters. If pockets of high seas were left as enclaves within the strait, then these could be absorbed as territorial waters, providing they were less than 2 nautical miles wide. Where the opposite shores are controlled by different states it was recommended that the maritime boundary lay 'down the centre of the strait' in those cases where it was narrower than twice the breadth of the territorial seas. This is the only reference in the Hague proceedings to the division of territorial waters between states, even though Adami and Lapradelle had referred to this issue in books published shortly before the conference.[43]

The fifth and most difficult subject related to the status of bays, and the sub-committee considered three questions: the definition of a bay, claims to bays on historic grounds, and the status of bays shared by states. It was agreed that bays would have to be defined by geographers and that the lawyers would then be able to apply the rules laid down and discuss what legal consequences followed. There were clearly two methods which could be employed to define bays. Either all potential bays could be examined and compared and lists prepared of those features which would be considered as bays for the determination of the territorial sea, or arbitrary mathematical definitions of bays could be created and then applied to actual situations. The second, easier method was adopted and two proposals were advanced. The first, made by the American delegation, was complicated and would have produced fewer legal bays than the second method which was suggested by French representatives. Both systems, which are shown in Figure 1, applied only to bays or parts of bays where the distance between the opposite headlands was not more than 10 nautical miles. In the American method a straight line was drawn across the mouth of the bay under consideration and measured. An envelope of arcs of circles, having a radius equal to one-quarter of the closing line, was then constructed from all points on the shore of the bay. A semicircle was then drawn on the landward side of the closing line, with a radius equal to one-quarter of the closing line. If the area enclosed between the envelope of arcs and the closing line was greater than the area of the semicircle the indentation was considered to be a true bay which

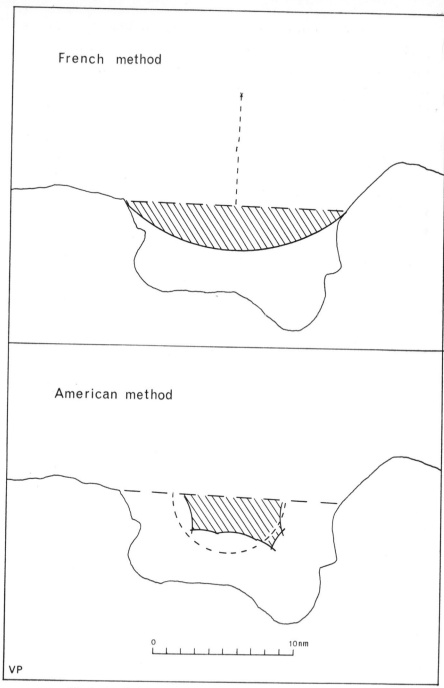

French method

American method

0   10nm

VP

Fig 1   Methods of defining bays proposed at The Hague in 1930

could be closed by a straight line from which the territorial waters could be measured. If that area was less than the area of the semicircle the feature was not considered to be a true bay, and the territorial sea would be measured from the low-water mark of the coast of the indentation.

The French method first required a bisecting perpendicular to be constructed on the seaward side of the closing line. An arc of a circle was then described on the landward side of the closing line, with its centre located half the length of the closing line along the perpendicular and its radius equal to the distance between the centre and the termini of the closing line. If the area of the bay between the coast and the closing line was greater than the segment of the circle between the arc and the closing line then the indentation was considered a true bay.[44] Figure 1 shows the operation of both methods in the case of the same bay and the different results achieved. According to the French method this bay could be closed, because the bay has a larger area than the shaded segment of the circle. According to the American method this bay could not be closed, because the semicircle is larger than the shaded area of sea. The French method would allow bays with a smooth profile to be closed with a straight line, even when the entire waters of the bay would be considered territorial waters if the minimum distance of 3 nautical miles was measured from all points around the shore of the indentation. The American delegation justified the use of the construction of an envelope on the grounds that this generalised the shape of the bay and made comparison easier than by using the detailed sinuosities of the coast. However, Boggs admitted that the proportion of one-quarter of the closing line might be too large a radius for the arcs, and he advocated experiments with various proportions to obtain a satisfactory definition.[45]

Although the initial discussion referred to the problem of islands in the mouth of the bay and the view was expressed that only the sea distance should be measured, there was no reference to this matter in the final report. The American delegation deliberately avoided mention of islands in the mouth of the bay, because it was considered that such complications prevented consideration of the shape of the real bay. This view was sustained by the belief that the variety of islands in and near the mouths of bays made it impracticable to treat them uniformly. One must respect the judgement of Boggs, but it is surprising that it was not specifically stated anywhere in the report that for purposes of calculation of area, islands in the bay were not distinguished from water surfaces. The Americans also justified the apparent neglect of islands in the mouths of bays on the grounds that they had other proposals designed to eliminate 'objectionable pockets of high seas', which took islands into account. Unfortunately this proposal was not included in the final report.

Although in the initial discussions there was reference to historic bays and shared bays there was no mention of them in the final report. It appears that the deliberations convinced the delegates that these matters were too difficult to allow any sort of agreement. It is true that the American proposal about the definition of bays was believed to apply to bays shared by two countries which had agreed on the division of the waters of the bay, but there was no indication as to how such a division could be achieved.

Shortly after the conference, Boggs published two papers containing new suggestions which were apparently based on the work he had done for the conference. The first dealt with the elimination of objectionable pockets of high seas and the second with the continuation of land boundaries through territorial seas.[46] When the territorial seas are drawn around islands, some areas of high seas may be left as enclaves within the territorial sea and other areas of the high sea may be left as deep indentations into the territorial sea. Such areas serve no useful purpose for navigation and they are usually so narrow that attempts to fish there are fraught with the dangers of trespassing into territorial waters. Boggs therefore recommended that such areas should be annexed in certain circumstances. It was recommended that any enclaves of the high seas should be annexed, although it will be recalled that in respect of pockets of high seas enclosed in straits, the report suggested that they should only be annexed if they were less than 2 nautical miles in breadth. In the case of indentations Boggs proposed a closing line of not more than 4 nautical miles. A semicircle should be constructed on the closing line, with its diameter equal to the length of that line. If the area of sea enclosed between the edge of the territorial sea and the closing line exceeded the area of the semicircle those waters could be annexed. If the area of waters enclosed were less than the area of the semicircle then such waters remained as part of the high seas. These situations are illustrated in Figure 2, where the enclave (A) and the indentation (B) could be annexed, while the other indentations (C and D) would remain part of the high seas.

Boggs proposed that land boundaries between adjacent states should be extended through the territorial waters along the median line, which he defined as 'the line every point of which is equidistant from the nearest points or points on opposite shores'. Prior to this suggestion it had been usual to recommend that boundaries should be continued through the territorial seas in one of two ways.[47] First, it was suggested that the last boundary section on land should be projected through the territorial waters. An alternative line was offered by a boundary which was drawn perpendicular to the general alignment of the coast. Both these lines had obvious disadvantages. The final alignment of the land boundary would be drawn without regard to the territorial waters and could operate very unfairly against one of the countries. In the case where the boundary followed a river to the sea the final course of the river might change from time to time, but it would be intolerable if the division through the territorial sea also altered. The problem of drawing a line perpendicular to the coastline rests in the fact that the general alignment of the coast may be very hard to fix. Should the alignment be determined for 5 miles on either

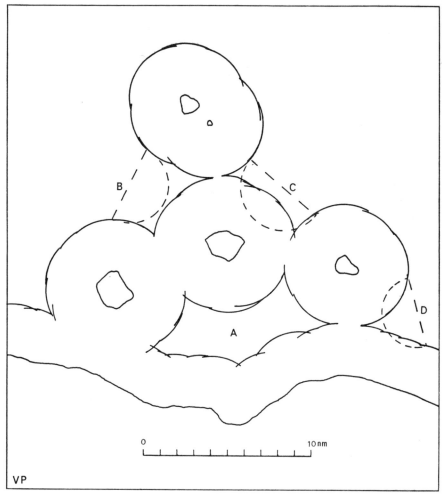

Fig 2   Proposals for eliminating objectionable pockets of high seas advanced by
S. W. Boggs

side of the land terminus, or for longer or shorter distances? The situation will vary with different coastlines, but as Figure 3A shows, it is entirely possible for one state (country A), to be deprived of territorial waters which lie outside the breadth of territorial waters claimed by a neighbouring state, whether the continuation is a direct line or perpendicular to the coast. Any system, where the fairness of the result fluctuates with the plan of the coastline, is defective. A system which is universally fair requires the construction of a median line, which is shown in Figure 3B. Boggs recommended the construction of the median line by trial and error, and this is certainly the easiest method of construction. With a pair of dividers locations which are equidistant from the nearest points on the shore of each state can be fixed. This is the technique which a navigator would use to ascertain the position of his vessel. This system works easily even when islands are present, although Boggs sensibly suggested that any median line which changed alignment frequently could be smoothed for easier administration.

The United Nations conference on the law of the sea in 1958 at Geneva, unlike its predecessor at The Hague, succeeded in codifying many regulations governing the delimitation of the territorial sea. The second section of the Convention of the Territorial Sea and the Contiguous Zone contains thirteen articles which deal with most of the major issues of delimitation. The official records of the conference provide detailed information of the role which different countries played in fashioning separate parts of this section.[48] The main provisions of the 1958 convention can be summarised as follows.

First, possession of territory adjoining the sea creates the right to territorial waters, whether that territory is part of the mainland or an island. In cases where the coast of such territory has a smooth plan the baseline from which the breadth of the territorial sea is measured is provided by the low-water line recognised by the coastal state. The outermost, permanent harbour works are considered as part of the coast and roadsteads used for loading, unloading and anchoring ships are

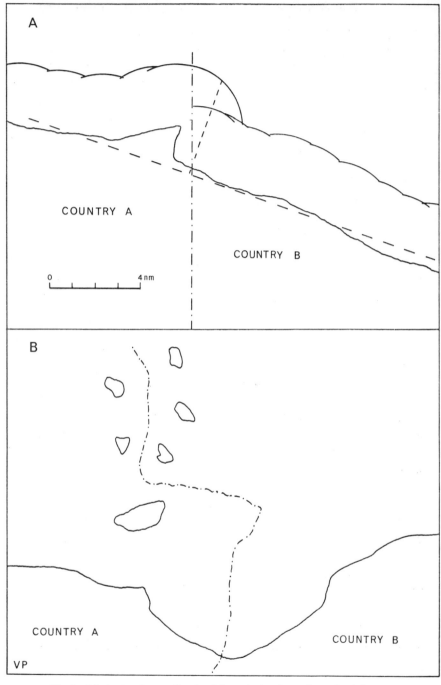

Fig 3   Methods of extending land boundaries through territorial waters

considered as lying within territorial waters, whatever their distance from shore.

There was very little discussion of these propositions. Some representatives tried to recommend a more precise definition of the low-water line. The term 'isobath zero' was suggested by France, but was rejected on the grounds that there was no equivalent term in English and that the line meant by the term might hold different meanings for different countries. The low-water line had a much more general currency and could be easily determined from all nautical charts. The Burmese delegate, presumably because of the presence of certain Thai islands in the mouth of the Kra estuary, recommended that alien islands within the territorial waters of another country should not create rights to territorial waters, but there was no support for this view.[49] So this definition of the normal baseline was less precise than that recommended at the Hague conference.

Secondly, in cases where the coastline is deeply indented or fringed with islands, as in the case of Norway, it is permissible to connect certain points by straight baselines from which the territorial sea will be measured. Such baselines may not depart to any appreciable extent from the general direction of the coast, they may not connect low-tide elevations unless some permanent structure has been built on them, they may not be constructed in such a manner as to separate the territorial waters of another state from the high sea, they must be drawn so that internal waters on the landward side of the baseline are closely linked to the land, and they must be clearly marked on published charts. The concept of straight baselines as opposed to the closing lines of bays was new and it was the subject of long debates, which focused on two main themes. The United Kingdom, the United States, Germany, Greece, Italy and Japan all sought to place a limit to the length of straight baselines. The United Kingdom suggested a length of 10 nautical miles, but later agreed, at Sweden's request, to increase the proposed limit to 15 nautical miles. The other states were also concerned to limit the distance of the baseline from the coast and recommended that no line should be more than 5 nautical miles from the coast.[50] The British recommendation was accepted and a maximum length of 15 nautical miles was laid down in the resolutions adopted by the First Committee. This provision, however, was deleted from the final convention by the full session of the conference. The major non-communist maritime powers were obviously fearful that certain states would abuse this provision, a fear which has subsequently been realised. In the next chapter cases will be noted where states have drawn straight baselines in situations where the normal low-water line would have been appropriate.

The second main theme of this debate, which was also continued when islands were discussed, concerned the applicability of these proposals to archipelagos, whether coastal, as in the case of Finland, or oceanic, as in the cases of Indonesia and the Philippines. The major powers were determined that this matter should be deferred for further consideration, and that was eventually done. However, the Philippines and Indonesia have proclaimed straight baselines surrounding their islands, and this must be considered one of the great unresolved questions concerning the delimitation of the territorial sea.

The provision that straight baselines must not isolate the territorial waters of another state from contact with the high seas was introduced by Portugal.[51] It seems a sensible proposal of importance to all small states existing as coastal enclaves on the shores of a larger country. The Portuguese possessions which fall into this category are Portuguese Timor and Macau. Other territories or states in similar positions include Singapore, Monaco, Hong Kong, Gambia and Walvis Bay.

The third major issue concerned the treatment of individual bays, as opposed to a series of deep bays which might give rise to the straight baseline already described. There were two ways by which the waters of a bay might be proclaimed internal waters, and a straight baseline drawn across the mouth of the bay. First, providing the water entrance or entrances to the bay total not more than 24 nautical miles, a straight baseline may be drawn across the mouth of the bay if the area of the bay, including any islands, is greater than a semicircle constructed on the closing line. In one sense this is a compromise between the American and French proposals at The Hague. The American method of drawing the semicircle on the closing line is preserved, but the French method of measuring the actual area of the bay, rather than the area of the generalised shape of the bay, is added. If the mouth of the bay is more than 24 nautical miles then such a line may be drawn at the first points where the bay narrows to that width. There was considerable debate on this subject with the major non-communist maritime countries seeking to limit the length of the closing line to 10 nautical miles. But the proposal of the Soviet Union, Poland, Bulgaria and Guatemala that the closing line should be 24 miles, that is twice the width of a 12 mile territorial sea, was adopted.[52]

Bays may also be proclaimed internal waters if the bay is considered to be historic. The concept of historic bays is well established, but no precise definition of such bays has ever been formulated and the 1958 convention did not resolve the matter. The Japanese delegate introduced an amendment to define historic bays in the following terms.

> The term 'historic bays' means those bays over which coastal State or States have effectively exercised sovereign rights continuously for a period of long standing, with explicit or implicit recognition of such practice by foreign States.[53]

Some states supported the Japanese view that the conference should try to produce a definition of historic bays, but the majority supported the resolution of Panama and India that the matter should be referred back to the United Nations General Assembly. This is the second major unresolved question connected with the delimitation of territorial seas.

Countries were also authorised by the convention to draw straight baselines across the mouths of rivers which flow 'directly into the sea'. Originally this article also included

E

reference to estuaries, by indicating that in such situations the rules for determining bays applied. However, the difficulty of defining estuaries led to the deletion of this qualification by the full conference. This excision means that the term estuary is not mentioned anywhere in the convention, creating a situation which might be abused. It is perhaps significant that Uruguay and Argentina have claimed the estuary of the Rio de la Plata on the grounds that it is a river flowing directly into the sea, which is patently not true, rather than on the grounds that it is an historic bay, which is at least a matter for debate.

One minor matter which was settled by the conference concerned low-tide elevations. Such features could be used to justify the extension of the territorial sea if they lay at a distance not exceeding the width of the territorial sea from the baseline. This resolution means that countries cannot claim extensive territorial seas on the existence of isolated reefs and rocks which are only visible above the surface at low tide.

Figure 4 illustrates the main rules decided at the 1958 Geneva Conference, for a territorial sea of 3 nautical miles. The smaller bay (A) can be closed by a straight baseline, because the area of the bay is larger than the area of a semicircle of 10 miles in diameter, which is the total length of the three openings. The larger bay (B) cannot be similarly closed, because the semicircle drawn on the first line, measuring 24 miles within the bay, is greater than the area of the bay landward of that line. The mouth of the river (C) can be closed by a straight baseline because it flows directly into the sea. The breakwaters (D) are considered as part of the coast from which the territorial sea is measured. The island (E) generates its own territorial waters, as does the low-tide elevation (F), which is within 3 miles of the island. The other low-tide elevations (G) are more than 3 miles from the island and cannot be used to justify an extension of the territorial sea.

The last important issue settled by the conference dealt with the division of territorial waters between states occupying opposite shores or adjacent coasts. It was agreed that neither

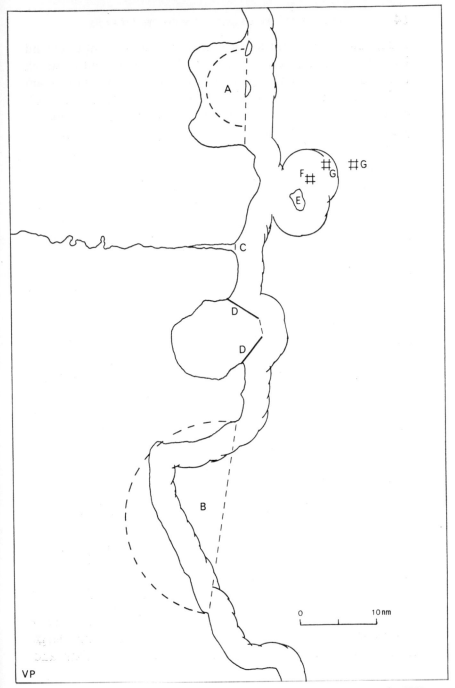

Fig 4 Rules for measuring the territorial sea established at Geneva in 1958

state, failing agreement to the contrary, had the right to extend its territorial sea beyond the median line, every point of which is equidistant from the nearest points on the baselines from which each state measures its territorial sea. Cambodia recommended the thalweg concept of the continuous line of greatest depth, but this received no support. Thus Boggs's proposal, which had not been adopted at the Hague conference, was accepted in 1958.

Despite the considerable progress made in 1958 there are a number of questions related to the delimitation of the territorial sea which are unresolved. In the next chapter, the examination of claims to territorial seas by individual countries will show how states have taken unilateral decisions in the absence of rules, which will make the eventual codification of such laws difficult. There are seven important unresolved questions.

First, the definition of circumstances under which straight baselines are appropriate is too imprecise, and the term 'deeply indented and cut into' is being interpreted very loosely by some countries. Secondly, the absence of any rules governing the acceptable baselines of archipelagos had led certain countries, such as Indonesia and the Philippines, to declare a system of surrounding straight baselines, which theoretically convert enormous areas of high seas into internal waters. Thirdly, the regulations about bays apply only to bays which fall entirely within the jurisdiction of a single state. There is no provision for shared bays yet there are many important shared bays around the coasts of the world. Fourthly, the concept of historic bays is as imprecise as it has ever been. This is an issue which individual states interpret to suit themselves, yet the concept is clearly important because it is mentioned in three places in the convention: in the articles on straight baselines, the definition of bays, and the division of territorial waters between states. Fifthly, the article dealing with rivers is again too imprecise to prevent abuses by states claiming large estuaries which could not be claimed as bays. The sixth and seventh problems are less important; they concern icebound coasts and objectionable pockets of high seas created by the territorial seas drawn around islands. Icebound coasts are not located on main shipping lanes but there are important fishing grounds off some of these areas, and it would be reasonable to establish a firm rule about whether the extent of the territorial sea is affected by the freezing or thawing of coastal waters. The record of the conference does not show that the elimination of objectionable pockets of high seas received significant attention. If, as appears to be the case, such pockets are useless for fishing or navigation, it would be sensible to eliminate them.

CHAPTER THREE

Claims to Territorial Seas

THIS chapter examines specific national claims to territorial seas and also considers some related questions. First, the pattern of claims is described, together with recent trends, and the arguments used by states to justify particular attitudes in this matter; secondly, the use of straight baselines and the claims to historic bays by various states are analysed; thirdly, particular cases where adjoining states have drawn boundaries separating their respective territorial seas are considered. The endorsement and application of the archipelago concept by a number of countries forms the fourth topic of this chapter and the fifth section examines the problem of innocent passage through international straits which are entirely occupied by territorial seas, and the related question of passage through international canals.

THE PRESENT PATTERN OF CLAIMS TO TERRITORIAL SEAS

In 1973, Lebanon and Nicaragua were the only independent coastal states which had not formally proclaimed the width of their territorial seas. The remaining maritime countries had all established claims, which ranged from 3 nautical miles to 200 nautical miles. As Table 1 shows, the widths claimed most frequently were: 12 nautical miles by fifty-six states, 3 nautical miles by twenty-five states, 6 nautical miles by ten states and

TABLE 1 *Claims to territorial waters*

Breadth of territorial sea (nautical miles)	Number of states	Percentage of world's fish catch (a)	Percentage of world's merchant fleet (b)	Percentage of air traffic (c)	Percentage of world's coastline
3	25	26·4	38·9	62·8	27·2
4	4	6·2	12·8	4·2	2·6
6	10	6·3	11·3	10·5	5·2
10	1	0·1	0·6	*	0·2
12	56	35·9	31·6	19·6	52·6
18	1	0·1	*	*	0·1
30	3	0·2	0·1	*	0·6
50	1	*	*	*	*
100	1	*	*	*	0·2
130	1	*	*	*	0·1
200	8	21·9	4·1	2·9	6·5
Other	5 (†)	2·9	0·6	*	4·6

* Negligible percentage
† Korea, Maldives, Nicaragua, Lebanon, Philippines

Sources: (a) *United Nations Statistical Yearbook*, 1971, 137–8; (b) *World Almanack*, 1973, 433; (c) *International Civil Aviation Bulletin*, May 1973, 25

200 nautical miles by eight states. The claims show some distinct regional features; apart from Sierra Leone all the countries claiming seas of 200 nautical miles are located in South or Central America and six of the ten countries claiming 6 nautical miles have coasts on the Mediterranean. The impression of 6 nautical miles as a characteristic of Mediterranean lands is reinforced by the fact that Turkey, which is excluded from Table 1, claims waters 6 nautical miles wide in the Mediterranean, and 12 nautical miles wide on the Black Sea. Northwest Europe stands out as an area of narrow claims, because in addition to the states claiming 3 nautical miles, Iceland and the

Scandinavian states of Norway, Sweden, and Finland claim only 4 nautical miles. The largest group of states, which claim 12 nautical miles, shows no regional concentration and is represented on all continents except Australia. However, some of the countries in this group provide very long stretches of coast subject to uniform claims. Travelling north from the South African–Mozambique boundary to the Soviet–Norwegian boundary, claims only vary from 12 nautical miles on the coast of South Korea, South Vietnam and the former Trucial States on the southern coast of the Persian Gulf. By contrast, the coast which exhibits the greatest variety of claims occurs in West Africa, where eight different widths are found.

Since 1950, as the number of independent states has increased there have been important changes in the proportion of states claiming different widths, as Table 2 shows, and there has been both a proportional and absolute decline in the number of states claiming territorial waters of 3 nautical miles. Nineteen of the twenty-five states in this group are either located in north-west Europe or are countries which were formerly colonies of

TABLE 2 The changing pattern of claims to territorial waters

Territorial waters	Number of states		
	1950	1965	1972
3nm	40	32	25
4nm	4	3	4
6nm	9	16	10
9nm	1	—	—
10nm	4	2	1
12nm	3	26	56
18nm	—	—	1
30nm	—	—	3
50nm	—	—	1
100nm	—	—	1
130nm	—	1	1
200nm	1	1	8
Total	62	81	111

states in this area. If newly independent states such as Fiji, Barbados and Qatar follow the example of many other post-colonial states, they may not continue to be members of this group. Looking at the other countries in this category, only the inclusion of Cuba, which has not changed its claim since 1936, seems inexplicable. Japan plainly has many of the commercial characteristics and interests of states in northwest Europe; South Vietnam and Taiwan have been client states of the United States for many years, and this may have encouraged them to follow the American lead. Monaco and Jordan have the shortest coastlines of all the countries. There would seem to be no advantage, and only added responsibility for the authorities in Monaco, if a wider territorial sea was claimed, while Jordan's coastline at the head of the Gulf of Aqaba makes any claim in excess of 3 nautical miles pointless, because it cannot claim beyond the line of equidistance with Israeli and Egyptian waters.

For all practical purposes the countries claiming 4 nautical miles can be considered with this first group, because the variation results from the different definition of a league in Scandinavia and the rest of Europe. Apart from the conversion of Denmark, in 1966, from 4 nautical miles to 3 nautical miles, this group, consisting of the three Scandinavian states and Iceland, has remained unchanged in the period under review.

The number of states claiming territorial waters of 6 nautical miles reached a peak of sixteen in 1965, but since then it has declined to ten. This width is today particularly associated with the Mediterranean and, in 1958, the Israeli delegate to the conference on the law of the sea noted that his country had selected that width reluctantly for reasons of local conformity.[1] About the time of his statement this width was also popular in the adjoining regions of the Middle East, represented by Kuwait, Iran and the Somali Republic, and in West Africa, where Mauritania, Gabon, Cameroun, Gambia, Senegal, Equatorial Guinea and Spanish Sahara, then both colonies, and Ivory Coast, have now made claims to greater widths.

There have been two other trends since 1950. First, the number of countries claiming 12 nautical miles has shown a dramatic increase in both absolute and proportional terms. In 1950 less than 5 per cent of countries claimed this width; in 1972 that proportion had risen to 50·5 per cent. The members of this large group of fifty-six states possess a rich diversity of characteristics. The list includes the giant communist states of the Soviet Union and China, and some of the former's satellites in eastern Europe; the commercially powerful countries of France and Canada; the world's principal colonial power Portugal; and a variety of Third World states, ranging from the wealthy petroleum-producing countries of Libya and Saudi Arabia, to the impoverished states such as Yemen (San'a) and Equatorial Guinea, and from the giant states of India and Indonesia to the tiny countries of Nauru and Tonga. Thirty-nine of these states raised their claims to 12 nautical miles from narrower seas, generally of 3 nautical miles. The Soviet Union is the country which has claimed this width for the longest period, having established this rule in 1909.

The second trend reveals a significant increase in the number of countries claiming territorial seas wider than 12 nautical miles. In 1950 only Peru claimed more than 12 nautical miles. By 1965 it had been joined by Guinea and, seven years later, by another thirteen states. It is perhaps equally significant that eight of the fifteen countries in this group claim territorial waters of 200 nautical miles and two others claim more than 100 nautical miles. All these states are located in South America or West Africa.

While it is important to know the number of countries claiming different widths, it is also important to know which kinds of countries reveal a tendency either to maintain a constant claim or vary their claims. On this basis it is possible to distinguish three groups of states. First there are those states which, over a long period, have not varied the width claimed for their territorial seas. With the exception of the Soviet Union, which has a long history of claiming 12 nautical miles, the countries in this group claim 3, 4 or 6 nautical miles. They are mainly European states or regions of European colonisation, such as Australia, New Zealand and the United States. Sweden has maintained the same limit since 1779 and the United States since 1793. The inclusion of Japan in this group, with its powerful commercial interests, comes as no surprise; and the peculiar circumstances of Jordan and Monaco have already been noted.

The second group of states includes those which have increased their territorial waters a few miles and those which, by a single act, have increased their claim to a width not exceeding 12 nautical miles. This is a large group and includes the great variety of states described earlier, which claim 12 nautical miles. Most of them increased their claims from 3 to 12 nautical miles, but there were some smaller adjustments. For example, in 1970 Albania increased its territorial sea from 10 to 12 nautical miles and three years earlier Dominica doubled its territorial waters to a distance of 6 nautical miles.

The third group of states includes those which have either increased their territorial waters by several miles, or made frequent changes in the limits claimed. Many of them satisfy both these conditions, and they all claim more than 12 nautical miles. There are fifteen of these states and they are all located either in South or Central America and West Africa. The extreme case is Gabon which inherited a territorial sea 3 nautical miles wide when it became independent in 1960. In January 1963 the width was increased to 12 nautical miles and it was more than doubled to 25 nautical miles in August 1970. In January 1972 Nigeria's lead was followed and the territorial sea was made 30 nautical miles wide, but this claim only lasted six months, after which the width was increased to 100 nautical miles. The explanation for these dramatic changes appears to lie in a boundary dispute between Gabon and Equatorial Guinea over the ownership of the islands of Corisco and Elobey. The dispute arose over ambiguities in the Franco–Spanish treaty of 1900 and was sharpened by reports of possible oil fields on the neighbouring continental shelf.² Table 3 provides details of the changed claims by countries in this group.

A select group of three states have reduced their claims to territorial seas. In 1901 Cuba claimed a width of 4 leagues, or 12 nautical miles. This width was halved in 1934 and halved again in 1936, which means that Cuba makes the narrowest

TABLE 3 Countries which have increased their territorial seas often, or by considerable distances

Country	Claimed width in nautical miles and date of establishment
Argentina	3 (1869); 200 (1967)
Brazil	3 (1940); 6 (1966); 12 (1969); 200 (1970)
Cameroun	3 (1933); 6 (1962); 18 (1967)
Chile	3 (?); 50km (1948); 200 (1953)
Ecuador	3 (1930); 12 (1951); 200 (1956)
Gabon	3 (1933); 12 (1963); 25 (1970); 30 (1970); 100 (1972)
Gambia	3 (1878); 6 (1968); 12 (1969); 50 (1971)
Ghana	3 (?); 12 (1963); 30 (1972)
Guinea	3 (1933); 130 (1964)
Mauritania	3 (1933); 6 (1962); 12 (1967); 30 (1972)
Nigeria	3 (1964); 12 (1967); 30 (1971)
Panama	12 (1958); 200 (1967)
Peru	3 (1934); 200 (1947)
Sierra Leone	3 (1957); 12 (1965); 200 (1971)
Uruguay	3 (1914); 6 (1963); 12 (1969); 200 (1969)

claim of any communist state. Denmark, in 1966, reduced its claim from the Scandinavian league of 4 nautical miles to the southern European league of 3 nautical miles. In 1965 the authorities in Honduras reduced the territorial sea from 200 nautical miles, which had been established in 1951, to 12 nautical miles.

Table 1 also shows the proportion of the coastline along which different widths of territorial sea are claimed, and it is evident that there is a rough correspondence between the proportion of states claiming various widths and the proportion of coastline which they control. However, it is not possible to make much use of these figures, because of the varying nature of the coastline and coastal waters in each category. For example, 10 per cent of the coastlines occupied by states claiming 3 nautical miles is represented by the shores of Greenland, which are seldom navigated by commercial vessels, even though major fishing grounds are found south of the island. A significant proportion of the coasts where territorial waters are 12 nautical miles wide lie along the arctic fringes of Canadian islands and the Soviet Union. For this reason there is very little point in calculating the approximate area of claimed territorial seas or in estimating how much more of the high seas will be annexed if all states claimed 12 or 100 nautical miles. There is one other reason which discourages such computations. Many states do not measure their territorial seas from their coasts; they measure them from baselines at varying distances from the coast, which are either justified by the irregular nature of the coast or by the need to secure historic bays. However, before the incidence of straight baselines and historic bays is examined, it is necessary to review the arguments used by states in favour of the most popular widths claimed.

There are two sets of arguments which must be considered. First, there is the controversy over whether the width of the territorial seas should be uniform throughout the world, or left to the discretion of individual states. Secondly, there is the dispute over whether those seas should be comparatively narrow or comparatively wide.

It is the view of many governments, especially those which claim narrow seas, that a uniform width should be agreed amongst all countries. The opinion of the Swedish delegate to the 1958 conference on the law of the sea summarises this position.

Turning to the question of the territorial sea he emphasised that its breadth must be fixed by international law. If states were free arbitrarily to extend their territorial sea, the fundamental rule that no State might subject any part of the high seas to its sovereignty would be violated.[3]

Some other countries, including the Soviet Union, take a more flexible attitude and urge that states should be allowed to fix their own boundaries within fairly narrow limits.[4] Both these views are opposed by those governments which believe that each country has the right to determine the appropriate width on the basis of its historical, geographical, cultural, economic and strategic circumstances. Repeatedly throughout the general debate this point was asserted by representatives and it has now been taken up with enthusiasm by the representatives of the People's Republic of China.

> Natural conditions differ in various parts of the world. The length and curvature of the coastlines of coastal countries, the depth and inclination of the seabed along their coasts, the specific conditions of their coastal resources and the joining of neighbouring countries in the same sea area are diversified. Moreover, the needs of economic development and national security differ for the people of each country. It is, therefore, entirely proper, legitimate and irreproachable for coastal countries to delimit in a reasonable way their own territorial sea . . .[5]

Elsewhere in his speech on 20 March 1973, the Chinese delegate to the United Nations conference made it clear that his country supported claims by South American countries for territorial waters 200 nautical miles wide. There is no evidence to show how this basic disagreement will be resolved, but there is plenty of evidence to show that the South American states are determined to maintain their existing claims.

Turning now to the arguments advanced in support of wide or narrow seas, it is evident that they are based mainly on economic considerations. Those states urging narrow territorial seas are anxious to avoid diminution of the area of the high seas for two reasons. First, several of these states possess large fishing fleets which exploit grounds remote from their own shores, closer to other countries. The British and Japanese delegates in 1958 stressed the damage which would be caused to their respective economies by any extension of territorial waters over fishing grounds formerly located in the high seas. The British representative argued in the following fashion.

> The United Kingdom had to maintain a population of fifty million people, in a comparatively small area in which the density of population was very high. It did not produce all the food it consumed, and a large part of its foodstuffs had to be imported and paid for out of its earnings in foreign currency. A commodity such as fish which could be caught and marketed without spending any foreign currency and which did not need to be set off against corresponding exports, played a very important part in balancing the United Kingdom's economy. And a major part of the country's supply of fish was provided by its distant-water and middle-water fishing fleets, which would be grievously affected by a twelve-mile zone of exclusive fishing.[6]

Table 1 shows the importance of countries, claiming seas 3 and 4 nautical miles wide, in the world's fishing industry. The other arguments in favour of narrow territorial waters are related to aspects of air and sea communication. Because merchant vessels have the right of innocent passage through territorial waters, their extension should not theoretically make any difference to maritime navigation. It is evident, however, that the right of innocent passage may be withdrawn either because of fears of pollution through tanker disasters, or for political reasons. In addition, as the United States' representative noted in 1958, many ships wish to avoid entering territorial waters and such vessels would be required to make lengthy detours to avoid transit through wide territorial waters. These detours would have to be made without the benefit of coastal navigational aids and the vessels would probably not carry sufficient cable to allow them to anchor outside wide territorial seas. Any increases in costs which these changes caused would have to be borne by those countries dependent on maritime commerce.[7] Emphasis was also placed on the additional costs which would be involved in assuming sovereignty over wider territorial seas; costs which would strain the budgets of poorer countries. Further, in time of war, weak neutral states would experience difficulties in preserving the neutrality of wide territorial seas.

The British and American delegates to the 1958 conference drew particular attention to the importance of the breadth of the territorial sea to air navigation.[8] All legal authorities dealing with the law of the air agree that there is no right of innocent passage through national air space comparable with innocent passage through territorial waters.[9] However, two international agreements seem to modify this position. The first is the Chicago convention of 1944, by which signatory states grant to other states, and receive from them, the right for unscheduled, civil, international air services to make flights into, or to make non-stop transit flights across, national territory.[10] Territorial seas are considered as part of national territory. Such flights are subject to any safety regulations in respect of security zones. The second is the International Air Services Transit Agreement which was agreed at the same time as the Chicago convention.[11] The transit agreement allows scheduled international air services of signatory states to fly over the territory of other signatories and to make landings for non-traffic purposes. However, this right is exercised in accordance with the provisions of the Chicago convention.

> That latter treaty, however, provides that no scheduled international air service may be operated over or into the territory of a contracting state, except with the special permission or other authorisation of that state, and in accordance with the terms of such permission or authorisation. Since the exercise of the Transit Agreement freedoms is made contingent on prior permission of the subjacent state, it follows that the grant of overflying privileges under that agreement is actually illusory.[12]

It is also important to note that in the middle of 1972, thirty-two countries with coastlines had not adhered to the transit agreement. These countries included the Soviet Union and Indonesia, which both have very long coastlines, and Panama, Ecuador, Peru, Chile, Uruguay, Sierra Leone, and Brazil, which each claim territorial waters 200 nautical miles wide.[13] Certainly there are some bilateral agreements between states covering air transit through national air space, but the concern of the British and American governments over this matter can be understood. Table 1 reveals that the countries which claim narrow territorial seas are responsible for the largest proportion of civil, international air traffic, whether it is measured by total load carried unit distances or the number of passengers carried unit distances.

Although there was no specific reference to the security interests of major powers during the debates on the breadth of the territorial sea, such interests nevertheless exist. The United States is believed to be particularly concerned about the advantage which Soviet submarines will obtain from operations in wider territorial seas, where American surveillance is not permissible.[14]

There are three general arguments which are used by those states which advocate wider territorial seas. First, since many of these states have become independent after a period of colonial administration, there is an obvious antipathy to a rule established by colonial powers in earlier periods.[15] Secondly, several small and medium powers supported the extension of territorial waters because they would be better insulated from risks attached to incidents and conflict involving the navies of major powers.[16] Further, in view of the increased speed at which ships can travel, these states also maintained that a wider territorial sea was necessary to allow the interception of smugglers.[17] The third, and principal, argument used in favour of wider territorial seas rested on the perceived need of many states to have exclusive access to maritime resources.[18] This argument has a number of facets. Considerable importance is attached to the need for control of fishing grounds, through the extension of territorial waters, to prevent their destruction or

F

serious depletion. Claims to very wide territorial seas were justified by countries, such as Peru, on the grounds that such acts were sanctioned by American claims to the continental shelf in 1945.[19] It is plain that states using these arguments were trying to compensate themselves for possessing only a very narrow continental shelf. Finally, some countries, including Turkey, asserted that the territorial seas should be wide in the cases of those countries which had very limited resources on land.[20]

It proved impossible to reconcile these two sets of conflicting arguments in 1958 and 1960, and the next attempt is scheduled to be made at Caracas in 1974. The six preparatory meetings held for the 1974 conference during 1972 and 1973 failed to make any significant progress on this question.

CLAIMS TO STRAIGHT BASELINES AND HISTORIC BAYS

The fourth article of the convention on the territorial sea allows states to construct straight baselines, where appropriate, from which the breadth of the territorial sea can be measured.

> Article 4
> 1.   In localities where *the coast line is deeply indented and cut into*, or if there is a fringe of islands along the coast in its immediate vicinity, the method of straight baselines joining appropriate points may be employed in drawing the baseline from which the breadth of the territorial sea is measured.
> 2.   *The drawing of such baselines must not depart to any appreciable extent from the general direction of the coast*, and *the areas lying within the lines must be sufficiently closely linked to the land domain to be subject to the regime of internal waters*.[21]

It is immediately apparent that the language of these two sections is sufficiently vague to allow a multiplicity of interpretations, and it comes as no surprise to discover that by the end of 1972 47 countries out of 118 had proclaimed straight baselines along part or all of their coast. This total does not include countries which have proclaimed straight baselines around archipelagos, nor does it include some countries, such as Chile, which would seem to have a very good case for establishing a straight baseline. It should be stressed at this point that straight baselines are quite separate from closing lines on legal bays.

The language used in Article 4 evidently owes a great deal to the judgement of the International Court of Justice concerning the fisheries case between Norway and the United Kingdom; the words shown in italics in the quotation above occur in the judgement also.[22] The British government was challenging the right of the Norwegian authorities to measure their territorial sea from a system of straight baselines linking points on the outer line of the 'skjaergaard', which is the name given to the fringing islands, believed to number 120,000. The court found that the system, which had its origins in baselines drawn in 1869 and 1889, was not contrary to international law.

At one stage in the proceedings the British government alleged that certain sections of the baseline did not respect the general direction of the coast. The judges referred to this matter in the following terms:

It should be observed that, however justified the rule in question may be, it is devoid of any mathematical precision.[23]

This specific enjoinder applies generally to the other criteria by which baselines are fixed: indented coast, fringing islands, immediate vicinity, and close links between the land and the waters inside the baseline. In an effort to discover some simple mathematical test which would satisfactorily distinguish those situations where baselines are appropriate from those where they are not, twenty-five proclaimed baselines were examined. Table 4 shows the information collected for each case. After careful examination of each individual column and combinations of columns, it was regretfully concluded that they offered no simple mathematical test to distinguish genuine from spurious baselines. For example, the figures for Portuguese Guinea and Albania are similar, yet there can be no doubt that

TABLE 4 Proclaimed straight baselines, excluding archipelagos

	Number of segments	Number of legs	Average length of legs (*nautical miles*)	Longest leg (*nautical miles*)	Maximum distance between baseline and nearest coast (*nautical miles*)
Indented coasts					
Finland	1	179	4·4	8	6
France	11	77	9·1	39	20
Iceland	2	36	21·8	74·1	24
Ireland	6	44	10·8	25·2	10
Sweden	7	95	10·4	30	10
Turkey	2	119	5·2	23·5	9
United Kingdom	1	25	11·3	40·3	10
Fringing islands					
Denmark	19	72	4·9	17·8	7
West Germany	6	18	5·2	21·5	17
Mozambique	5	23	19·7	60·4	10
Portuguese Guinea	1	11	13·9	29	9
Thailand (islands of Phuket and Chang)	2	30	7·4	19·7	10
Yugoslavia	3	26	9·4	22·5	6·6
Debatable validity					
Albania	1	7	12·5	21·2	6
Argentina	3	3	103	120	105
Burma	1	21	39·3	222·3	75
Dominican Rep	4	4	12·7	22·7	4
Ecuador	1	4	86·2	136	52
Guinea	1	1	120	120	17
Haiti	1	10	37·2	111	40
Madagascar	1	37	42·7	123·1	25
Mauritania	1	1	89	89	34·2
Mexico	10	22	16·2	39·4	13
Portugal	1	2	26·4	31·25	21
Thailand (Phangan I)	1	15	8·4	33·75	33
Venezuela	1	1	98·9	98·9	22

the straight baseline is appropriate in the case of Portuguese Guinea, with its multitude of islands which fringe almost the whole coast, and inappropriate in the case of Albania's uncomplicated coastline. The point is also illustrated by the comparable figures for Mexico and the United Kingdom. In this case the British authorities have invoked straight baselines in order to tie the fringing Hebrides to the deeply indented Scottish mainland, while the Mexican government has drawn baselines from a smooth coast to isolated islands in order to close the head of the Gulf of California.

The Geographer of the United States government, apparently conducting a similar search for mathematical precision, has calculated the ratio of land to sea between the straight baseline and the coast. Such ratios have been calculated for a number of countries, including Norway and the United Kingdom (1:3·5), eastern Thailand (1:5) and Burma (1:50). Such an index is a useful guide since it will be generally true that baselines which create a high value will be of doubtful validity. Unfortunately, this is a very laborious index to calculate in most cases, especially along the Finnish, Danish and Yugoslav coasts. Further, in those instances of obvious abuse of the system, as in the case of Burma and Ecuador, it is unnecessary to make the calculation.

In order to compare the effect of the baselines of different countries, it is necessary to make the calculations for a standard breadth of territorial sea, and to relate the increase to the length of the baseline. For example, Ecuador has a mainland straight baseline system of 345 nautical miles; when the present claim of Ecuador to a territorial sea of 200 nautical miles is plotted from the baseline, instead of the coast and adjoining islands, an additional 1,569 square nautical miles are abstracted from the area of high seas. If Ecuador had claimed a breadth of 12 nautical miles, 4,485 square nautical miles would have been annexed from high seas. Calculations to show the erosion of high seas by baselines, assuming a territorial sea 12 nautical miles wide, were made for nine baselines, and the answers were then divided by the length of the baselines. The resulting ratio of area of high sea annexed per mile of baseline is shown for the nine cases in Table 5. This index is easier to calculate than the land-to-water ratio, and it is generally true that a high index suggests that the baseline has been constructed in contravention of the principles laid down in Article 4. Unfortunately, it is also

TABLE 5 *Index to show the erosion of the high seas by selected straight baselines. The method of calculation is described in the text*

Portuguese Guinea	1
Thailand (Chang Island)	1
Thailand (Phangan Island)	4·5
Portugal	4·9
West Germany	6·8
Guinea	9·6
Haiti	10·6
Venezuela	10·6
Ecuador	13

true that the improper use of straight baselines to close very shallow indentations of the coast will annex only small areas from the high seas. For example, although the Portuguese straight baseline causes less erosion of the high seas than the German line, it is obvious that the German line is properly drawn to connect the fringing Frisian Islands, while the Portuguese baseline closes the shallow bays near the mouths of the Tagus and Sado Rivers.

It therefore appears that there is no simple mathematical test which will establish the extent to which particular straight baselines conform with or abuse the principles laid down in Article 4. Each case must be examined separately and judgement made with regard to the unique geographic, historic and economic circumstances. Nevertheless a general profile of both proper and improper baselines can be described. Proper straight baselines usually have a number of segments, each composed of several legs, interspersed with sections of the low-water mark of island and mainland coasts. These are necessary qualifications if the line conforms to the general direction of the coast. The length of individual legs is short and the baseline is rarely more than 24 nautical miles from an exposed coast. These baselines do not usually enclose a high proportion of water to land, and they do not extend the outer limit of territorial waters far into areas of the high seas. By contrast improper straight baselines generally have few segments composed of few legs, and are rarely interspersed with sections of the low-water mark. Individual legs of the baseline may be very long, as Table 4 shows, and may be distant from the exposed coast. Such straight baselines often enclose a high ratio of water to land, and cause the annexation of large areas of the high seas.

It is now proposed to examine examples of proclaimed straight baselines to illustrate these general points, and those cases where baselines seem appropriate will be considered first.

The first group of straight baselines which need illustration are those which have been drawn along deeply indented coasts. Although such coasts also often possess some fringing islands, the best examples are found in northern Norway, western Iceland, the Brittany peninsula, the northwest coast of Scotland, the western Mediterranean coast of Turkey, western Ireland and the Baltic coasts of Sweden and Finland. If the classification of these coasts by McGill is examined, it is apparent that the first five occur in complex hilly or mountainous areas; all except the Turkish coast was fashioned primarily by the action of ice, and in Iceland there has been the added complication of volcanism.[24] The west coast of Ireland includes both glacial hill and plain areas, while the Finnish and Swedish coasts are complex glacial plains which experienced extensive post-Wisconsin marine submergence followed by subsequent emergence caused by isostatic rebound. The Irish straight baseline was proclaimed on 20 October 1959 from Scart Rocks, Malin Head in the north, to Carnsore Point in the southeast.[25] As Figure 5 shows, the line consists of six segments connected together by four sections of mainland or island coast. The six segments are composed of forty-four legs, the longest of which is 25·2 nautical miles long,

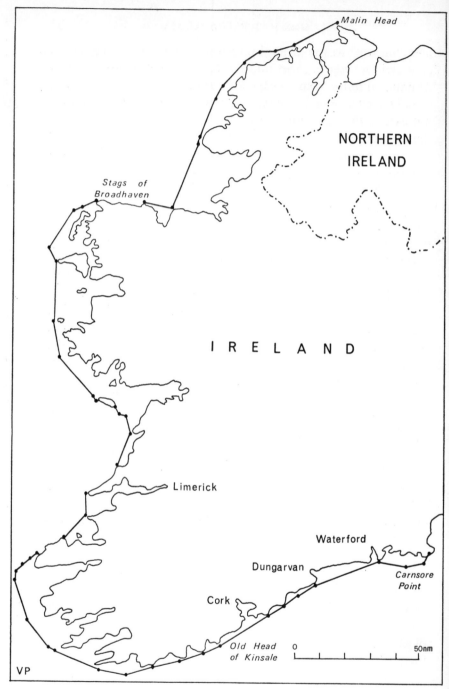

Fig 5 Ireland's straight baselines

enclosing Dungarvan Bay and Waterford Harbour. Twenty-one of the specified points are on the mainland of Ireland and a similar number are on islands. The remaining eight are set on rocks which are permanently above water. The straight baseline preserves the general direction of the coast and it is noteworthy that, unlike the Norwegian government, the Irish authorities have not used the outermost islands in each case. Tory Island in the north, the Stags of Broadhaven in the west, and Fastnet Rocks in the south lie outside the straight baseline. It is evident, even on small-scale maps, that the west coast of Ireland is much more deeply indented than the south coast, and a case could be made out for using the low-water mark east of the Old Head of Kinsale supplemented by bay or estuary closing lines at Cork, Waterford and Youghal.

The straight baseline in northwest Iceland, which stretches for 76 nautical miles from Horn to Bjargtangar, provides a good example of the use of such a system on a deeply indented coastline (Figure 6). The Finnish declaration of straight baselines on 18 August 1956 was unusual because it enunciated the principles on which the turning points were selected.[26] First, the points are designed to create the largest area of 'inner territorial waters' possible. These are presumably internal waters. Secondly, consecutive points must not be further apart than twice the breadth of the territorial sea; at present this distance is 8 nautical miles. Thirdly, the location of the points will be reviewed every thirty years.

The second group of straight baselines are those drawn along the outer edges of islands fringing the coast. Straight baselines related to islands have been proclaimed by the governments of West Germany, Denmark, Yugoslavia, Thailand, Mozambique and Portuguese Guinea, and these six examples provide a variety of fringing island forms. The east and north Frisian Islands, which lie off the coasts of West Germany and Denmark between the German–Dutch border and the Skallingen peninsula, mark the outer line of dunes which once fringed this entire coast. They were submerged during late Quaternary times and

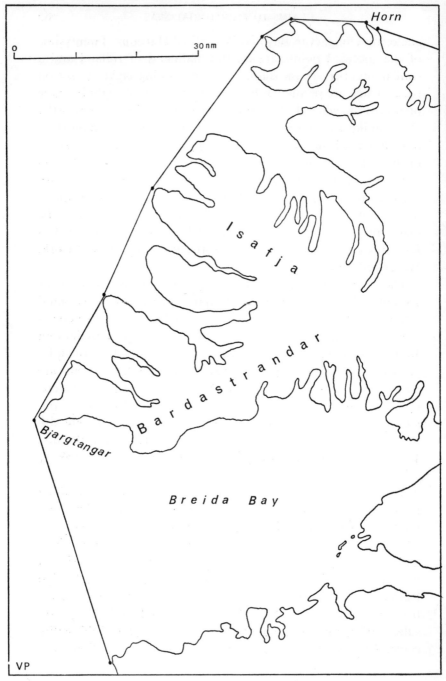

Fig 6   A section of Iceland's straight baselines

divided into several linear islands, such as Fano, Romo, Sylt and Langeoog. The east coast of Denmark has resulted mainly from the advance and retreat of ice-sheets over the shallow platform on which the Danish archipelago stands.[27] Lobes of the ice-sheets gouged channels, which have been subsequently filled by the sea, such as the Little Belt, and morainic deposits were laid down between the lobes as low hills. The islands off the coasts of Yugoslavia and Thailand are associated with complex mountains which drowned during the Quaternary changes in sea-level. Along the Yugoslavian coast, sea-level in early Quaternary times was probably 400 feet below its present level. The subsequent rise has drowned the basins and valleys, leaving the outer ranges, folded during the Tertiary period, as islands still reflecting the grain of the Dinaric Alps.[28] The northern coast of Mozambique is fringed with coral reefs and islands, while the islands masking the coast of Portuguese Guinea were formed in the swampy estuary of the Geba and Corubal, where mangroves abound. The Yugoslav straight baseline was proclaimed on 23 April 1965, between Capes Zarabaca and Kastanija; it consists of three segments totalling 244·7 nautical miles, which are connected by the low-water marks of the island of Mljet for 22 nautical miles and the island of Dugi Otok for 26 nautical miles. The three segments comprise twenty-six individual legs. Six low-tide elevations mark turning points along the straight baseline and each has a lighthouse on it, in accordance with the conditions of Article 4. Part of the Danish straight baseline, proclaimed on 21 December 1966, tied the Baltic islands of Samso, Fyn, Langeland, Aero and Als to the mainland. This was achieved by seven segments linked by sections of the low-water mark of each of the islands, as Figure 7 shows. The nine individual legs, which total 68·6 nautical miles, preserve the direction of the coast very closely. In some studies the Geographer has introduced the concept of fringing islands screening the coast. In the case of the Danish baseline mentioned above the islands screen 73 of the 80 nautical miles of the coast of Jutland.[29] This is another helpful guide to the

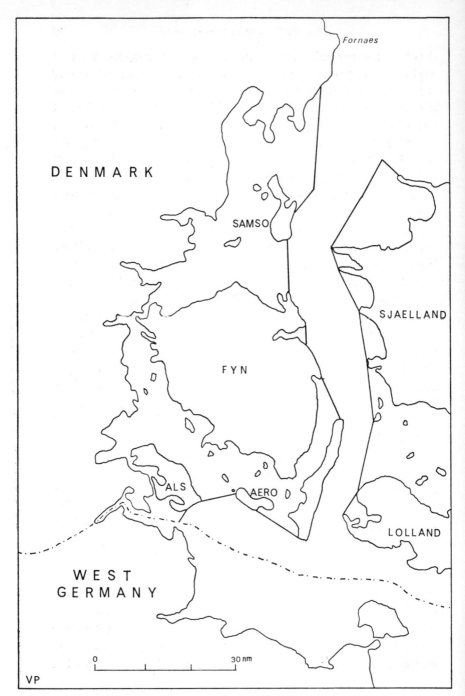

Fig 7   A section of Denmark's straight baselines

proper interpretation of fringing islands, but there are two disadvantages which prevent it from being completely reliable. First, even with identical patterns of islands, different measures would be obtained on coasts which had differing degrees of embayment or indentation. Secondly, this measure is unable to take account of the degree of association between the islands and the mainland, which must be an important consideration.

Before examining those cases where countries have proclaimed straight baselines which do not seem to accord with the principles laid down in Article 4, it is necessary to note that there are cases where states combine segments clearly permissible in terms of the Article with others of doubtful validity. The smoother nature of the southern coast of Ireland compared with the west coast has already been noted; other countries which may have extended their straight baselines further than they should include Madagascar, Thailand and Mozambique. The government of Madagascar has drawn a single straight baseline 2,029 nautical miles long around the south, west and northeast coasts of the island from Sainte Luce to Foulpointe. A straight baseline can be justified on the northwest coast between Cape d'Ambre and Cape St Andre because of deep indentations, and along the remainder of the west coast as far as Point Fenambosy because of the widespread coral reefs, but elsewhere the coastline is too smooth and the coral reefs too narrow to justify drawing straight baselines. However, it must be conceded that the baselines along the south and east coast do not cause any significant annexation of the high seas.

The Thai straight baseline was declared in three areas of the coast on 12 June 1970. The segment along the Thai coast of the Malacca Strait stretches for 156·1 nautical miles between the border with Malaysia and the island of Phuket. This straight baseline encloses seven large islands and a myriad of small islets, which undoubtedly fringe the coast. It is also significant that the outermost islands have not been used in every case. The second segment is 66 nautical miles long and ties the islands of Chang and Kut, together with several smaller islands, to the Thai coast just west of the Cambodian border. Once again these islands screen more than three-quarters of the coast with which they are closely associated. However, the third segment on the west coast of the Gulf of Siam is difficult to justify. This segment is 126·5 nautical miles long and joins Cape Yai in the north with Cape Kho Khao in the south, as Figure 8 shows. From the northern terminus to Hin Bai Island, a distance of 76 nautical miles, the baseline connects seven isolated islands, which cannot be described as fringing the coast. From the island of Phangan southwards the baseline follows an outer line of large islands, which, together with another line further west, centred on Phaluai Island, effectively screen the Thai coast. The straight baseline of Mozambique consists of five segments, of which only the two longest are considered here. The first, occupying 140 nautical miles from Cape Delgado to Point Maunhane, encloses a coast which is both embayed and fringed with numerous small islands and reefs. The second segment, which stretches for 244 nautical miles between the Bay of Conducia and the mouth of the Moniga River, encloses a coast which is generally smooth and which has too few islands to justify drawing a straight baseline.

Since 1 March 1960, when Albania proclaimed a straight baseline along a gently embayed coast, a number of other states have established straight baselines which fail to satisfy the principles of Article 4. Various arguments, associated with the form of the individual coasts, have been used to justify these actions.

The Albanian coast between the mouth of the river Bojana and Cape Gjuhezes, which is the section contained by the straight baseline, offers a sharp contrast with the Yugoslav coast to the north. The grain of the Albanian topography is transverse to the coast, whereas the Dinaric grain and coast are roughly parallel. Low limestone spurs covered with garrigue occur as headlands, such as Capes Rodonit and Lagit, and they alternate with smooth bays with alluvial coasts laid down by the discharge of rivers, such as the Drin and Shkumbin, which

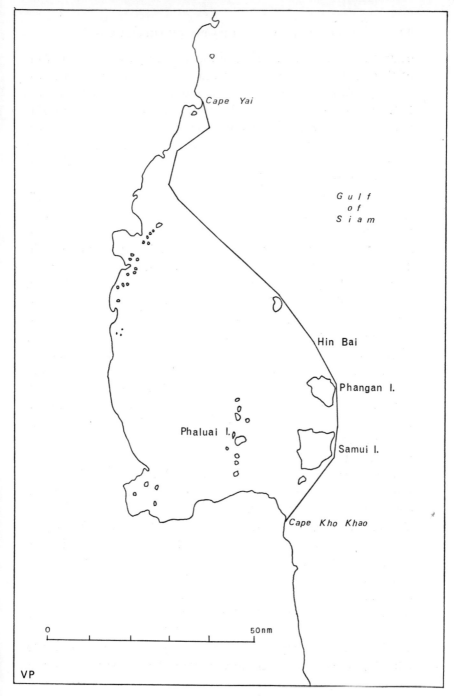

Fig 8   A section of Thailand's straight baselines

drain the interior mountains. With the exception of the island of Sazan, the baseline passes from headland to headland, enclosing two bays which satisfy the requirements of the convention and five which do not. However, because the bays do not penetrate deeply into the coastline, the effect on the outer boundary of the territorial waters is very slight.

The authorities in Argentina, Haiti, and the Dominican Republic have used straight baselines to close bays, which did not meet the requirements for legal bays in the convention and which they presumably judged could not be claimed as historic bays. On 6 September 1967, the Dominican government proclaimed straight baselines closing various bays; four of which do not meet the legal requirements of a bay. These four bays—Yuma, Andres, Ocoa and Esenada de los Aguilas—all have mouths smaller than 24 nautical miles, but they fail to satisfy the semicircular test. The government in Buenos Aires, on 29 December 1966, announced straight baselines closing three distinct bays, of which only the Nuevo Gulf satisfies the requirements for a legal bay. San Matias Gulf requires a closing line of 65 nautical miles and the Gulf of San Jorge is 58 nautical miles wider. The concept of straight baselines was not meant to be used in such situations and Argentina would have to establish claims to the status of historic bays for these features to conform with the convention.

The government of Haiti, on 6 April 1972, proclaimed, by implication, a straight baseline of ten segments. The regulation designated, on a map with the scale of 1:5 million, the outer limits of Haiti's territorial sea by ten straight lines, which began at the northern terminus of the boundary with the Dominican Republic and ended at the southern terminus. Since Haiti claims a territorial sea of 12 nautical miles, it follows that the baseline from which this sea is measured lies 12 nautical miles landward of the outer limits. One of the segments closes the Gulf of La Gonave, which has a mouth 89 nautical miles wide. The large island of La Gonave effectively closes the head of this gulf, but the straight baseline pushes the outer limit of the territorial sea 40 nautical miles further from the coast of the island.

The common coastal feature associated with the straight baselines of Mauritania and Guinea is a wide area of shallow water on a gently embayed coast. On 3 June 1964 the administration of Guinea announced that the territorial sea would be measured from a straight line 'passing by' the southwest of Sene Island in the north and Tamara Island in the south. These two points lie 120 nautical miles apart but, if it is assumed that the line is continued in both directions to the parallels declared by Guinea to separate its territorial sea from those of its neighbours, it will be 42 nautical miles longer. The straight baseline lies very close to the outer limit of shoal water, except opposite Taboria, where shoal water lies 14 nautical miles inside the line. There are certain Guinean islands, such as Alcatraz, which lie outside the straight baseline and, because of this and the wide territorial seas claimed by Guinea, the straight baseline does not cause much erosion of the high seas.

The Mauritanian straight baseline, decreed on 21 January 1967, stretches for 90 nautical miles between Capes Blanc and Timiris.[30] The line encloses a gently curved bay, which contains a dozen islands. The entire bay is filled by the Arguin Bank, which is generally less than 15 metres (8 fathoms) deep, and the baseline includes two-thirds of the bank as internal waters of the state. Both these shallow regions off Guinea and Mauritania are important local fishing grounds, and the baselines enable both countries to increase the area over which they possess exclusive fishing rights.

Four states—Argentina, Portugal, Venezuela and Burma—have established straight baselines which appear to be designed to close large estuaries or bays fed by important rivers. Uruguay and Argentina, on 30 January 1961, jointly claimed the waters of la Plata estuary, by drawing a straight line between Punta del Este in Uruguay and Punta Rosa in Argentina. This line is 120 nautical miles long, and it is justified by these two states under Article 13 of the territorial seas convention which allows river

G

mouths to be closed by a straight line. This argument is presumably employed because the estuary is too wide at the mouth to satisfy the conditions for a bay, and because it would be more difficult to establish claims to the status of an historic bay, even though it is listed as such in a memorandum on historic bays.[31] No reputable geomorphologist would fix the mouth of la Plata River in .he location selected by the two states. Between Capes Raso and Sines the Portuguese authorities have drawn a straight baseline which seals the two bays at the mouths of the Sado and Tagus Rivers. The Tagus Bay could be considered a legal bay if the waters of the estuary were considered part of the sea, but the estuary is too distinct for this to be a reasonable suggestion. The Sado Bay is too wide to count as a legal bay, because the mouth is 31 nautical miles wide. Even if the closing line was drawn at the maximum width of 24 nautical miles, the isolated waters of the Sado estuary would have to be counted as sea for the bay to satisfy the convention's requirements.

By a presidential decree dated 10 July 1968, the government of Venezuela drew a straight baseline 99 nautical miles long across the mouth of the bay into which the river Orinoco flows. The very shallow waters, generally less than 7 metres (4 fathoms), between the baseline and the coast, give this claim some common features with the claims of Guinea and Mauritania. The world's longest baseline segment was drawn by the Burmese government on 15 November 1968, when the Gulf of Martaban was closed by a line 222 nautical miles long. This gulf receives drainage from the Irrawaddy and Salween Rivers. The entire Burmese baseline is justified on the grounds of 'geographical conditions' and the need to safeguard the vital economic interests of coastal inhabitants but it is hard to see what arguments would justify this particular segment, which at one point is 75 nautical miles away from the nearest land.

Two countries have made use of islands, which are clearly not fringing islands in the sense intended by Article 4, as the basis for straight baselines. The Burmese baselines on the Tenasserim coast, between Long and Cabusa Islands, and on the Arakan coast, between Cheduba and Koronge Islands, lie off smooth coasts exposed to the open sea without the benefit of screening islands. On 30 August 1968, the Mexican government established a system of straight baselines in the Gulf of California, consisting of ten segments. Seven of these segments connect isolated islands to the smooth coast on the western coast of the gulf, another segment serves the same function on the eastern side, and the remaining two close the head of the gulf as Mexican internal waters, at the island of San Sebastian. This arrangement excludes areas of high seas that previously existed near the head of the gulf.

One of the best examples of a baseline contravening Article 4 is provided by Ecuador. The government of Ecuador proclaimed a system of straight baselines on 28 June 1971, part of which enclosed the entire mainland coast, while the remainder surrounded the Galapagos Islands. Figure 9 shows that the mainland baseline is 345 nautical miles long and consists of four legs, the shortest being 56 nautical miles long. There are four reasons why this baseline seems to be at complete variance with the conditions of Article 4. First, the line does not conform with the general direction of the coast. With such a small number of long baselines it is obviously very difficult to satisfy this condition. The most obvious departure from the alignment of the coast concerns the leg which joins Point Santa Elena with a location on latitude 3° 23′ 33″ south. There appears to be no good reason why a series of shorter baselines could not have been drawn to preserve the shape of the Gulf of Guayaquil. Secondly, the coast of Ecuador is not deeply indented or cut into. Thirdly, one of the turning points of the baseline is on the island la Plata. This is an isolated island, 14 nautical miles from the coast; in no sense can it be considered part of a group of fringing islands in the immediate vicinity of the coast. Fourthly, the southern terminus of the straight baseline is neither a high-tide elevation nor low-tide elevation surmounted by a permanent structure, it is simply a point on the surface of the sea. It is not difficult to predict that if the straight baseline along the mainland of

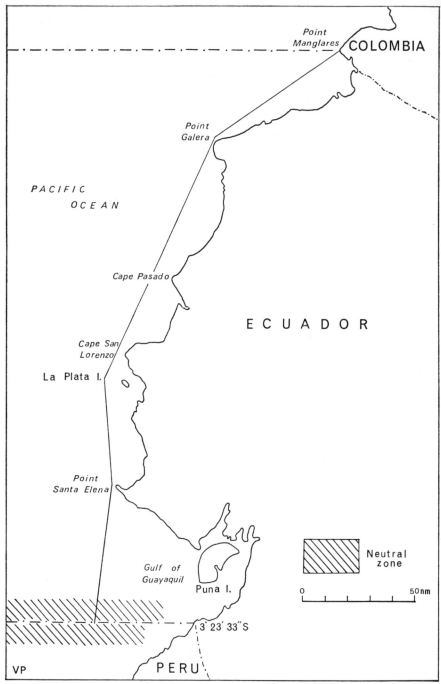

Fig 9 Ecuador's straight baselines

Ecuador is generally accepted by other states, there will be increasing abuse of the provisions of Article 4, to a point where it becomes irrelevant.

Article 7 exempts historic bays from the provisions relating to the definition of legal bays and straight baselines. Strohl suggests that the earliest use of the term 'historic bay' occurred in 1910, when Drago dissented from the North Atlantic Coast Fisheries Arbitration.[32] The concept has caused much debate amongst international jurists, and the best accounts of the various legal issues and opinions are provided by Strohl and Bouchez.[33] The niceties of the legal controversies do not concern the geographer, who is more concerned with the practical results of state actions. In this sense the significance for geographers of the concept of historic bays can be easily stated.

Recourse to proclamations of authority over historic bays allows states to escape from the provisions concerning the drawing of straight baselines and the definition of legal bays. This escape is simplified by the lack of codification of international law regarding historic bays. This means that there is no bay which cannot be claimed on one basis or another. The importance of this situation rests in the fact that the waters of historic bays fall within the internal waters of the state; there is no right of innocent passage through them.[34] Although there is no codification of international law which describes the characteristics of historic bays, or the processes by which they can be challenged, there is some agreement about the conditions under which claims to historic bays should be considered valid. First, there must be a formal claim to the bay by the state concerned; secondly, the state should have exercised an overt sovereignty in the waters for a sufficiently long period; and thirdly, other states should have acquiesced in the exercise of that sovereignty.

Table 6 lists the bays which are generally considered to have been claimed on historic grounds. It was compiled from the United Nations Memorandum on Historic Bays, the specific studies of Bouchez and Strohl, and the publications of the Geographer of the United States State Department.[35] The list

TABLE 6 Historic bays listed by various authorities named in the text

Australia	Blue Mud Bay	Roebuck Bay
	Broad Sound	St Vincent's Gulf
	Buckingham Bay	Shark Bay
	Coffin Bay	Spencer Gulf
	Exmouth Gulf	Storm Bay
	Hervey Bay	Streaky Bay
	Investigator Strait	Upstart Bay
	Moreton Bay	Van Diemen Gulf
	Oyster Bay	
Bulgaria	Burgas Bay	Stalin Bay
Canada	Chaleur Bay	Hudson Bay
	Conception Bay	Miramichi Bay
China	Gulf of Po Hai	
Congo (Brazzaville)	Luango Bay	Pointe Noire Bay
Dominica	Escocesa Bay	Samana Bay
	Negba Bay	Santo Domingo Bay
	Ocoa Bay	
France	Granville Bay	
Gabon	Cape Lopez Bay	Gabon Estuary
	Corisco Bay	Mondah Bay
Guatemala	Amatique Bay	
Kenya	Ungwana Bay	
Netherlands	Zuider Zee	
Norway	Varanger Fjord	Vest Fjord
Panama	Gulf of Panama	
Portugal	Sado Bay	Tagus Bay
Sweden	Laholm Bay	Skeldervieen Bay
Territory of Afar and Issa	Tadjoura Bay	
Tunisia	Gulf of Gabes	Gulf of Tunis
Union of Soviet Socialist Republics	Chukchi Sea	Peter the Great Bay
	East Siberian Sea	Riga Bay
	Kara Sea	Sea of Azov
	Lapteu Sea	
United Kingdom	Bristol Channel	
United States of America	Chesapeake Bay	Monterey Bay
	Delaware Bay	Penobscot Bay
	Long Island Sound	Santa Monica Bay

contains a great variety of bays and some arctic seas, which stretch the meaning of the word beyond recognition. In size the features vary from Hudson Bay with an area of 472,000 square miles to the Bay of Luango with an area of only 37 square miles. With the exception of the Gulf of Panama between Points Mala and Jaque, the bays do not form important parts of ocean routes unconnected with the state making the claim. In this sense Hyde was correct when he made the following judgements:

> . . . the geographical relationship of those waters to that State were generally deemed to be such as to justify assertion and to discourage foreign opposition to it. Thus, the situation, that made the bay geographically a part of its territory, was the decisive factor . . . What, however, still weighs the scale in favor of the freedom of the individual State is the circumstance that its assertions of dominion do not necessarily extend over areas that in a geographical sense constitute a part of the high sea, and are chiefly confined to acts which in their application are primarily local and involve little interference between foreign States generally.[36]

All the historic bays on the list, with the exception of the Gulf of Panama, would only affect traffic travelling to and from the claimant state. However, the proclamation of historic bays also excludes alien fishing vessels and warships from the waters. It does seem that the majority of historic bays have been claimed on economic grounds connected with fishing, or for strategic reasons. One other important fact about the list of historic bays is that only two have been claimed or come to notice as probable claims since the United Nations memorandum of 1958. On 22 September 1959, the government of Thailand proclaimed the Bight of Thailand, north of parallel 12° 35′ 45″ north, to be an 'historical gulf'. In the same year a Chinese author, Fu Chu, noted that the Gulf of Pohai could be claimed on historic grounds.[37] By contrast, a number of countries, which were listed in 1958 as claiming historic bays, have subsequently closed those bays by systems of straight baselines, without any reference to their special status. The Portuguese, Swedish and French proclamations of straight baselines made no mention of the historic bays listed in Table 6, although they all are contained within the respective baselines. The Dominican government, when creating its straight baseline, declared that the Bays of Santo Domingo and Escocesa were claimed on historic grounds, but made no mention of the Bays of Samana, Ocoa and Neyba, which had been credited to the Dominican Republic in 1958.

It is possible that states have not attempted to claim historic bays in recent years because it is easier to proclaim straight baselines. It is almost certain, if the imprecise language of Article 4 had not allowed states to circumvent the regulations dealing with legal bays, that countries such as Burma and Ecuador would have laid claim to historic bays instead.

THE DIVISION OF TERRITORIAL WATERS BETWEEN STATES

States which share a coastline, and states separated by seas which are narrower than the combined width of their territorial seas, must draw boundaries to separate their territorial waters. Article 12 requires states to reach agreement in such cases but, in the absence of agreement, neither state may extend its control beyond the line of equidistance. Although Boggs had enunciated this principle in 1930, the technique had been used before that. In 1920, the Versailles powers drew such a boundary between the territorial waters of Germany and Denmark in the North Sea. There are many more cases of land boundaries being extended through the territorial seas between 1930 and the creation of the convention in 1958: for example, the Soviet Union and Finland had agreed on boundaries separating their territorial waters in both the Baltic and Barents Seas in 1940. The boundary in the Barents Sea was abandoned in 1944 by the Petsamo cession of 1944, but the initial boundary of 22·4 nautical miles in the Baltic was extended for another 7·4 nautical miles on 20 May 1965.[38] On 15 February 1957 the Soviet Union and Norway agreed on a boundary separating their territorial waters. The boundary was drawn as a straight line linking Buoy 415, which is situated just off the coast and marked the end of the boundary in 1947, to the intersection of the territorial waters claimed by both countries. Now since the Soviet Union claims 12 nautical miles and Norway claims only 4 nautical miles, it would seem that this scheme favours the Soviet Union. However, the Norwegian territorial sea is measured from a straight baseline which closes the mouth of Varanger Fjord, which is classed as an historic bay. In order to remove all possibility of confusion, it was specified that the Soviet territorial sea would be measured from a particular cape.

Along coasts which are not complicated by the presence of numerous islands, states are tending increasingly to draw simple continuations of their common land boundaries through territorial waters. For example the boundaries separating the territorial waters of Cyprus and the British Sovereign Base Areas are fixed by a series of lines defined by bearings from true north and distances in nautical miles, which represent generalised lines of equidistance. No terminus has been set for these four boundary segments, shown in Figure 10, and it must be presumed that this is designed to avoid the possibility that either government might increase its territorial sea to a point which encloses the territorial sea of the other government. However, it should be noted that while the two lines defining the territorial waters of the western British territory diverge from each other as they recede from the coast, the lines bounding the eastern area meet 34 nautical miles off the coast. It is also possible that the lines have been left without a definite terminus because of the possibility that the continental shelf may be exploited beyond the limits of territorial waters.

The governments of the United States and Mexico adopted a novel solution to the problem of the irregular shifting of the land terminus of their common boundary on the coast of the Gulf of Mexico. The terminus coincides with the centre of the mouth of the Rio Grande, wherever that happens to be. In

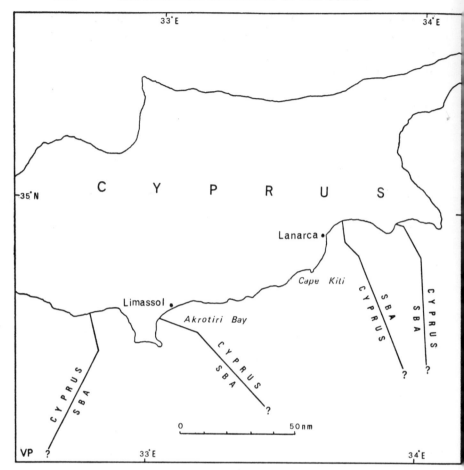

Fig 10 Division of territorial waters between Cyprus and British Sovereign Base Areas

order to avoid the need to change the boundary, as the mouth of the river shifts its position, the governments have agreed to a fixed point, 2,000 feet (610 metres) due east of the centre of the mouth as it existed on 23 November 1970, when the agreement was concluded. The permanent boundary is then drawn from this fixed point, which has the co-ordinates 25° 27′ 22·18″ north and 97° 8′ 19·76″ west, to another fixed point, with the co-ordinates 25° 58' 30·57" north and 96° 55' 27·37" west, 12 nautical miles off the coast. As the mouth of the Rio Grande shifts, the short section of boundary between the closest fixed point and the centre of that mouth will hinge about the fixed point.[39]

Chile, Peru and Ecuador have agreed that the boundaries between their respective territorial waters will be drawn along the parallels which intersect the coast at the termini of the land boundaries. It has also been agreed that, beginning at a distance 12 nautical miles from the coast, a special zone 20 nautical miles wide will be constructed astride the boundary. This zone is designed to avoid problems associated with accidental intrusion by the nationals of neighbouring countries in foreign territorial waters. A parallel of latitude is of course an arbitrary line, and because of the general direction of the coast, Peru forfeits territorial waters to Ecuador. Such a loss is obviously considered minor compared with the benefit of having a clear boundary, easily determined by mariners. The situation is rather different in the case of Guinea. That country declared unilateral limits to its territorial sea, and selected parallels of latitude. The southern parallel 9° 3' 18" sacrifices territorial waters to neighbouring Sierra Leone. However, the northern parallel 10° 56' 42·55" cuts deeply into waters which can be legitimately claimed by Portuguese Guinea as a basis of equidistance. It even places within Guinean waters the island of Poilao, which forms part of the straight baseline system of Portuguese Guinea. Venezuela is another country which has made a unilateral declaration regarding the extent of its territorial waters at the expense of its eastern neighbour Guyana. Venezuela claims part of western Guyana and has fixed the eastern terminus of its straight baseline across the mouth of the Orinoco River 25 nautical miles east of the present terminus of the common land boundary at Playa Point.

Boundaries between states holding the opposite shores of narrow straits have also been drawn on the basis of lines of equidistance. On 17 March 1970 Indonesia and Malaysia agreed to a common boundary separating their territorial waters through the Malacca Strait. The boundary consists of two segments, a short one of 4 nautical miles long at the eastern end of the strait and another 130 miles long through the western reaches. These lines are drawn equidistant from the straight baselines on either side. The strait at one point widens slightly and the territorial waters measured from each side do not meet. This leaves a small area of high seas measuring 40 square nautical miles. The Swedish and Danish authorities in 1932 drew a boundary separating their territorial waters through the entrance to the Baltic Sea. The northern and southern termini of this boundary, together with some of the points along it were fixed strictly on the basis of equidistance. At other parts of the line, however, it was decided to ignore the presence of certain islands, such as Ven, and draw a boundary equidistant from the Danish and Swedish mainlands.

ARCHIPELAGOS

Problems concerned with the territorial waters of mid-ocean archipelagos proved too difficult to solve at the 1958 conference, just as they had earlier defeated the 1930 conference.[40] The problem of coastal archipelagos appears to have been solved, because many states, such as Norway and Finland, have simply tied them to the coast by a series of straight baselines. Support for the special treatment of mid-ocean archipelagos, by surrounding them with a system of straight baselines connecting their outermost islands, was led at the 1958 conference by Indonesia and the Philippines, which are the two states most concerned. Opposition came principally from the United States and the United Kingdom, which were apparently anxious to avoid the conversion of large areas of the high seas to internal waters.

Mid-ocean archipelagos possess a considerable diversity of geographical characteristics and differing degrees of integration between the islands and the intervening seas. For the purposes of this discussion it is sufficient to suggest a simple, subjective classification of archipelagos based on the size of constituent islands, and the nature of their distribution. First, there are archipelagos where all the islands are small; secondly, there are archipelagos which consist of one or two large islands, surrounded by several small ones; and thirdly, there are archipelagos which contain several large islands. In each category there are two possible distributions: the islands may form a compact or a scattered group. The categories are represented in Table 7, which also includes examples of each.

TABLE 7 A suggested classification of archipelagos

Composition	Distribution Compact	Scattered
Small islands	Laeso (Denmark)*	Tonga
	Sjelland (Denmark)*	Solomon Islands
	Faroes (Denmark)*	Canary Islands
	Bear Island (Norway)*	Azores
	Dahlak (Ethiopia)*	Bahamas
		Maldives*
One or two large islands and several small islands	Sri Lanka	Galapagos (Ecuador)*
	Cuba	Hawaii (USA)
	Fiji	Mauritius?
	Greenland (Denmark)	New Zealand
	Iceland*	Trinidad and Tobago
	Madagascar*	
	Puerto Rico	
	Taiwan	
	United Kingdom	
Several large islands	Japan	Indonesia*
	Philippines*	Papua New Guinea

* Straight baselines proclaimed
? Position uncertain

Now it is probable that straight baselines surrounding compact archipelagos of the first and second groups do not really give concern to the opponents of the provisions for special consideration. Such baselines do not reduce the area of the high seas significantly. Reservations might be held against this generalisation by individual states, depending on the location of the archipelago and the nature of its offshore resources. Thus the presence of important sea routes near even small archipelagos may make maritime states think that straight baselines are inappropriate. Presumably British trawling interests would have preferred the Icelandic exclusive fishing zone to be measured from the low-tide mark rather than existing straight baselines across Faxafloi Bay.

The other four categories involve situations where large areas of the high seas would be transferred to the status of internal waters. For example, Indonesia's straight baseline system of 8,167·6 nautical miles, proclaimed on 18 February 1960, encloses 666,000 square nautical miles of internal waters; and the Philippines' straight baseline, measuring 8,174 nautical miles, encloses 148,921·5 square nautical miles of internal waters. This alone would encourage resistance by the maritime states, but there is the additional factor that Indonesia and the Philippines are located athwart important trade routes between Japan and Europe.

By the middle of 1973 twelve archipelagos, controlled by ten countries, had been surrounded by straight baselines. It seems increasingly probable that the debate about this matter in future will centre less on the legality of such action, and more on the status of the waters within the baselines. Providing that the right of free passage is maintained through the former high seas, now located within the straight baselines, there will be a chance of compromise between the contending states.

PASSAGE THROUGH INTERNATIONAL STRAITS

One of the important results of a general increase in the breadth of the territorial seas to 12 nautical miles would be the elimination of corridors of high seas through a number of international straits. The United Nations Secretariat listed thirty-two such straits.[41] The major non-communist maritime countries have expressed concern at this possible development which would affect them in three ways. First, there would be no right of unrestricted flight over the straits occupied by territorial waters. Secondly, the unrestricted freedom of navigation through the strait would be replaced by innocent passage in compliance with the regulations of the coastal state. Thirdly, the right of warships to pass through the strait, without consent, would be in dispute. These major maritime states have urged that vessels should have a clear and secure right to pass through such straits, a view which is opposed by many other riparian states which believe that the right of innocent passage is sufficient. This matter was not resolved at the conferences held in 1958 and 1960, and there has been no general agreement in the preparatory meetings for the 1974 conference.

Table 8 lists the straits involved and distinguishes those controlled by the major non-communist maritime powers and their associates from all others. It seems fair to assume that the fears of the maritime states regarding this question are groundless in respect of the eighteen international straits controlled by members of their group. Turning to the other fourteen international straits, it is apparent that they fall into three groups. First there are the six straits which are not important for international traffic and for which alternative routes exist. This group includes the Straits of Magellan, Zanzibar, Hai-nan and Palk, and the Dragon's Mouth and the Serpent's Mouth. Such straits have only local significance and none of the major maritime states would be seriously inconvenienced if restrictions were placed on their use. Secondly, there are five straits which are important for international commerce and for which there are alternative, albeit much longer, routes. This group consists of the Straits of Singapore, Malacca, Sunda, San Bernadino and Surigao. If restrictions were placed on these straits, much international commerce would be seriously disrupted. It will be noticed that all these straits are located off the shores of Asia, and traffic from Europe and the Middle East to Japan would have to travel via Bass Strait if impossible restrictions were placed on innocent passage through them. There is no obvious reason why the riparian states involved should wish to

TABLE 8 International straits entirely occupied by territorial waters 12 nautical miles wide

Straits in which major maritime state or dependency has riparian rights	Straits in which major maritime states have no riparian rights
Bonifacio	*Minor straits*
Chosen	Dragon's Mouth
Cook	Hai-nan
Dominica	Magellan
Dover	Palk
Foveaux	Serpent's Mouth
Gibraltar	Zanzibar
Juan de Fuca	
Kaiwi	*Important straits which have*
Karpathos	*alternatives*
Kithera	Malacca
Martinique	San Bernadino
Messina	Singapore
Minorca	Sunda
Oresund	Surigao
St George	
St Lucia	*Important straits without*
St Vincent	*alternatives*
	Bab al Mandab
	Dardanelles
	Hormuz

create unnecessary difficulties, but the maritime states would prefer that the opportunities for disruption did not exist. The only restrictions imposed to date have concerned oil tankers. Tankers with a capacity in excess of 200,000 dead weight tons may not pass fully loaded through the Malacca Strait, thus giant tankers plying between the Persian Gulf and Japan may only use the strait in ballast. When fully laden they must use the Lombok Strait, which increases the journey by 950 nautical miles, making the journey three days longer. Tankers in excess of 500,000 dead weight tons will have to use the Lombok Strait in both directions, which increases the journey by six days.

The three remaining straits are all important routes and there are no alternative sea routes. The strait consisting of the Dardanelles, the Sea of Marmara, and the Bosporus is of particular importance to the countries bordering the Black Sea, and passage through these waterways is governed by the Montreux convention of 1936. This convention allows the untrammelled passage of commercial vessels, and distinguishes between the warships of states bordering the Black Sea and other states. Apart from aircraft carriers and submarines, the warships of Black Sea states may pass through the straits without hindrance. Only the light warships of other states may pass through the straits, subject to restrictions about the tonnage of such vessels, the number of units in the area at any time, and the duration of the cruise. In times of war, when Turkey is neutral, the straits are closed to all warships.

The Strait of Bab al Mandab has four riparian states, and it is of great international importance when the Suez Canal is open. The existence of four riparian states means that it would be difficult to obtain concerted action regarding the regulations governing passage through the strait, and navigation is possible on either side of the line of equidistance drawn through the Large Strait, between Perim Island and the African coast. The close association of France with the districts of Afar and Issa give the major maritime states some influence in this area. Since the closure of the Suez Canal in 1967, the volume of traffic through this strait has declined significantly. If the Suez Canal is reopened, it seems likely that Egypt would discourage any interference with traffic through this strait, which might have an adverse effect on canal revenue.

The Strait of Hormuz is of particular importance to the maritime countries, because it provides the outlet for tankers exporting oil from the Persian Gulf. Since November 1971, when Iran took advantage of the British withdrawal to seize control of three islands in the strait, Iran has effectively controlled this outlet. There is no evidence that Iran would wish to interfere with traffic through the strait except to exert pressure on Iraq,

H

with which Iran has a number of boundary disputes associated with the Shatt al Arab, the land boundary through Kurdish areas, and the division of the continental shelf at the head of the Persian Gulf. It is noticeable that maritime countries, and especially the United States, have been at pains to establish cordial relations with Iran.

It therefore appears that in the contemporary situation this question of passage through international straits occupied by territorial waters is potential rather than actual. However, the maritime states, aware that claims to territorial waters in excess of 12 nautical miles will extend this potential difficulty to a large number of international straits, would prefer such problems to be removed.

INTERNATIONAL CANALS

There are four international canals which are effectively artificial international straits; they are the Suez, Panama, Kiel and Corinth Canals. These canals have some important common features. They were all built before World War I by maritime states associated with Europe and the North Atlantic in order to shorten commercial and strategic journeys. They have all suffered from the problem that an increasing number of large vessels are unable to use them. On geographical grounds the four canals can be divided into two groups. The Suez and Panama Canals may be characterised as continental canals, which were constructed across the isthmuses between pairs of continents; they offered much shorter routes to those existing at the time of their construction. The Kiel and Corinth Canals were constructed across the bases of peninsulas, and they did not offer the same saving in terms of time and distance over alternative routes. As Table 9 shows the peninsular canals are much less important than the continental canals in terms of shipping tonnage, although the peninsular canals record a greater number of smaller ships in transit.

It is the continental canals which are most important in terms of international traffic and as sources of international friction, and each canal must be examined separately.

From the time the Suez Canal was opened in 1869, until 1956, when it was nationalised by the Egyptian government, it was

TABLE 9 *Traffic on international canals*

	Number of transits	Cargo tonnage
Panama Canal (1971)	14,617	121·0 million tons
Suez Canal (1966)	21,250	274·4 million tons
Kiel Canal (1968)	80,204	43·4 million tons
Corinth Canal (1972)	6,919	4·9 million tons

considered of vital commercial and strategic importance to Britain and other maritime, colonial powers such as France. This belief underlay the Anglo-French intervention at Suez in 1956. Since that time, however, this view has been destroyed, and four developments explain this change. First, Britain and France have shed their colonial and strategic responsibilities in Asia; and such military assistance as Britain might render to Singapore and Malaysia would be provided by air rather than sea transport. Secondly, it now appears that the Soviet Union, with its naval forces in the Black Sea, the Mediterranean, and the Indian Ocean, would have the greatest strategic interest in preserving the operating capacity of the Suez Canal. Thirdly, the construction of crude oil carriers too large to pass through the canal meant that they had to travel around the longer Cape of Good Hope route. Fourthly, because of the interruptions to transit through the canal in 1956 and 1967, many shipping firms, which previously used the Suez Canal, would prefer to use the more secure Cape route.

It did seem, when the canal was closed in June 1967, that there would be pressure on both Israel and Egypt to arrange for it to be reopened as soon as possible. First, it seemed that the maritime states would encourage Israel to take a conciliatory position, because of the very severe problems the closing of the canal created. This development did not occur because the problems were not severe, and adjustments were easily made. Secondly, the importance of canal dues in contributing to Egyptian revenue seemed likely to encourage that country to seek an early settlement. This likelihood did not occur because Saudi Arabia and Kuwait have supplied grants to cover Egypt's financial loss.

If the canal was reopened without any modification it would be able to accommodate tankers of 60,000 dead weight tons fully laden, and tankers of 150,000 dead weight tons in ballast. In 1967 oil represented more than 70 per cent of the cargo by weight carried through the Suez Canal. The Suez Canal Authority announced in 1973 that the canal could be cleared and operating within four months of the commencement of operations, and that plans existed to deepen the canal so that vessels with a draught of 67 feet could pass through. This would represent laden tankers of 250,000 dead weight tons. It was estimated that this programme would be completed in six years. There is some evidence that events may have overtaken any such development. In December 1972, 37 per cent of the world's tanker tonnage consisted of ships too large to pass through the Suez Canal as it existed in 1967. This figure will rise to 54 per cent within three years, because 79 per cent of tanker tonnage on order consists of vessels in excess of 150,000 dead weight tons.[42] Couper also makes the important point that the cost of the expansion programme for the Suez Canal would have to be financed from increased dues.

> It should be noted in this connection that the cost of using the canal, at 1966 levels of dues, plus the cost of ship's time on canal transit and waiting for convoys, etc., almost equals the cost of additional mileage for a 200,000-ton vessel going around the Cape of Good Hope with cargoes for Europe. This close comparison means that any significant increase in dues could confirm the Cape route for the now common size of ship above 200,000 tons.[43]

If the canal is unable to recapture a very large proportion of its former oil traffic, it will be necessary to increase dues still further for other vessels, which might then be deflected from the canal by comparative costs.

There is one other advantage which has recently accrued to the Cape route. To promote safety of shipping the world's oceans are divided into regions of seasonal load-lines. This simply means that vessels in summer regions may carry more cargo, using a deeper draught, than when they are passing through winter regions.[44] In 1966 Cape Town was placed in a permanent summer region, which allows vessels using this route to carry the maximum amount of cargo all the year. On the basis of all this evidence it is impossible to disagree with Couper, when he suggests that on economic grounds alone, the future influence of the Suez Canal on the pattern of world shipping has been significantly reduced.[45]

The Panama Canal is a source of international friction because of Panamanian demands that the United States should renegotiate the treaty of 1903, by which it acquired the Canal Zone, with a view to returning this territory to Panama. These demands are raised every time there is a presidential election in Panama and, since 1971, they have attracted considerable support from the People's Republic of China and several countries in South America. The maritime countries would presumably feel that access to the canal was more secure under American rather than Panamanian administration. It certainly seems probable that the Panama Canal will retain a considerable measure of international importance for a much longer period than the Suez Canal. There are a number of reasons for this. First, most of the traffic through the Panama Canal is carried on ships of less than 30,000 dead weight tons, and oil, where the advantages of bulk carriers have been most obvious, accounts for less than one-quarter of the cargoes by weight carried through the canal. Second, bulk carriers of 67,000 dead weight tons can use the Panama Canal, and such vessels, known as Panimax ships, are still being constructed for trade between the Gulf areas of the United States and Japan. Third, in 1971 the annual number of transits through the canal was 15,000; this figure could be raised to 20,000 before delays would begin to occur because of excess traffic. However, Couper notes that some mammoth carriers already take coal from Hampton Roads, on the east coast of the United States, to Japan via the Cape of Good Hope. He also suggests that an increasing volume of traffic may cross the United States by land, instead of being carried by coastal vessels.[46]

Because of concern that the present canal might prove inadequate in the future it has been suggested on several occasions that the Panama isthmus should be pierced by another, sea-level canal. There are four sites where such a canal could be constructed. The shortest route, of 40 miles, lies east of the present canal near San Blas. Further east a route linking the Sasardi and Menti Rivers stretches for 60 miles across the isthmus. Another route, covering 100 miles follows the narrow neck of land through the Gulf of Uraba and the Truando valley in northern Colombia. Finally, a fourth route is possible along the border between Nicaragua and Costa Rica, skirting the south of Lake Nicaragua; this course is 140 miles long.

There have been several suggestions that an international canal should be constructed to pierce the Kra isthmus of Thailand. In 1793 a proposal was made to cut a small canal to facilitate naval operations against the Burmese. Afterwards, at irregular intervals, similar schemes were proposed, and Levine has published an account of these.[47] Before World War II the Japanese government was in favour of constructing a Kra Canal, but the British government, in firm control of the Malacca Strait and the Singapore naval base, opposed any suggestions along these lines. In 1946, the peace treaty between Britain and Thailand prohibited the construction of a Kra Canal, and this prohibition lasted until 1960. The idea was revived by a consortium, including the then ruling Revolutionary Party, but it was feared that the physical separation, which the canal might create between the southern and northern provinces, would encourage the Malay irredentist movement. For this reason these plans were abandoned. In July 1971, the Japanese government, with the approval of Thai authorities, surveyed three possible routes for an oil pipeline. The final report in March 1972 recommended the southern route between Ban Datu on the west coast and Ban Boso, near Songkhla on the east coast. This 65 mile pipeline would be extended 20 miles under the sea at both ends, in order to cater for giant tankers. The report also noted that such a pipeline would only be economically attractive if it could transfer 150 million kilolitres each year; this volume represented about half of Japan's annual imports from the Middle East at that time. The proposals were later circulated to a variety of Japanese firms, but there was no positive commitment from any Japanese organisation. This apathy to the project is known to have disappointed the Thai National Energy Authority. In July 1972 new investigations into the financial possibility of constructing a canal were ordered by the Thai government. After these investigations, it was announced in the same year, that a 97 mile long, five-lock canal would be built between Phangnga and Ban Don Bay, at an estimated cost of $US450 million (£189 million). Some private Thai authorities are known to favour the shorter, sea-level canal near Songkhla, even though it would cost much more to construct. By conventional excavating techniques a canal to take 500,000 dead weight ton tankers would cost $US6,000 million (£2,521 million); nuclear excavations would cost $US3,800 million (£1,597 million). But the advantage of this canal is that it could take very large crude carriers, whereas the northern canal could only take vessels less than 100,000 dead weight tons, and this would require transhipment operations at each end of the canal. There has been even less enthusiasm for either of the proposed canals amongst Japanese firms, than there was for the proposed pipeline. The Thai government was believed to be still hopeful of completing the project, and its fears that any canal would encourage southern secession have been supplanted by hopes that the economic activity which the canal would generate will reduce discontent in the southern provinces.

CHAPTER FOUR

Fishing Zones

On 18 March 1973, the first live rounds were fired in the third Cod War between Iceland and the United Kingdom. This dispute was precipitated seven months earlier, when Iceland announced an exclusive fishing zone stretching 50 nautical miles seaward of the country's straight baselines. The British government protested against, and resisted, this unilateral declaration on the grounds that it would exclude British fishing fleets from waters where they normally caught 60 per cent of their cod, haddock and plaice. The two earlier Cod Wars had occurred in 1952 and 1958. In the first instance Iceland's proclamation of a series of straight baselines had excluded foreign fishermen from areas of the high seas which were converted to territorial waters and internal waters. In the second case, Iceland extended its exclusive fishing zone for 8 nautical miles beyond the outer limit of its territorial waters, giving a total breadth of 12 nautical miles.

The Anglo-Icelandic dispute is only the most publicised of a series of contemporary fishing disputes, but it should not be thought that fishing disputes are a recent occurrence. Perhaps the first reference to measurement of the territorial sea by cannon fire occurred in 1610 during a dispute between Holland and Great Britain, over herring fisheries off eastern Scotland. Twelve years earlier Denmark, which then controlled Iceland, proclaimed an exclusive fishing zone of 2 leagues around the island's shores, to reduce the activities of foreign fishermen in the rich cod fishing grounds.

There are several reasons why fishing disputes are becoming more common, and perhaps more critical, in modern times. Some of these reasons are of long standing, while others represent a new development.

THE CAUSES OF INTERNATIONAL FISHING DISPUTES

The most obvious cause of fishing disputes results from the very uneven distribution of fish stocks throughout the area of the oceans and seas, and the fluctuations of those stocks over a period of time. At first, with the limited range of fishing craft, only the coastal dwellers closest to the best fishing grounds were able to exploit them. Gradually, neighbouring coastal inhabitants would also begin to exploit these grounds and then, as the range of craft began to increase, fishermen from distant countries began to harvest the resources of the rich grounds. Today there is no practical obstacle, although there may be economic limitations, to the activities of modern trawlers, equipped with radar and fish-detecting equipment, in association with larger, well-equipped factory ships, in waters thousands of miles from their home ports. Thus Russian trawlers have caught shrimps in the Gulf of Carpentaria; Japanese trawlers catch tuna near Mauritius; and Spanish fleets operate off the coast of South West Africa, which is also called Namibia by the United Nations.

A large number of factors, interrelated in a complex way, influence the location of any particular fish stock at any particular time. It is only necessary here to consider the most important. The basic food source for fish is phytoplankton, which consists of microscopic plants. The location of phytoplankton varies significantly across the surface layers of the oceans and seas. The Geographer has produced an excellent map, on a Mercator projection, showing the average daily production of phytoplankton in the world's seas and oceans north of latitude 60° south.[1] The most striking feature of the map is the concentration of high-yielding areas around the world's coasts. The richest phytoplankton pastures lie within 200 nautical miles of continental masses; by contrast the central areas of the oceans are comparative phytoplankton deserts, relieved by only a few small oases associated with parts of the mid-ocean ridges and some island groups. Phytoplankton need a supply of mineral salts and sunlight for growth. Sunlight and salts such as sodium chloride and calcium carbonate are commonly available in the upper layers of the oceans and seas. Therefore it is the availability of phosphates and nitrates, which are unevenly distributed throughout the oceans, which are critical in influencing the production of phytoplankton. These salts are most readily available in deep waters, where they have accumulated as a result of the decay of unused phytoplankton, and they become available in the upper layers where there are strong vertical and horizontal movements of water. Several situations will encourage or discourage such movements. They are obviously encouraged over continental shelves, where the shallow depths allow a much more rapid recycling of the critical nutrients. The effects of tides and deep waves are not available in areas of very deep water. Stormy weather will also encourage the development of waves and facilitate vertical movements, whereas the areas of light winds in the central parts of tropical oceans will lack this advantage. The absence of marked temperature differences between deep and surface waters will encourage vertical water movements. The lowest temperature gradients in the oceans will be found in the temperate and subarctic areas. In tropical regions the surface waters may be as much as 10° C warmer than the deep waters, and the resulting thermocline discourages the vertical movement of water. Strong currents and streams in the oceans will improve the chance of vertical mixing; such movements are strongest near the continents. Finally, strong, persistent offshore winds will promote the upwelling of cold waters from deep basins near the coast.

It is therefore possible to describe the characteristics of the most favourable areas, in terms of the vertical and horizontal exchange of waters, which will create concentrations of phosphates and nitrates. Such areas would be located over continental shelves or mid-ocean banks, in temperate regions where the thermocline between surface and deep waters was either very shallow or absent, where the tidal range was considerable and storms prevalent for part of the year, and across the path of major streams and currents. These characteristics are found over extensive areas of the northern littorals of the Atlantic and Pacific Oceans. Deep upwelling associated in some cases with the major circulatory movements of the oceans, and persistent offshore winds, provides favourable conditions for the growth of phytoplankton off the west coasts of continents in lower latitudes. This is particularly true of the west coast of Africa from the Canary Islands to Ivory Coast and from Gabon to South West Africa, of the west coast of the American continents between California and the Tropic of Capricorn and of the eastern coasts of the Arabian peninsula.

The significance of temperature does not end with consideration of the thermocline between surface and deeper waters; absolute temperatures also impose physiological limits on particular species of fish. For example, the main concentrations of north Atlantic cod are found in waters where the temperature range is from 2° C to 5° C.[2] The main concentrations of hake occur in waters with a temperature range of 4° C to 7° C, and the bluefin tuna shows much more tolerance by occurring in economic concentrations in waters varying from 5° C to 29° C. Coull notes that variations in salinity are mainly important in enclosed or semi-enclosed seas, where comparatively high or low levels of salinity may alter the types of fish found there.[3]

Fluctuations in the location of any fish stock occur over short and long periods. The short-term changes may be due to migrations associated with different stages of the life cycle: for example, the northern North Sea herring stock generally spends winter near the western edge of the Norwegian Trench. In spring, melting ice and snow cause a marked increase in the flow of fresh water into the Baltic Sea, and cause an outflow of cold water, rich in nutrients. The shoals move westwards feeding on the new plankton pastures and spawn off Shetland. From September, the herrings move slowly back to their winter quarters in the Norwegian Trench. Coull has collected many similar accounts of fish migrations in European fishing grounds.[4] There are also longer-term fluctuations in the location and size of fish stocks, but these have not been satisfactorily explained, and there is a risk that the easy answer of over-fishing will be accepted, even though such changes have occurred in historic times without any evidence of over-fishing.

When fishermen of different nationalities begin to compete for these rich, localised fisheries, it is possible for disputes to arise. Although this competition has existed in important fishing grounds such as Iceland, since the fifteenth century, there are a number of factors which make the occurrence and scale of disputes more serious in modern times.

First, the number and size of distant fishing fleets increased during the 1960s. Distant fishing fleets are those which operate in waters remote from their home ports. They are usually larger vessels than those employed in the domestic fisheries, and they generally spend longer at sea on any voyage. In some cases the fleets include factory ships, which allow the processing of fish at sea. Most of the developed countries, such as the Soviet Union, the United States, Japan, and the industrial countries of Europe, have both distant and domestic fishing fleets; in contrast most developing countries rely principally on domestic fleets. Improvements in the design and construction of vessels allow fleets from increasingly remote countries to compete in particular areas. Thus Japanese fleets operate off Iceland, Korean fleets off the coast of South West Africa, and Russian fleets fish off the coast of Argentina. Ranke has even suggested that Iceland can no longer be considered as a distant fishing ground for European countries.[5] He shows that the true distant fishing grounds are now located in the northwest Atlantic from west Greenland to New England, off northwest Africa between Capes Jubi and Verde, near the coast of South West Africa between Cape Fria and Luderitz Bay and off the mouth of la Plata River. The Spanish fleet operating near South West Africa now makes the largest catches of hake of any European fleet and, in 1967, 35 per cent of the Soviet fishing fleet was operating in areas other than the northeast Atlantic and northwest Pacific.

It is difficult to obtain precise information about the operation and distribution of distant fishing fleets, but one simple analysis gives useful approximate results. Each year the United Nations publishes statistics of fish catches, and they contain details of the catch by each country in a number of statistical divisions of the world's oceans.[6] If it is arbitrarily assumed that the catches of countries which are not riparian to the particular area under consideration are made by distant fishing fleets, the following pattern emerges. In 1971, the area of the east central Atlantic, off the coast of west Africa, was fished by eighteen distant fishing fleets, which was the highest total for any region. Apart from the northwest Atlantic, between the west coast of Greenland and the northeast coasts of Canada and the United States of America, where fourteen distant fleets were operating, all other regions had less than nine distant fleets. It should be noted that one of the reasons why the numbers of distant fleets is not higher involves the existence of remaining European colonies and overseas territories scattered around the world. Fragments of territory, such as the French islands of Saint Pierre and Miquelon, the Netherland's Antilles and Portuguese Timor, give the metropolitan states riparian status in distant waters. The areas of the northwest Pacific and the Mediterranean and Black Seas are not fished by any distant fleets, according to the definition used here.

If the proportion of catch won by distant fleets is considered for each area, it is clear that their presence has different levels of importance. There are five areas where distant fleets caught more than 40 per cent of the total for 1971. In descending order, they were the east central Atlantic (59 per cent), the northwest Atlantic (49 per cent), the northeast Pacific (47 per cent), the southwest Pacific (45 per cent) and the southeast Atlantic, off the coast of South West Africa (40 per cent). Only the western Indian Ocean falls into the intermediate range with 17 per cent of the catch attributed to distant fleets in 1971; in all other areas the proportion was less than 10 per cent. In 1971, the Soviet Union's distant fleets accounted for 41 per cent of all fish caught by such fleets defined in the above terms, and the Japanese distant fleets caught 25 per cent of the total haul.

The second main factor, which has operated in two ways, has been the process of decolonisation since World War II. First, decolonisation in Africa and Asia has greatly increased the number of independent countries, each able to pursue fishing policies tailored to their own needs. Secondly, this post-colonial period has been characterised by an increasing awareness of the economic disparity between developed and developing countries. This awareness has induced some measure of economic nationalism amongst the developing countries, and this has been evident in the fishing industry, where the differences between the distant and domestic fleets in waters off developing countries have been entirely obvious. Many developing countries with rich offshore fishing grounds have extended either their territorial seas or exclusive fishing zones, or both, to exclude foreign fishermen. The cases of Peru and Iceland have received most publicity, but there are several other cases. For example, Senegal, in 1967, claimed an exclusive fishing zone of 12 nautical miles. The fishing grounds off Senegal are particularly rich.[7] South of Cape Verde organic material provided by the Saloum, Gambia and Casamance Rivers is supplemented along the Petite Côte by upwelling waters from the ocean bottom throughout the year. These waters abound in herring, sardine and tuna. North of Cape Verde the river Senegal provides important supplies of nutrients, and elsewhere, along the dry coast, cold, enriched waters upwell from the continental shelf between 75 metres and 200 metres deep during the period from December to June. The main fish stocks are demersal species, such as cod, grouper and bass, which move south from Port Etienne between December and April, and north again between April and July. In 1967, the Senegalese fleet consisted almost entirely of skiffs, which landed 83 per cent of the total Senegalese catch, but such vessels rarely ventured deliberately more than 25 nautical miles offshore, and usually fished within the exclusive fishing zone. Outside these limits distant fishing fleets from Israel, Japan, Norway, the Soviet Union, Italy and Poland spent five months of each year making large catches of herring and tuna. In 1969, Nguyen-Van-Chi-Bonnardel wrote an article warning that Senegal, which depended upon its fisheries for a major contribution to the population's supply of protein, would have to consider restricting alien fishing activities.[8] Before the article was published, Senegal had increased its exclusive fishing zone to 18 nautical miles, and four years later on 10 April 1972, this zone was increased to 110 nautical miles measured from the outer edge of the territorial sea, which was 12 nautical miles wide. To demonstrate that the number of similar claims is increasing, it can be noted that in 1972 and 1973 South Vietnam, Oman, and Iceland created exclusive fishing zones 50 nautical miles wide, while Morocco and Costa Rica created similar zones 70 and 200 nautical miles wide respectively.

In the earlier discussion of distant fishing fleets, it was noted that there are four areas where the distant fishing fleets of developed countries catch significant proportions of the total catch taken off the shores of developing countries. These areas are the east central Atlantic, the southeast Atlantic, the southwest Pacific, including New Zealand, and the western Indian Ocean, which includes the Persian Gulf and the Red Sea. In the southwest Pacific, the proportion of the catch taken by distant fleets was stable, at 45 per cent, for the period between 1964 and 1971. In the other areas the proportion increased dramatically. In the east central Atlantic the proportions rose from 3 per cent in 1964 to 49 per cent in 1971. The comparable figures for the southeast Atlantic were less than 2 per cent and 40 per cent, and for the western Indian Ocean 4 per cent and 17 per cent. Thus in 1971, these were the three major areas where a conflict of interest between developed and developing countries seemed likely.

The third factor which contributes to the more frequent occurrence of disputes is the contemporary concern with issues of conservation and resource management. Some scientists and many more governments are quick to detect what they believe to be over-fishing of some areas. These fears are particularly prevalent at this time as the demand for fish products increases, and as more efficient means are devised for detecting and catching fish.

The fourth factor concerns the increased attention which is being paid to the sea as one of the two remaining frontiers of exploration and as the greatest remaining source of unclaimed and untapped wealth. The scramble for control of the littoral seas during the current period matches the competition for colonies amongst the European countries in the second half of the nineteenth century.

This section leads to two main conclusions. First, disputes may arise when fishermen of different nationalities begin to compete for a single fish resource fairly close to the shores of one of the nations. These disputes occur either because the riparian state wishes to obtain a larger share of the total catch, or because it wishes to extend the apparent economic life of that particular fish stock by introducing conservation measures. Secondly, the disputes fall into two major categories. The first category of dispute occurs between countries which occupy the opposite shores of comparatively narrow areas of sea: the best recent examples of such disputes are provided by disagreements between Japan and the Soviet Union, and between Japan and South Korea. The Japanese–Soviet dispute arises over the Soviet declaration in 1957 that Peter the Great Bay, near Vladivostok would be closed by a straight baseline.[9] The Japanese–Korean dispute was concerned with Korean claims to wide exclusive fishing zones.[10] The second category involves disputes between domestic and distant fishing fleets. These disputes occur between developed countries, such as Japan and the United States of America and Canada, and between developed and developing countries, in the eastern Atlantic off the coast of Africa, in the southwest Pacific, where there are a myriad of small islands not yet independent, and in the western Indian Ocean. In all these cases the distant fishing fleets which are most vitally concerned are those of Japan and the Soviet Union.

PROBLEMS IN MEASURING THE IMPORTANCE OF FISHERIES

Any attempt to solve fishing disputes must take into account the relative importance of fisheries to the states concerned. Therefore the problems of measuring the relative importance of fisheries must be considered before the various attempted solutions to fishing disputes are examined. There are three obvious aspects of fishing industries which can be compared to show their relative importance to different countries; they are the total catch, the employment and investment involved in the industry, and the importance of fish products in national trade.

The weight of the catch is often the statistic most readily available, but unfortunately this is not an accurate measure of importance. The value of the catch is much more useful. This is a harder figure to obtain and in any case, as one United Nations report noted, the calculation of comparative values on the basis of official rates of exchange may not give a true picture when applied to domestic fish products.[11] If this problem is discounted it is then necessary to relate the value of fish products to the economic value of other activities in the state, so that the significance of the fisheries contribution can be gauged. There are twin difficulties about this operation. First, in many developing countries the accuracy of figures referring to total national income is unsatisfactory. Secondly, in many developed countries it would be hard to establish the importance of all

I

activities related to fishing, including processing, manufacturing and distribution. The calculation of these ratios will favour the developing countries, because their secondary and tertiary sectors are less developed than those of industrial countries. It is also possible to argue that fish catches by developed countries such as Japan and the United Kingdom, which have limited areas, include the concealed value of saving foreign exchange for food imports. This foreign exchange would have to be expended on fish imports if the operations of their fleets were restricted.

The importance of fisheries to the national economy can also be measured by the numbers of workers they employ. Again, these raw statistics, which are not always available, may give a misleading impression. First, in some countries fishing is a seasonal occupation for men who farm for the rest of the year. This situation occurs in countries with very different characteristics. For example, the communities of Kayar, in central Senegal, are engaged in fishing from December to June, during the dry season, and on their farms for the rest of the year.[12] In Norway and Ireland respectively the proportions of part-time fishermen were 55 per cent and 70 per cent in 1966.[13] Secondly, simple employment statistics will vary with the degree of capital investment in the industry. For example, in 1970 Peruvian fishermen caught nine times as much fish by weight as Spanish fishermen, but there were at least 100,000 Spaniards employed in the industry, compared with 20,000 Peruvians.[14] In Europe, West Germany and Iceland possess the most capital-intensive fisheries.[15]

Only a tiny fraction of the world's catch of fish is traded internationally and in only very few cases does fish constitute a major item of export. The two most obvious cases are Iceland and Peru, which respectively obtained 75 per cent and 32 per cent of their exports by value from fish products in 1971. The volume of domestic trade in fish products will in most cases exceed the volume entering international trade by a very large margin; therefore trade figures will not be a very useful criterion for measurement, except where countries such as Iceland and Peru and areas such as the Faroes are concerned.

There are two further points which must be made in this section. First, while this discussion has been framed in terms of countries, because disputes arise between countries, it must be realised that fishing is a very localised industry and that in many cases there will be discrete, small regions of the state where fishing is of paramount importance. When the British government protested about the extension of Iceland's exclusive fishing zone in September 1972, they complained that over 100,000 workers and dependants would be adversely affected in the North Sea ports of Lowestoft and Grimsby. In Denmark the value of fish products represents less than 1 per cent of national income, but on the Faroe Islands, which form part of Denmark, the regional figure is 30 per cent. Helin has noted that fishing employs half the labour force of Murmansk and generates three-quarters of its revenue.[16] It is not unreasonable for countries which may be adversely affected by unilateral actions of other states to stress the severe personal hardship which these actions may cause to whole communities in particular regions.

Secondly, it is plainly not sufficient for a country to justify extensions of exclusive fishing zones by demonstrating that fishing is an important economic activity by one or more of the measures discussed above. It is essential that it should also show that the fishing grounds, from which aliens will be excluded, form an important part of the area exploited. Senegal's claim to an exclusive fishing zone, stretching 122 nautical miles from the country's baseline, includes fishing grounds which skiffs will never be able to exploit. Yet, in the late 1960s, skiffs accounted for 83 per cent of the Senegalese catch. In 1971, the catch of Australian fishermen was worth about $A57 million (£26 million). It is important to note, however, that 74 per cent of that total was provided by catches of molluscs and crustaceans taken comparatively close to shore.

This discussion suggests that each dispute will have to be settled after taking into account a large number of different factors, which will combine in individual ways in each case. There is no simple measurement of the economic importance of fisheries to any particular country.

THE RESOLUTION OF FISHERY DISPUTES

It was noted earlier that fishing disputes normally arise when fishermen of different nationalities are competing for a single fish stock. The aim of the state initiating the dispute is either to secure rights to a larger share of the stock, or to introduce conservation measures which will extend the economic life of that fishery. Because of the current respectability which attaches to conservation measures, it is usual for states to advance these as the reason for introducing restrictions on foreign fishermen. The regulations may be concerned with exclusion from certain areas, prohibition on fishing in certain seasons, the outlawing of various kinds of fishing gear, and restrictions on catching certain kinds of fish. It would be possible to examine each of these types of regulation in turn but, since political geography is vitally interested in relations between states, it seems more appropriate to examine attempted solutions from this point of view. Basically there are three distinct situations. First, states may act unilaterally to settle a fishing dispute in their own favour. Secondly, with one or more states, they may come to a multilateral agreement which resolves the matter. Finally, the world community of states may agree on general rules to govern the operation of international fisheries. The categories of unilateral, multilateral and international actions correspond closely to Johnston's categories of unshared exploitation, modified exploitation and shared exploitation.[17] It would be ideal if these were chronological steps towards complete international agreement on the regulation of fisheries, but unfortunately this is not so. Unilateral actions and multilateral agreements have existed for centuries and they are both in particular evidence at present. Indeed, since the unsuccessful international conference on this question in 1960, there have been more effective unilateral actions than there have been multilateral agreements. In addition, the measures of international agreement recorded in the Convention on Fishing and Conservation have had very little impact on the actions of fishing states. It is now necessary to look at each of these categories of government action in turn.

Unilateral actions have involved the establishment of control over areas of the oceans previously considered to be high seas. Without controlling the area, states clearly have no ability to compel fishermen of other nationalities to observe regulations dealing with seasons, fishing gear and species caught. This annexation of the high seas has been achieved by three common processes. First, in some cases straight baselines have been drawn across large bays in order to enclose that bay and, at the same time, to push outwards the boundary between the high and territorial seas. This technique was used by British authorities in 1609 to close the Moray Firth and various other large bays to Dutch fishermen. More recently Iceland and the Soviet Union have safeguarded coastal fisheries by similar means. Mention was made in the last chapter of the Icelandic decision to close Breida and Faxafloi Bays by straight baselines in 1952, an act which precipitated the first Cod War. On 21 July 1957 the Soviet Union announced that Peter the Great Bay would be enclosed as Soviet internal waters by a straight baseline 108 nautical miles long between the Tumen River and Povorotnyy Point.[18] Peter the Great Bay is part of the area which Morgan has described as the most important fishing area in the world.[19] Bêche-de-mer and molluscs are found there in considerable quantities in addition to herring, which appear during three periods between November and April. Japanese fishermen began to replace Koreans and Chinese as the dominant fishing group in Peter the Great Bay after 1885, during a period when Russia seemed disinterested in this fishery. As Russia began to develop its Pacific provinces its interest in these coastal waters increased and in 1900, rent had to be paid by the foreign fishermen for particular fishing areas and a tax paid on the weight of fish caught. After the Russo–Japanese war a fisheries agreement closed part of Peter the Great Bay to Japanese fishermen. This line is shown in Figure 11. A new convention in 1928 did not alter this limit. On 30 March 1944 a new Soviet–Japanese agreement drew a line about 160 nautical miles long between Oposny Island, which lies east of Povorotnyy Point, and the mouth of the river Tumen. Japanese fishermen were prohibited from fishing west of this line for the duration of the war. Technically the war ended on 19 October 1956, and on 10 April 1957 the first Japanese fishing boats commenced operations west of the wartime line. Three months later the Soviet government reached its decision to close the bay by the new closing line, on the grounds that Peter the Great Bay was an historic bay. Now, as Figure 11 shows, although the 1957 line lies west of the 1944 line, when the territorial sea of 12 nautical miles is measured from the new line the area from which Japanese craft have been excluded is increased.

Because countries have exclusive fishing rights within their territorial waters, many countries have extended their territorial waters in order to exclude alien fishermen from particular areas. Such states seem unconcerned by the responsibilities connected with defence and supervision which these extended claims legally incur; it is sufficient that their nationals have exclusive access to particular fisheries. The extension of territorial waters was considered in the last chapter and there is no need to provide the same examples again. The longstanding Peruvian claim to territorial waters 200 nautical miles wide has been very effective in reserving fisheries for the domestic fishing fleet. Since 1963 the proportion of fish caught in the southeast Pacific by distant fishing fleets has declined significantly. Cameroun and Gabon are two West African states which have increased their territorial seas to promote local fishing industries. By 1967, Cameroun had increased its claim to 18 nautical miles and with the assistance of an American firm was establishing a prawn and fish export industry at Douala. Gabon, with four increases in nine years, eventually claimed 100 nautical miles in 1972, only

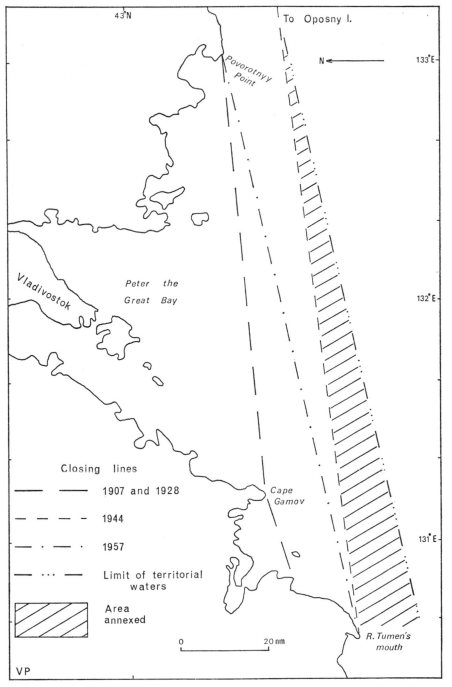

Fig 11   Closing lines across Peter the Great Bay

six months after announcing development plans for a fish processing industrial area at Owendo. As in the case of Cameroun, shrimp and fish exports will be the main product. Sierra Leone, Guinea and Gambia are other West African countries which have recently claimed much wider territorial waters in order to secure exclusive rights to offshore fishing grounds.

Attempts were made in 1958 and 1960 to secure international agreement on a fixed breadth of territorial waters and an exclusive fishing zone lying between the territorial waters and the high seas. These attempts narrowly failed, but the declaration of exclusive fishing zones has become a common feature of the political geography of the oceans. The advantage of using exclusive fishing zones, rather than extending the territorial sea, is that this introduces less interference with the rights of other countries to use the same area for air and sea navigation and research, and reduces the responsibilities incurred by the claimant state. By the end of 1973, thirty-two countries had proclaimed exclusive fishing zones outside their territorial waters. With the exception of Sri Lanka, which made its declaration in 1956, the others were made after 1961. Twenty-two of these countries place the outer edge of their exclusive fishing zone 12 nautical miles beyond the baseline from which the territorial sea is measured. Only the United Kingdom has a narrower claim of 6 nautical miles. Apart from Sri Lanka's claim, which is related to the continental shelf rather than a specific distance, the other eight zones vary from 15 to 200 nautical miles wide. The full list of these states and their respective claims is provided in Table 10. When Morocco announced in January 1973 that an exclusive fishing zone would be established 70 nautical miles wide, it was estimated by the Moroccan authorities that about 23,000 fishermen from the Canary Islands and southern Spain would be excluded from their former fishing grounds. Spanish fishing interests in the narrow seas between the Canary Islands and the African coast were first established in the fifteenth century. At the close of that century annexation of the Canary Islands gave the Spanish authorities a considerable measure of influence and

TABLE 10 Countries claiming wider exclusive fishing zones than territorial seas

Country	Territorial waters (nautical miles)	Exclusive fishing zone (nautical miles)
Australia	3	12
Belgium	3	12
Congo (Brazzaville)	12	15
Costa Rica	12	200
Denmark	3	12
Dominican Republic	6	12
Haiti	12	15
Iceland	4	50
Ireland	3	12
Italy	6	12
Ivory Coast	6	12
Malta	6	12
Monaco	3	12
Morocco	12	70
Nauru	3	12
Netherlands	3	12
New Zealand	3	12
Norway	4	12
Oman	12	50
Poland	6	12
Portugal	6	12
Senegal	12	110
South Africa	6	12
South Vietnam	3	50
Spain	6	12
Sri Lanka	12	continental shelf
Sweden	4	12
Taiwan	3	12
Tunisia	6	12
United Kingdom	3	6
United States	3	12
Yugoslavia	10	12

control in these waters, which abound in demersal and pelagic species of fish. That control was strengthened during the period 1476–1524 by the occupation of a fort near Ifni. In 1860, Spain, by means of a treaty with the Sultan of Morocco, obtained territory around Ifni which would be 'sufficient to set up a fishery, such as Spain had there formerly'. The proclamation of a Spanish Protectorate over the area of Spanish Sahara in 1884 further cemented Spain's territorial domination in this region. After World War II, pressure from Morocco began to reduce the extent of Spain's African territories. In 1958 the strip of Spanish Sahara north of latitude 27° 40′ north was ceded to Morocco, and in 1969 Spain retroceded Ifni to Morocco in exchange for permission for Spanish fishermen to fish within Moroccan territorial waters. It was in 1969 that Morocco had increased the breadth of its territorial waters from 3 to 12 nautical miles. Spanish trawlers were harassed in Moroccan territorial waters in the first half of 1972 and Moroccan trawlers were forbidden to land their catches at the Spanish port of Mellila, which is the only port of the eastern segment of the Moroccan Mediterranean coast. When the exclusive fishing zone was established it was noted that certain states would be able to enter into agreement with Morocco to fish in areas between 12 and 70 nautical miles off the coast. It is known that at least one French concern has reached an agreement of this type. Argentina, Brazil and Uruguay are three other countries which are prepared to license fishing by aliens in zones within the wide territorial waters they have claimed.

On 18 December 1970 the Canadian government resurrected the seventeenth-century British device of denying bays to foreign fishermen by closing them with straight lines. By drawing straight lines Canada preserved the Gulf of Saint Lawrence, the Bay of Fundy, Queen Charlotte Sound, the Dixon Entrance and Hecate Strait for Canadian fishermen. These lines, which enclosed about 80,000 square nautical miles, are not straight baselines and they do not alter Canada's claims to territorial waters.

There are several examples of fishing agreements between two or more states in the last century. For example, in 1839 Britain and France agreed on certain simple rules governing their fishermen, after disagreements over the activities of British trawlers in dredging for oysters between Jersey and the French coast.[20] The agreement reserved for each country the coastal waters 3 nautical miles wide, and set conditions regarding gear and the identification of fishing boats in the high seas. The agreement was not very successful because Belgian fishermen persisted in fishing oyster beds within 3 nautical miles of the French and English coasts, and because Irish oyster beds extended beyond the 3 nautical mile limit. The North Seas Fisheries Convention of 1882 was more successful. The conference was attended by representatives from Belgium, the Netherlands, Germany, France, Britain, Denmark, Norway and Sweden, and all except the last two countries signed the convention. Fulton has noted that it had the effect of reducing tension in the North Atlantic fisheries.[21] A feature of some recent agreements has been the provision for phasing out the activities of distant fishing fleets from areas claimed by coastal states. Such provisions as those between Norway and the United Kingdom in 1960 afford the distant fleets time to search for new grounds. Under the Anglo–Norwegian agreement, Britain approved the extension of Norway's exclusive fishing zone to 12 nautical miles, and in return was given permission to fish the outer 6 nautical miles until 31 October 1970.

In 1964, after the United Kingdom had served notice that it intended to withdraw from the 1882 convention, a new conference was held and delegates from thirteen European countries attended. The important provisions of the new convention laid down that each country was entitled to exclusive rights in a zone 6 nautical miles wide. In the coastal zone between 6 and 12 nautical miles of the shore only the coastal state and those nationals which had fished the waters between 1953 and 1962 were entitled to operate. In addition these favoured aliens were prohibited from fishing for species which they had not previously caught and the coastal state had the right to enforce any conservation measures, providing that they did not discriminate against any fishermen in the area.[22]

Between 1952 and 1954 South Korea proclaimed certain exclusive fishing and conservation zones which adversely affected the activities of Japanese fishermen in areas which had previously been considered high seas. The dispute dragged on for eleven years before a successful compromise was reached. The compromise gave each country an exclusive fishing zone 12 nautical miles wide and created an extensive joint control zone in which precise regulations were laid down about the operations of mackerel trawlers.[23] This bilateral agreement seems to have satisfied both sides and worked very well.

There have also been fishing agreements which referred to particular species. One of the best documented concerns the Pacific halibut, which lives over the continental shelf from California to the Bering Strait.[24] This fish is caught almost entirely in areas of the high seas, and American and Canadian fleets began to exploit this resource in 1888. By 1915, the total annual catch had risen to 31 million kilogrammes, but thereafter, despite increasing numbers of boats and longer periods spent at sea, the catch began to decline to 23 million kilogrammes in 1917. In 1923, an American–Canadian agreement established a three months' closed season and created facilities for research into the fishery. This research established the existence of two main areas near Cape Spencer, in Alaska. In 1931 a further agreement changed the closed seasons, divided the fishery into areas and limited the catch taken from any area. In 1932 the halibut region was divided into four zones and two nursery areas were established. During subsequent years restrictions were placed on fishing gear which took a heavy toll of young fish. Further agreements in 1937 and 1953 have refined the regulation of this fishery.

Anadromous species of fish, which live in the sea but return to fresh water to spawn, provide opportunities for serious disagreement between countries exploiting high seas and coastal fisheries. Because salmon lose condition quickly after spawning, they can be caught in their best condition as they leave the salt water and enter fresh water. It is also at such points that the concentration of salmon is greatest, and therefore it is not surprising that the earliest commercial salmon fisheries were established near the mouths of these rivers. In Alaska, an important salmon fishery was established in Bristol Bay. Since the salmon run in the summer months, it is necessary to freeze or can the fish quickly and the factories which perform this operation require large capital investment. Minghi has written a comprehensive account of the disagreements which developed between the United States and Japan over salmon fisheries when Japanese boats began to catch salmon outside American territorial waters in Bristol Bay during the late 1930s.[25] In 1953, Japan agreed to refrain from catching salmon spawned in Alaskan streams but, since such salmon cannot be distinguished from salmon spawned in Siberian rivers, it was necessary to fix an arbitrary dividing line. That line was fixed at 175° west, and Japan has refrained from catching salmon east of that line. Unfortunately for the American fishermen in Bristol Bay, their catches continued to decline in 1958 and it has been assumed by many Americans that the dividing line should have been moved further west. The Japanese, not surprisingly, declined to agree to any westward movement of the line until scientific evidence had been provided to show that such a movement was appropriate. That evidence has never been assembled and the matter has not been resolved. However, the decline in Bristol Bay catches, which persisted to 1966, was then dramatically reversed.

Logan has described an agreement between Canada and the United States concerned with salmon fishing near the border of British Columbia and Alaska.[26] As a result of complaints by Canadian fishermen that Americans were catching salmon trying to reach Canadian rivers, a series of surf lines were selected along the coasts of Washington, Oregon and British Columbia and salmon net fishing was prohibited seawards of these lines. The Canadian authorities then discovered that the Alaskan surf lines were actually 3 nautical miles off the coast, whereas the other surf lines lay much closer to the coast and in some cases coincided with the shore. This seaward projection of the Alaskan surf lines favoured the American fishermen operating off Noyes Island and infuriated the Canadian fishermen who still insist that Canadian salmon are being caught in this area.

International conventions agreed at the 1958 conference on the law of the sea deal with fishing in three distinct areas. First, the Convention on the Territorial Sea gives the coastal state the right to exclusive use of fisheries within territorial waters. Secondly, the Convention on the Continental Shelf gives the coastal state the exclusive right to catch sedentary species of fish which at the harvestable stage are either immobile on or under the seabed, or unable to move except in constant physical contact with the sea floor. This definition clearly includes oysters and coral; it is less clear whether it also includes crabs and lobsters. This last point was an issue between the Brazilians and French who were fishing off the Brazilian coast in 1962.[27] Thirdly, the Conventions on the High Seas and Fishing and Conservation refer to fishing outside territorial waters. The former convention simply states that there is freedom of fishing on the high seas, the second convention then qualifies that freedom by making it subject to existing treaty obligations, the interests of coastal states and the need for conservation. It is this second convention which must now be examined in more detail.

The Convention on Fishing and Conservation is based on an important biological concept of optimum sustainable yield. When a virgin stock of fish is being exploited by an increasing number of fishermen, it is possible to predict the important trends which will occur. As the weight of the catch increases, the total number of fish in the stock, the total weight of that stock, and the average age of the fish in that stock will decline. These trends will continue to a point which is called the optimum sustainable yield. Unfortunately that point cannot be detected, until it has been passed. This is because, once the point has been

passed, the yield of the fishery will also decline, despite any
increase in fishing effort.[28] The point of optimum economic
yield will always occur before the optimum sustainable yield as
Figure 12 shows. In that figure the optimum sustainable yield
occurs at point S, on the top of the curve. The optimum economic yield will occur at point E, where the distance is greatest
between cost and revenue. Evidently, if it were possible to halt

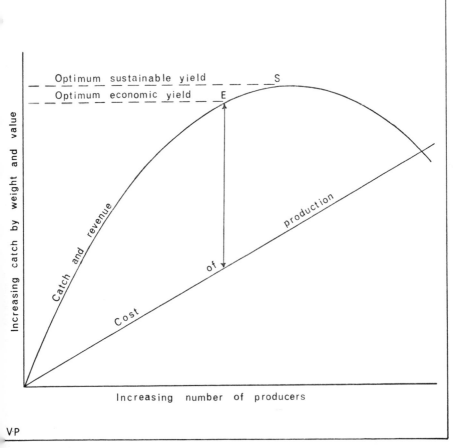

Fig 12 The relationship between optimum sustainable and economic yields
(after Coull)

the expansion of the fishing activities when the optimum economic yield was reached, there would be some wastage of food because more fish could be caught. If a halt to expansion is delayed until the point of optimum sustainable yield is identified, economic waste has already occurred. In taking the biological standard, rather than the economic standard, the convention seems to discount the fact that fishing is an economic activity and that unilateral actions and multilateral agreements have been primarily based on economic considerations.

The convention makes provision for conservation in three situations. First, where a single country is exploiting a high seas fishery it has the responsibility for introducing any necessary conservation procedures. Secondly, where two or more countries are exploiting the same high seas fishery any one country can request negotiations to introduce conservation regulations. Thirdly, the coastal state is given a special position regarding high seas fisheries adjacent to its territorial seas. Coastal states are eligible to take part in any conservation discussions regarding such areas, even though its nationals do not use this resource. Coastal states may request negotiations, with a view to introducing conservation regulations in the high seas adjacent to its territorial seas, and states using those high seas may not introduce conservation measures which conflict with those already adopted by the coastal state. Finally, the coastal state may, if negotiations have proved inconclusive after six months, introduce unilateral measures of conservation, providing three other conditions are met. First, there is an obvious need for such action; secondly, the action is based on appropriate scientific findings; and thirdly, that such actions do not discriminate against foreign fishermen. The convention also describes machinery which may be used in order to resolve any disputes which may arise. Unfortunately, this convention has not proved very useful. There appear to be two reasons for this. States are generally more interested in obtaining higher returns from fishing activities than in achieving the optimum sustainable yield. Some coastal states seek higher returns through excluding foreign fishermen from high seas fisheries. With no legal restriction on the width of territorial waters it is easier to extend this width rather than carry out research to establish the need for conservation. In any case, the extension of the territorial sea discriminates most effectively against foreign fishermen, which is forbidden in introducing conservation measures. To the end of 1973 there has not been a single case where a coastal state has applied conservation measures in adjacent high seas, under the terms of the convention, by providing convincing scientific research findings.

It may prove impossible to establish more useful rules to govern the general operation of this industry which creates the opportunity for international discord, given the mobility of fish stocks, the inadequacy of statistical data relating to fish stocks, and the differing levels of economic development of countries which have different political philosophies. In that case there will have to be a continuing dependence on multilateral, regional agreements which are capable of dealing with specific situations. One idea which has been canvassed increasingly in recent years concerns the preferential right of coastal states in respect of adjacent high seas fisheries.[29] This preference might operate in four distinct ways:[30] by excluding foreign fishermen from certain areas; by giving coastal fishermen exclusive rights in certain seasons and exclusive rights to catch certain species of fish; or it might be regarded as a proportion of the total catch. There seems no reasons to doubt the view that at the end of 1973 trends in international consensus on these matters were running in favour of coastal states and to the disadvantages of states such as the Soviet Union and Japan, which have very important distant fleets. The future for such operations may well involve co-operative ventures with developing coastal states.

K

CHAPTER FIVE

The Continental Shelves

THERE are important similarities between national claims to exclusive fishing zones and continental shelves. Both claims begin at the outer edge of the territorial seas and both are made to place valuable resources under the control of the coastal state. Moreover, these claims do not interfere with the rights of aliens to use the waters in the fishing zone or above the continental shelves for navigation and research. Exclusive fishing zones generally are concerned with fish that swim, while claims to the continental shelves reserve the right to harvest sedentary species of fish and to exploit mineral resources.

Effectively, states have controlled the continental shelves underlying territorial waters for as long as those waters have been claimed. The legal nature of territorial waters prevented aliens from operating in those waters with a view to collecting sedentary species or searching for mineral deposits, although it is only comparatively recently in the history of the law of the sea, that techniques have been developed to exploit mineral resources from vessels. It is therefore not surprising that the initial claims to parts of the sea floor were concerned with sedentary species.

Legal historians believe that they have detected claims to the sea floor as early as the sixth century BC.[1] During the nineteenth century a number of claims were made regarding sedentary fisheries. For example, in 1811 the British government acted to exclude foreign fishermen from pearl beds outside the territorial waters of Sri Lanka.[2] This prohibition was renewed at intervals thereafter, and in 1890 sedentary fisheries were preserved east of a line drawn from a point 6 nautical miles west of Talaimannar to a point 6 nautical miles west and 2 nautical miles south of Tailavilla. At one point this line was 25 nautical miles from the Sri Lanka coast.[3] In 1839, the British and French governments reserved areas of Granville Bay for the sole use of French oyster fishermen.[4] The Sea Fisheries Act of 1868 authorised Irish commissioners to regulate the dredging of oysters within 20 nautical miles seaward of a straight line joining Lanbay Island and Carnsore Point.[5] There were also regulations governing pearl fisheries off the shores of Queensland and Western Australia during the last century, although these only applied to British boats. O'Connell notes that some authors have overestimated the extent to which these claims involved areas beneath the high seas because they did not correctly appreciate the extent of Queensland's territorial waters.[6] Some declarations regarding sedentary fisheries defined the exclusive area by depths. Thus the Tunisian authorities, in 1904, assumed control over sponge fishing between the outer limit of the territorial sea and the 50 metre (27 fathom) isobath. In a similar way, the Sri Lanka authorities in 1925 defined pearl banks as areas bounded by the 3 fathom and 100 fathom (5 metre and 180 metre) isobaths.[7]

It is clear that these claims were to living organisms, but that since these organisms were more or less permanently attached to the sea floor, it was sensible to claim the sea floor where they might be found. Claims to mineral resources on the continental shelf became common only after 1942, even though minerals had been mined from the continental shelf much earlier. Wenk refers to galleries driven under the sea floor off west Scotland in 1620 to extract coal, and Gidel has provided a list of mines in Cornwall, Cumberland, Nova Scotia, Vancouver, Australia, Chile and Japan, which penetrated beneath the territorial sea.[8] In 1858, a British Act of Parliament stated that all mines and minerals below the low-water mark under the open sea adjacent to Cornwall formed part of the possessions of the British queen. Petroleum was first extracted from under the sea in 1899 by pipes driven from a pier attached to the land. By 1933, 9 million barrels were produced each year off the Californian coast. Just prior to World War II techniques allowed the use of drilling rigs on ships to operate in sheltered waters. During the Hague Conference in 1930, the Colombian delegate requested a wide territorial sea so that his countrymen could exploit pearl fisheries and petroleum.[9] In 1942, without specifically mentioning minerals, the British and Venezuelan governments agreed on a boundary dividing the 'sea-bed and sub-soil outside of the territorial waters'. This agreement was plainly made so that the authorities of Venezuela and Trinidad could regulate the underwater search for petroleum. Thereafter declarations concerning the minerals of the continental shelf were made in rapid succession by a large number of countries. In January 1944, the government of Argentina deemed the epicontinental sea to be a temporary zone of mineral reserves and then, in September 1945, President Truman made his famous declaration, which included the following phrases.

> Having concern for the urgency of conserving and prudently utilizing its natural resources, the Government of the United States regards the natural resources of the subsoil and seabed of the continental shelf beneath the high seas but contiguous to the coasts of the United States as appertaining to the United States, subject to its jurisdiction and control.[10]

This claim triggered off similar claims, first from the countries of South and Central America, and then from countries throughout the world. Claims were so widespread by 1958, that the Conference on the Law of the Sea produced a convention dealing with the continental shelf.

The Convention on the Continental Shelf is the shortest of the four conventions agreed in 1958. This fact, and the absence of sharp and bitter disagreements during the debates at the committee stage, are probably explained by the contemporary nature of the subject.[11] The first six of the fifteen articles comprising the convention are the most important for political and economic geographers. The first article defines the continental shelf as the seabed and subsoil of submarine areas adjacent to coasts, but outside the area of the territorial sea, to a depth of 200 metres or beyond that limit where the depth of water allows exploitation of natural resources.[12] It is evident that this is an imprecise definition, which depends upon the technical skills available to any country at a particular time. During the debate on this article some countries urged greater precision. The French and Lebanese delegations sought to delete the reference to exploitability beyond 200 metres (109 fathoms); Yugoslavia's representative suggested that the outer limit should not be more than 100 nautical miles from the coast, and an Indian proposal recommended that the limit should be the 550 metre (300 fathom) isobath.

The second article gives the coastal state sovereign rights over the continental shelf whether or not its nationals are engaged in exploiting the shelf's resources. It also defines the resources of the shelf as mineral and non-living materials, together with living organisms belonging to sedentary species. These living organisms are further defined as being immobile or unable to move except in direct contact with the continental shelf in the harvestable stage. It was made quite clear in debate that crustacea were not considered to be sedentary species, although an attempt to include this reference in the convention was rejected. According to the Australian delegate, sedentary species included 'coral, sponges, oysters, including pearl shell, the sacred chank of India and Ceylon, the trochus and plants'.[13]

The third article confirms that the rights of the coastal state over the continental shelf do not affect the rights of other countries in the waters or air space above those waters. The laying of submarine cables is the subject of the fourth article, and coastal states, subject to taking reasonable measures for the exploration and exploitation of the continental shelf, are prohibited from interfering with the laying or maintenance of submarine cables by other countries. The fifth article similarly preserves the freedom of other nationals to navigate, fish and conduct research for publication, in the waters over the continental shelf. The sixth article dealt with the division of the continental shelf lying between two countries or adjacent to two countries. In each case it was stipulated that the boundary should be the line of equidistance between the nearest points on the baseline from which the territorial sea is measured, although it is also permissible for the states concerned to agree to some other line. This article also required continental-shelf boundaries to be defined by charts and geographical features as they existed at a particular date, and by permanent identifiable points on land. There were a number of alternative suggestions concerning this article but they were all rejected. For example, the Italian delegation recommended that where there were offshore islands the line of equidistance between opposite countries should be drawn between the coasts of the mainland. This interpretation would be to Italy's advantage in the Adriatic Sea, because the Yugoslav coast is fringed by a number of islands, while the Italian coast is devoid of such islands. The Iranian delegation requested that a clause should be included making it permissible to draw the line of equidistance between high-water marks, rather than low-water marks from which territorial seas are normally measured. This suggestion was rejected, but the reasoning of the Iranian representatives was transparent. The submarine areas in the Persian Gulf shelve much more steeply off the Iranian coast than off the coast of Saudi Arabia, Bahrain, Qatar and the various emirates. This means that there is only a slight horizontal distance between high-water and low-water marks along the Iranian coast, compared with considerable horizontal differences between these two levels along the opposite coast.

Since 1958 a number of countries have applied the terms of this convention in a variety of ways and a number of problems have arisen. It is proposed to defer discussion of particular national claims and specific problems until the next chapter. The remainder of this chapter examines general questions connected with the political and economic geography of the continental shelves of the world.

WHY DO STATES CLAIM AREAS OF THE CONTINENTAL SHELF?

This fundamental question has already been briefly answered: states claim sovereignty over areas of the continental shelves because they might contain valuable resources. It is now necessary to explore the nature of these resources in more detail.

The resources of the shelf are conveniently divided into living and inanimate categories. The living resources include seaweed, coral, molluscs and bêche-de-mer. Each of these commodities may be locally of some importance, but the total value of such products is only a tiny fraction of the value of non-sedentary species caught in the waters above the continental shelf. It is also true that some of these commodities had more commercial importance in the past than they have today. Seaweed is harvested in Japan for the preparation of certain foods and, in 1971, the total collected was 212,000 metric tons. In parts of Ireland and western Scotland seaweed is used as a fertiliser. Trade in natural pearls and pearl-shell was more important in the past than today. Reputedly the best natural pearls are found in the Persian Gulf, along the coast between Oman and Qatar, where the Mohar variety of *Meleagrina vulgaris* occurs. Large fleets of dhows still search for pearls in these waters between May and September each year. Pearl fisheries off the coast of Sri Lanka, in the Gulf of Mannar, are now less important than they were, but the collection of chank shells is still of local significance. The chank is a gastropod producing a thick, heavy shell. This shell is used as a religious symbol associated with the worship of Vishnu, and some of the shells are fashioned into bangles and other ornaments and sold throughout Sri Lanka and southern India. Some of the best waters for collecting pearl-shell occur off the northern coasts of Western Australia and Queensland, and around Papua New Guinea. The shell of the *Pinctada margaritifera* grows to considerable size, but, as Table 11 shows, the pearl-shell industry of Northern Australia has shown a distinct decline since World War I. The value of natural pearls exported in 1971 was $A18,000 (£8,367), compared with the value of cultured pearl exports which stood at $A2·1 million (£976,108) in the same year, and cultured pearls are now a much more significant item of the world's international commerce than natural pearls.

TABLE 11 *Selected figures to show changes in the Australian pearl-shell industry*

	1920	1933	1971
Number of boats	515	237	28
Men employed	3,738	2,339	416
Production (tons)	2,126	1,675	593
Export (tons)	1,570	1,650	580
Value	£320,000	£198,000	$A601,000*

* £279,352
Source: *The Australian Yearbook*

The inanimate resources of the continental shelf may be usefully divided into three types. First, there are accumulations of the remains of living organisms; secondly, there are the mineral deposits which lie on, or just below, the surface of the shelf in unconsolidated deposits; and thirdly, there are mineral deposits lying deep below the surface of the continental shelf, in consolidated or unconsolidated material.

The most useful remains of living organisms are coral reefs and shell beds. Mero has described the commercial use of shell beds in Iceland and Texas.[14] A deposit of crushed shells was discovered 10 nautical miles offshore in Faxafloi Bay on the west coast of Iceland, in 1949. The shells are washed off rocky areas to the southwest during winter storms and are pulverised as they are washed eastwards. The beds vary from 1–4 metres (3–13 feet) in thickness and are found in water which does exceed 40 metres (130 feet) deep. Since more shell is washed into the area each year than is mined, the deposit would seem to have an excellent future. Layered shell deposits are found in the Gulf of Mexico off the south coast of the United States, and Texan companies extracted 45 million tons of shell in the first twenty years after World War II. Crushed coral can also be used in the manufacture of cement and lime in those volcanic islands where limestone is scarce.

Mineral deposits on or close to the surface of the continental shelf are found in concretions or sedimentary layers. The best-known concretions are of phosphorite nodules which vary in size and occur either as flat slabs or irregular masses; they have been described by a number of authors.[15] Although the exact method of formation is not understood, the environment where nodules generally occur has been identified. They are found in areas where large numbers of small marine organisms are killed either by fluctuations in temperature, caused by the mixing of cool and warm water, or by fluctuations in salinity caused by the discharge of large rivers in flood. Off California the nodules are found on the walls of submarine canyons, on fault scarps, and on the outer edge of the continental shelf close to the beginning of the continental slope. These are all areas where there is normally very little deposition because of the concentration of ocean currents. Since there is no evidence to the contrary, it is assumed by Mero that the nodules form deposits only one layer thick.[16] An American vessel, *Glomar Explorer*, began operations in October 1973 to collect manganese nodules from the sea floor in areas lying within the triangle marked by southern California, Hawaii and Panama in waters as deep as 4,000 metres (2,190 fathoms). The nodules are sucked from the floor of the sea by pipes with a diameter of 40 centimetres (16 inches). It has been estimated that a square mile of the sea floor could yield 50,000–75,000 tons of nodules. Mero also describes barium sulphate concretions which have been located off Colombo in the Indian Ocean, near the Kai Islands of Indonesia and off the southern end of San Clemente Island of California.[17] He judges, however, that extensive deposits of these nodules are unlikely to be found.

The sedimentary layers on the continental shelf are composed of material derived from the land catchment or the outer edge of the continental shelf. There is no known mechanism for raising sediments from the abyssal plain to the continental shelf via the steep continental slope or submarine canyons. Plainly the material moved shorewards from the outer edge of the continental shelf may be former terrestrial deposits laid down in an earlier geological phase or material eroded from bedrock on the sea floor.[18] It follows from this that the geological composition of the land and submarine catchments will be one of the most important variables determining the location of continental shelf deposits. It is generally considered that the most-valuable surface sedimentary deposits have been mainly derived from terrestrial sources. They include diamonds, gold, platinum, tin, and heavy mineral sands such as ilmenite, monazite, rutile and zircon. These valuable minerals will be released from the solid rock on land by the normal processes of denudation and weathering, and they will then be transported by rivers to the sea. The valuable proportion of the river's load will be deposited fairly close to the mouth, and from there it may be moved and sorted by wave action. Bird has described two distinct situations in which sorting occurs.[19] Where the sandy deposits overlie a shallow rock platform backed by a cliff, wave action will stir the whole mass and heavier minerals will accumulate in the lower levels of the deposit, in contact with the platform. Where the sand deposits are much thicker, they will be subject to alternations of erosion by high energy waves during stormy weather, and of renewal by the action of gentle swells during calm weather. This alternation of cutting and filling in what is called the sweep zone creates variable laminae of the heavier minerals, and these laminae will be resorted and reformed on many occasions. Extreme storm waves will throw deposits of heavy minerals above the mean high-tide level. On beaches that are prograding, these heavy mineral deposits may form discontinuous seams for considerable distances. Now it is evident that these processes will be creating useful mineral deposits near certain coasts and well within the outer limit of the narrowest territorial waters. But the relevance of these processes to the present subject stems from major sea-level changes during the Quaternary period. During the glacial periods sea-levels fell as increasing volumes of water drawn from the oceans were retained as ice on the land; during the inter-glacial and post-glacial phases sea-levels rose as water was returned to the oceans faster than it was evaporated. This means that during the glacial periods considerable areas of the present continental shelves stood above the sea and the coasts were located seaward of the present position. There is still debate about the maximum extent of the sea's retreat and the issue is complicated by subsequent tectonic movements, but there is some consensus on a level 300–450 feet below present sea-level.[20] This means that the locations of former beaches are now under varying depths of water on the continental shelf. Whether these former beach sites are occupied by surface sedimentary deposits depends upon a number of interrelated and variable factors. First, the climate over the land catchment would play a major role in influencing the volume of sediment delivered to the coast. Humid climates would encourage the formation and flow of rivers, which would be largely absent in coasts off tropical deserts and polar and temperate ice-caps. The amount of sediment generated would also be influenced by the major gradients obtaining throughout the catchment. The rate of marine transgression in the inter-glacial and post-glacial periods would also be an important factor. Where the rise in sea-level was rapid there would be less opportunity for the critical zone of wave action to destroy the drowned, thick beach deposits. This would be particularly true where the beach deposits were protected by overlying dunes. A slower rate of marine transgression would allow the wave zone to move the drowned beach deposits landwards. It should be noted, however, that a rapid rise in sea-level across a rock platform backed by a cliff would leave the feature as a notch in the sea floor where subsequent accumulation of sediment could take place. The location of mineral deposits on the continental shelf would also be affected by tectonic movements, by the growth of coral reefs which would reduce wave energy along the coast, and by the headward and lateral extension of submarine canyons.

The rivers which delivered sediment to glacial shorelines, excavated valleys in the continental shelves which they crossed. During the drowning process these lower river courses have been filled with sediment carried by the river and by unconsolidated material on the continental shelf which has been displaced along the coast by currents and waves. Mero refers to some of these drowned valleys extending 300 miles beyond the present coast.

A few illustrations will indicate the potential value of offshore surface mineral deposits. Tin is mined from the continental shelf, in water depths of 60–130 feet (18–40 metres), off the coasts of Thailand and Indonesia. The Indonesian operations occur near the islands of Belitung, Bangka and Singkep.[21] Diamonds are mined in important quantities off the coast of South West Africa. Presumably they were carried to the continental shelf by the Orange River, when the sea-level was considerably lower, and have been distributed northwards by the Benguela Current. The extensive occurrence of these deposits is indicated by the strict prohibitions on entry to the coastal areas of South West Africa. Mero predicts that platinum deposits will be mined in the drowned lower reaches of the mouth of Salmon River in Alaska, which he estimates extend more than 100 miles beyond the coast. At present, however, the value of sand and gravel dredged from coastal waters exceeds the value of other surface mineral deposits. Emery estimates that the total value in 1969 was \$US200 million (£84 million).[22] This material was used for filling sites, for road construction and for the manufacture of concrete aggregate. Such deposits will generally be drawn from the continental shelf within territorial waters.

To conclude this brief review of the surface mineral deposits of the continental shelf, mention must be made of glauconite. Mero describes this authigenic material as 'a hydrated potassium, iron, aluminium silicate', and it is potentially important because it could be used as a source of potash or potassium. Glauconite grains are generally found in muds and oozes along coasts where there are no major rivers and where sedimentation from terrestrial sources is very slow.

Probably every type of mineral resource is represented somewhere under the surface of the continental shelf. However, the additional expense of finding and mining resources on the continental shelf, compared with similar deposits on land, probably means that only a small proportion of these occurrences will be developed. Because there is a lower incidence of igneous intrusions on the continental shelf than on the land, the occurrence of metallic minerals is limited. Such deposits occur at the contact between igneous and other rocks, in fissured zones, and in igneous intrusions. It is also a disadvantage that metallic minerals are often harder to mine than mineral deposits in sedimentary rocks. Both sedimentary and vein deposits are mined by galleries driven from land. Reference was made earlier to coal-mines driven under the Northumbrian and Scottish coasts. In the Gulf of Finland tabular veins of magnetite are mined from tunnels driven between Jussaro and Stenlandet Islands.[23] But the most important fuels obtained from beneath the surface of the continental shelf are crude petroleum and natural gas. According to industry estimates, 14 per cent of the world's natural gas production and 18 per cent of the world's crude petroleum production was obtained from the continental shelf. Although it is not possible to distinguish what proportion was obtained from outside the narrowest territorial waters of 3 nautical miles, Tables 12 and 13 list the most important offshore producers of oil and gas. The petroleum and gas deposits may be trapped in anticlines formed during the tectonic warping of parts of the shelf, or by traps created by salt domes. These salt structures occur in large numbers along the American coast of the Gulf of Mexico. As the salt dome thrusts upwards through overlying strata it drags the sedimentary layers upwards, forming traps along its edges and on the top of the plug. In some limestone cappings over these domes sulphur has been discovered as Mero has described for the Grand Isle sulphur deposit off the Louisiana coast.[24] In March 1972 the deepest petroleum-producing well on the continental shelves was also located off Grand Isle. The Hunt Oil Company drilled their number one well in Block 15 to a depth of 6,740 metres (22,115 feet), and produced a commercial flow of petroleum from the interval between 6,230 metres (20,440 feet) and 6,248 metres (20,500 feet).[25] There is every reason to suppose that the rapid developments in drilling technology will soon allow that record to be surpassed.

TABLE 12 *Production of natural gas from the continental shelf*

| Country | Million cubic feet/day produced gas | | | |
	1970	1971	1972	1971–2 change mc/ft
United States	8,591·78	10,046·58	9,110·62	−935·96
Iran	3,500*	3,578·9	4,500*	+ 921·1
United Kingdom	1,086·30	1,794·25	2,560·36	+ 766·11
Saudi Arabia	494·80	587·12	690·17	+ 103·05
Neutral Zone	193·97	201·10	204·13	+ 3·03
Australia	60·55	98·10	121·77	+ 23·67
Qatar	107·12	130·60	121·71	− 8·89
Angola/Cabinda	78·63	105·75	109·67	+ 3·92
Peru	64·66	62·75	61·17	− 1·58
Trinidad/Tobago	10·96	10·69	10·69	—
Total	14,188·77	16,615·84	17,490·29	+ 874·45

* Estimated

Source: *Offshore*, 20 June 1973

TABLE 13 *Production of crude petroleum from the continental shelf*

| | Thousand barrels/day | | | Change | Per cent |
Country	1970	1971	1972	1971–2	change
Venezuela	2,761	2,803	2,886	+83	+ 2·96
United States	1,577	1,692	1,664·58	− 27·5	− 1·63
Saudi Arabia	1,251	1,210	1,490·7	+280·7	+ 23·0
Iran	322	444	467·8	+ 23·8	+ 5·3
Neutral Zone	(*)	380	409·8	+ 29·8	+ 7·8
Nigeria	275	361	409	+ 48	+ 13·2
Abu Dhabi	269	342	345·2	+ 3·2	+ 0·9
Australia	216	262	303	+ 41	+ 15·6
USSR	258	250	236	− 14	− 5·6
Brunei–Malaysia	146	138	218	+ 80	+ 58·0
Qatar	172	207	209	+ 2	+ 0·9
Egypt	257	121	157	+ 36	+ 29·8
Trinidad/Tobago	76	123	155	+ 32	+ 26·0
Angola/Cabinda	96	131	137·4	+ 6·4	+ 4·9
Dubai	70	126·5	129·5	+ 3·0	+ 2·4
Indonesia	—	32	69·9	+ 37·9	+118·4
Gabon	29	27·2	43·6	+ 16·4	+ 60·3
Mexico	35	37	38	+ 1	+ 2·7
Norway	—	22	32·3	+ 10·3	+ 46·8
Peru	—	22	23·8	+ 1·8	+ 8·1
Italy	12	10·9	10·9	—	—
Brazil	8	8·2	8·2	—	—
Congo	—	0·5	7·9	+ 7·4	+148
New Zealand	—	—	2·7	+ 2·7	− 1
Japan	3	2	1·1	− 0·9	− 45·0
	7,833	8,752·3	9,456·38	+704·08	+ 8·0

* Neutral zone included with Saudi Arabia in 1970 compilation
Source: *Offshore*, 20 June 1973

It is also possible that some states are interested in claiming sovereignty over the continental shelf, because it gives an opportunity to install defensive equipment, such as radar and sonar equipment. There is nothing in the convention which specifically sanctions such actions: sovereignty is exercised for the purpose of exploring the shelf and exploiting its natural resources. There does not seem to have been much consideration of this issue. Franklin reaches the view that states would be acting legally if they established weather stations and radar equipment on installations built originally to explore and exploit the resources of the continental shelf.[26]

This discussion of the reasons why states claim areas of the continental shelf leads naturally to questions about the political problems which such claims create.

WHAT POLITICAL PROBLEMS ARE RAISED BY CONTINENTAL SHELF CLAIMS?

There are four related political problems connected with national claims to areas of the continental shelf. First, there is the difficulty of determining the shelf's outer edge. Secondly, there is the dispute about the extent to which states can claim sovereignty over detached parts of the continental shelf, separated from other parts by deep trenches. Thirdly, there is the difficulty of dividing the continental shelves which are shared by adjacent or opposite states; and finally, in federal countries, there are the disagreements over ownership between the federal and state authorities.

The first article of the convention defines the area to which it applies in the following terms.

For the purposes of these articles, the term 'continental shelf' is used as referring (a) to the seabed and subsoil of the submarine areas adjacent to the coast but outside the area of the territorial sea, to a depth of 200 metres or, beyond that limit, to where the depth of the superjacent waters admits of the exploitation of the natural resources of the said areas; (b) to the seabed and subsoil of similar submarine areas adjacent to the coasts of islands.[27]

Many lawyers have written long and complicated analyses of this article from the legal point of view.[28] The inconclusive legal debate will be avoided here, and the following analysis is made simply from the point of view of political and economic geography. It is apparent that coastal states have the right to exercise sovereignty, in accordance with the convention, over submarine areas outside their territorial waters to a depth of 200 metres (109 fathoms), whether those territorial waters are measured from the mainland or an island. There is no evidence in this article that the term 'continental shelf' is used in a geological sense, and the absence of any geological definition of its limits suggests that the term was used only in a legal sense. This view is confirmed by reference to the discussions which led to the adoption of this phrasing. The International Law Commission undertook the preparatory drafting work for the 1958 Geneva Conference and Brown made the following judgement after examining the records of the commission's work.

> There can be no doubt then that the ILC *as a body* recognised that the legal Continental Shelf might extend beyond the geological continental shelf . . .[29]

Since the term 'continental shelf' is used in this imprecise fashion, the other qualifying phrases must be examined in an effort to discover whether any limit is envisaged to the continental shelf claims. The limits of exploitation are obviously not fixed. They will move seawards as technical advances are made. It was noted earlier that the new *Glomar Explorer* is capable of collecting manganese nodules from depths in excess of 3,000 metres (1,640 fathoms). It is also not clear whether the convention requires that exploitation is an economically profitable operation, or whether the subsidised collection of mineral samples constitutes exploitation. Finally, on this point, it is uncertain whether each state is entitled to claim the submarine areas to depths capable of exploitation by the best techniques available anywhere in the world, or only the techniques available to the claimant state. The latter interpretation would act against the interests of the poorer countries of the world.

The only other clue to the possible location of the outer edge of the continental shelf is the adjective 'adjacent'. Brown makes an exhaustive analysis of this term but reaches the conclusion that it does not define any outer limit of the shelf. All that can be certain is that 'adjacent' refers to uninterrupted contact

L

between the coast and the continental shelf. Thus, for example, it would not be possible for Poland to make any claims to the continental shelf of the North Sea.

The geographer must therefore conclude that the convention does not provide any outer limit to the legal continental shelf. However, it is clear that the United Nations believes that there are limits to national claims on the continental shelf. On 17 December 1970, the General Assembly adopted a declaration dealing with the seabed and ocean floor which contained the following statement:

> *Affirming* that there is an area of the sea-bed and the ocean floor, and the subsoil thereof, beyond the limits of national jurisdiction, the precise limits of which have yet to be determined.[30]

The problem of fixing the outer limits of the continental shelf is a serious one. It is entwined with the width of the territorial sea, because this convention only applies outside territorial waters. States which want to avoid debate about the legality of their claims to outer areas of the shelf can simply extend their territorial waters to the desired distance, a technique which has been used to secure exclusive fishing zones. It also seems probable that there will be different interpretations over the outer limits of the continental shelf between those countries which possess unlimited adjacency to the middle of the oceans, and those which are landlocked or possess only small areas of continental shelf. If the deep seabed is to be used for the benefit of all countries, these latter states have a vested interest in seeing that the unclaimed area is as large as possible.

The second political problem concerns claims to detached parts of the continental shelf which are separated from the coastal sections by depths well in excess of 200 metres. This type of configuration may create a situation where detached exploitable areas lie seaward of unexploitable areas. The language of the first article does not make it clear whether such areas may be claimed. This situation is a comparatively common one. The two clearest cases involve Norway and the island of Timor which is shared by Indonesia and Portugal. In each case a trench in the seabed close to the coasts severely restricts the extent of the continental shelf covered by waters less than 200 metres deep. The Norwegian Trench has depths of 500 metres (275 fathoms) and the Timor Trough has maximum depths of 3,000 metres (1,640 fathoms). Beyond these depressions a broad continental shelf stretches towards the coast of opposite countries; the United Kingdom in the case of Norway, and Australia in the case of Timor. After initially arguing that these depressions marked the dividing line between their respective continental shelves, the United Kingdom and Australia made concessions to the other countries concerned. In other cases only a single country is involved. For example, there are extensive detached areas off the northern coasts of Norway and Svalbard, and between the Soviet possessions of Novaya Zemlya and Franz Joseph Land. The Sulphur and Rodger's Banks off the east coast of Brazil, in latitude 17° south, are separated from similar coastal areas by channels more than 2,000 metres (1,090 fathoms) deep. The Penguin Bank, located in the South China Sea, is separated from the coastal shelf by depressions with a depth of 2,500 metres (1,366 fathoms). The increasing number of accurate bathymetric charts are revealing numerous cases where detached exploitable areas lie seaward of areas which are unexploitable because of their excessive depth. Examination of a recent chart of the northern Pacific Ocean shows several of these areas in the Sea of Okhotsk, in waters east of the Kuril Islands and west of Hawaii, and off the Californian coast.[31] Barry has described claims by the United States to the Cortez Bank since 1967.[32] This bank is situated about 38 nautical miles southwest of San Clemente Island, from which it is separated by channels over 1,100 metres (600 fathoms) deep. The United States government asserted claims to the area when a private consortium decided to create an artificial island on the bank in 1967. Several other governments have also made it clear that they do not regard unexploitable depressions in the general area of the continental shelf as marking the edge of legitimate claims. In 1956, the Venezuelan authorities ruled that channels, depressions and irregularities in the seabed of the continental shelf 'shall not constitute a break in the continuity of that shelf'. In 1968, the Soviet Union specifically incorporated deep depressions in the shelf as part of the continental shelf. Two years later the Canadian government followed the Venezuelan example and declared that accidental features, 'such as a depression or a channel', would not interrupt claims to a continuous continental shelf.[33] The Canadian claim was probably made with the shelf south of Nova Scotia and the Bay of Fundy in mind. The continuation of the land boundary between the United States and Canada, along a marine line of equidistance, passes south of the main channel leading to the Bay of Fundy, and allocates to Canada part of George's Bank. The United States takes the view that the boundary should follow the deepest part of the submarine canyon leading out of the Bay of Fundy, as shown in Figure 13.

Detailed charts show that the morphology and scale of these presently unexploitable depressions varies considerably. It would be very difficult to produce a logically valid rule which determined that depressions with specific depths and widths terminated continental shelf claims, while shallower and wider or narrower depressions could be ignored by the claimant state. It seems probable that states will increasingly disregard channels and depressions in the surface of the continental shelf when establishing their areas of sovereignty.

The third political problem arises from the need to divide the continental shelf between opposite and adjacent states. The procedure for this division was laid down in the sixth article of the convention.

1. Where the same continental shelf is adjacent to the territories of two or more states whose coasts are opposite each other, the boundary of the continental shelf appertaining to such states shall be determined by agreement between them. In the absence of agreement, and unless another boundary line

is justified by special circumstances, the boundary is the median line, every point of which is equidistant from the nearest points of the baselines from which the breadth of the territorial sea is measured.

2. Where the same continental shelf is adjacent to the territories of two adjacent states, the boundary of the continental shelf shall be determined by agreement between them. In the absence of agreement, and unless another boundary is justified by special circumstances, the boundary shall be determined by the application of the principles of equidistance from the nearest points of the baselines from which the breadth of the territorial waters is measured.[34]

Essentially these definitions are the same. The reference to the median line between opposite states is proper, since the line is drawn through the middle of the waters between them, but such a line is also equidistant.[35] Once again lawyers have written at length about the legal interpretations of this article, but this discussion examines only the geographical implications.[36]

It appears that two distinct situations are envisaged. The first is where the boundary is drawn along the line of equidistance; the second is some other line justified by 'special circumstances'. There are geographical problems of interpretation associated with each. The line of equidistance, either between adjacent or opposite states, is an easy line to find once a detailed map has been prepared showing the territory of each state. This is a unique line, and different cartographers working with identical maps would draw the same lines. The problem therefore relates not to drawing the line, but to the baselines from which it must be constructed. It is obviously possible for a state, by the creation of straight baselines, to increase its share of the continental shelf by deflection of the equidistant line. There is no record of any dispute based on such actions, but the straight baseline proclaimed by Haiti increases its share of the continental shelf which lies between Haiti and Cuba. Figure 14 shows the equidistant line drawn between the territory of the two countries and the equidistant line which results from the baseline closing La Gonave Gulf. The area between these two lines is approxi-

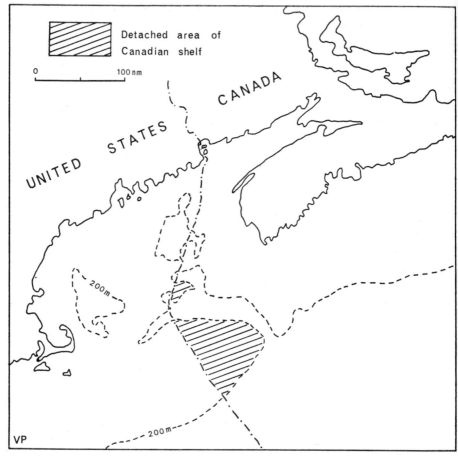

Fig 13   Division of the continental shelf in the Bay of Fundy

mately 350 square nautical miles. The French government showed itself alert to this problem when it acceded to the convention on 14 July 1965. The reservation was then made that France would not be bound by any straight baselines established after the first signature of the convention on 29 April 1958. During the 1958 Conference the German delegate noted that he interpreted any exceptional delimitation of territorial waters to constitute special circumstances. Figure 15 shows other hypothetical situations, where the construction of straight baselines would allow a state to secure a larger share of the continental shelf than would accrue from a line of equidistance between low-water marks.

The problem associated with boundaries justified by special circumstances is to decide which geographical conditions provide special circumstances. In the final report of the International Law Commission of 1956 it was noted that provision must be made for departures from the equidistant line necessitated by any exceptional configuration of the coast, as well as the presence of islands and navigable channels.[37] During the debates at the 1958 Conference, which effectively adopted the Law Commission's recommendation on this matter, there was further debate on the need to overcome the disproportionate effect of tiny, isolated islands on the allocation of the continental shelf. Alien islands, close to the shore of a country, can deprive that country of considerable areas of the continental shelf, if the island is used in drawing the line of equidistance. It was awareness of this possibility which prompted the French government to declare, when making its reservations about Article 6, that it considered special circumstances applied in the Bay of Grandville where the British Channel Islands are located. The Venezuelan authorities consider that special circumstances exist in the area between the Venezuelan coast and the Dutch island of Aruba.[38] The Greek islands close to the Turkish coast, and the Australian Ashmore and Cartier Islands near the Timor coast, restrict the claims to the continental shelf by Timor and Indonesia. It would obviously be possible for states concerned in these situations to agree that the boundary should be drawn without giving full effect to the rights attached to the isolated islands; in the next chapter some specific examples of this solution are discussed.

Some countries which are shelf-locked believe that this condition creates special circumstances which require a boundary other than the line of equidistance. A state may be considered to be shelf-locked, when the continental-shelf claims of its

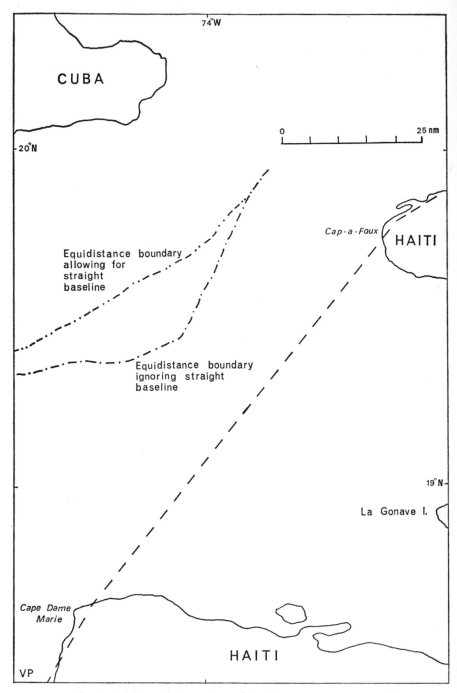

Fig 14   Division of the continental shelf between Cuba and Haiti

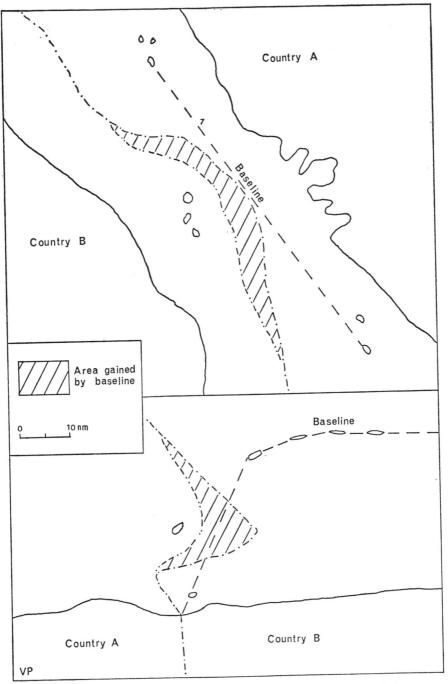

Fig 15 The influence of straight baselines on continental shelf boundaries

neighbours converge comparatively close to its coast and deny the state access to the edge of the shelf and the abyssal plain, or to the middle of an enclosed sea, such as the North Sea and the Persian Gulf. This problem occurs in two situations. First, it may occur because the shelf-locked state has a very narrow coastline, as in the case of Iraq, Jordan, Monaco, Togo and the Casamance area of Angola. Secondly, states which have con-cave coasts may also be shelf-locked; this situation occurs on the continental shelves claimed by West Germany, Cambodia, North Vietnam and North Korea, although it only affects the west coast of North Korea. The only shelf-locked territories which do not fit either of these categories are West Malaysia and Singapore. Claims by these territories to the surrounding continental shelf are curtailed because they are surrounded by the territories of neighbours such as Indonesia, Thailand and South Vietnam.

The circumstances of West Germany are of particular interest because of a case brought before the International Court of Justice, whereby the governments of West Germany, Denmark and the Netherlands requested the court to decide what prin-ciples and rules of international law are applicable to the de-limitation of the continental-shelf boundaries between them. The dispute arose when the Danish and Dutch governments agreed on a boundary between their continental shelves in the North Sea, on 31 March 1966, which clearly imposed limits on the area available to West Germany. Further, both before and after that date, both these governments had urged the West German government to settle its continental-shelf claims on the basis of lines of equidistance. The boundaries in question are shown in Figure 16. The record of pleadings in the case form a mine of information for the political geographer who has the patience to separate the geographical gems from the legal dross.

During this legal contest the German side asserted that the aim of the continental-shelf boundary was to provide a just and equitable share for each state. It followed that the line of equi-distance would only satisfy this condition on a straight coast-

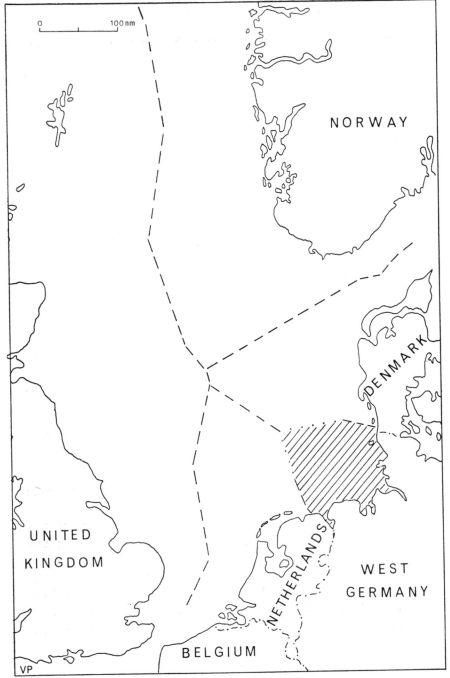

Fig 16 West Germany's shelf-locked position before 1968

line, and therefore on all coastlines which are not straight, special circumstances apply.[39] The other two governments rejected this view and insisted that each state was entitled to the continental shelf which appertains to its territory, and that the line of equidistance is the fairest way of determining such divisions. The West German government wanted a larger share of the North Sea continental shelf than the lines of equidistance would provide and it also sought access to the areas near the centre of the North Sea, where the prospects of finding commercial oil and gas fields were considered better. The German authorities therefore proposed a sector theory, which would interpose German areas of the continental shelf between the Dutch and Danish areas.

The court concluded that the line of equidistance was not an obligatory method of delimitation, and that delimitation should be by agreement in accordance with equitable principles so as to leave to each state as much as possible of the continental shelf which constitutes 'a natural prolongation of its land territory into and under the sea'. The court indicated that, where this method produced overlaps, these were to be divided between the states in agreed proportions or, failing agreement, equally. Finally the court noted some of the factors which should be considered in reaching boundary agreements on the continental shelf. They include the general configuration of the coast, the physical and geological structure of the continental shelf, and the length of respective coastlines, which ought to be in reasonable proportionality with the extent of the continental shelf acquired by each state.[40]

The decision of the court has been criticised by a number of writers, amongst whom Brown and Friedmann have been prominent.[41] The main criticisms centre on the views that the court has tried to establish a measure of distributive justice which will open the door to litigation between states; that the factors listed for consideration by the court will not necessarily guarantee a just delimitation; and that the court has indicated the goals without indicating certain methods by which they can be reached. It does seem very likely that any state which feels disadvantaged by the configuration of its coast and those of its neighbours will find support in the judgement for opposition to the lines of equidistance. It is hard to understand why the court relied mainly on the length of coastline when other factors, such as wealth of the state, dependence on continental-shelf resources, the poverty of land resources, and population numbers, are also factors which should be considered in any equitable apportionment of the continental shelf. Friedmann makes a very telling point about the court's attitude to nature, which is of interest to geographers, when he asks why a concave or irregular coastline should be considered unnatural while a straight coastline is natural.[42] It is indeed a puzzle why the court should try to compensate for a geographical disadvantage, namely a convex coast, which they judge unnatural, when they apparently accept so many other inequalities, which could be defined as unnatural by the same logic. So long as the earth's surface is divided amongst sovereign states there will be geographical inequalities and some states will benefit from the facts of geography and others will be placed at a disadvantage. Would the court consider it natural and equitable that Switzerland should have no claim to any continental shelf, and that Zaire, a large, populous country, should only be able to claim a small sliver of a very narrow continental shelf? It is hard not to join Brown in regretting that the court has handed down a judgement which 'can only add to the confusion over delimitation of the continental shelf'.[43]

As a result of the judgement, West Germany was able to negotiate agreements with the Dutch and Danish governments which gave West Germany a sector of the continental shelf, stretching to the middle of the North Sea. These agreements, together with others, are considered in the next chapter.

There is one problem which has not been explored by lawyers about the question of drawing boundaries between adjacent areas of the continental shelf. The continental-shelf boundary begins outside territorial waters. Now there seems to be general agreement that the equidistance line is the proper boundary to separate territorial waters: even proponents of the German case before the International Court accepted this view, as did the judges who prepared the majority report.[44] Therefore, by extending claims to territorial waters, one state can compel its neighbours to adopt a line of equidistance which also divides the continental shelf. This technique would be effective where a neighbouring state claimed that special circumstances made some boundary other than the line of equidistance appropriate between adjacent areas of the continental shelf. Figure 17 gives an imaginary example of how the extension of a territorial sea would adversely affect the claims of a country to a continental-shelf boundary based on special circumstances. If country B claimed only 12 nautical miles of territorial waters, country A could argue for a special continental-shelf boundary beginning at point X to offset the existence of island M. If country B increased its claim to territorial waters 50 nautical miles wide, any continental shelf boundary would have to begin at point Z.

The last political problem associated with ownership of the resources of the continental shelf applies only to federal states. In Canada, Australia, West Germany, Malaysia and the United States of America, there have been various disputes between the federal and state authorities over such matters as control of licensing exploration and exploitation, regulations for sedentary fisheries, and the payment of royalties by mining companies. These problems are of a constitutional, rather than geographical nature, and there is a considerable legal literature dealing with this entire issue.[45] The geographer's interest centres on any territorial arrangements which are made in solving this constitutional matter. For example, in 1969, the government of Canada established certain 'mineral resource administration lines' on the continental shelves. Landward of these lines the coastal provinces administer mining operations and acquire all the revenue generated by these activities. The continental shelf seaward of the dividing lines is administered by the Canadian government, which has undertaken to allot half the revenue

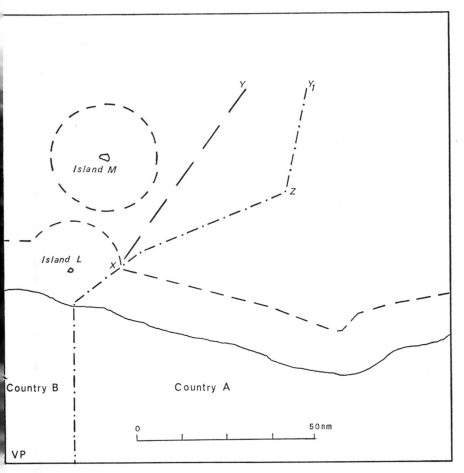

Fig 17   The effect of the width of territorial waters on continental shelf boundaries

gained to a common fund, which will be divided amongst the provinces in an agreed proportion.

HOW DOES THE NATURE OF THE CONTINENTAL SHELF BEAR UPON THESE POLITICAL PROBLEMS?

The final question to be examined in this chapter concerns the extent to which the political problems described above are made easier or more complex by the nature of the continental shelf.

Most continental submarine margins consist of a continental shelf, bounded on the seaward edge by a continental slope, which is linked to the abyssal plain by a continental rise. A section through a typical submarine margin is shown in Figure 18. The average continental shelf is 40 nautical miles wide and

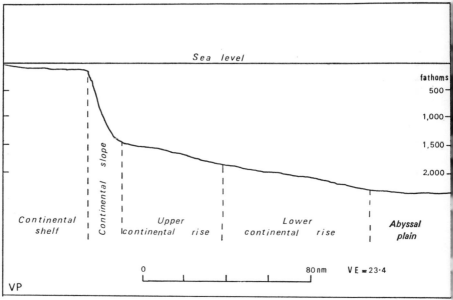

Fig 18   A section through an average continental margin

it descends at a gradient of 0° 7′ to a water depth of 132 metres (72 fathoms) at its outer edge. The average continental slope occupies a horizontal width of 12 nautical miles, and descends at an angle of 4° 17′ to a water depth of 2,925 metres (1,600 fathoms). The average continental rise, which consists of an apron of debris masking the junction between the continental slope and the abyssal plain, stretches for about 100 nautical miles, with gradients varying from 1° 26′ at its landward edge to 0° 4′ at the junction with the abyssal plain.[46]

If only a typical submarine continental margin existed over

considerable lengths of the world's coastlines, some of the political problems described above would be made much less difficult. Unfortunately, the outstanding characteristic of the submarine margin's morphology is its wide variation. The detailed description of the margin by Shepard shows that the variation occurs in respect of every facet of its morphology. The width of the continental shelf varies from 700 nautical miles in the Barents Sea to less than 20 nautical miles west of the Niger Delta. The depth of water at the outer edge of the shelf reveals a range from 20 metres (11 fathoms) to 550 metres (300 fathoms), and the transition from the gentle gradients of the shelf to the steeper gradients of the continental slope may occur over distances of 1–5 nautical miles. The gradient of the continental slope varies from less than 1° off the coast of northwest Australia to 45° off Santiago, where the slope descends to the Barltett Trough. The width of the slopes similarly varies from less than 10 nautical miles to 20 nautical miles. Finally, the continental rise is not present where the slope descends into troughs, and elsewhere this mantle of debris may extend as much as 400 nautical miles seaward from the base of the continental slope, as it does off Dakar in West Africa.

This brief description demonstrates the difficulty of setting linear morphological boundaries at the outer edge of the continental shelf. Obviously the easiest solution to this problem would be to set a maximum distance from the coast, within which the coastal state had sovereignty over the resources of the seabed. Clearly this distance would have to be set at least at the maximum width of the continental shelf, which, as noted earlier, is located in the Barents Sea. Some states might argue that the distance should represent the maximum known width of the submarine continental margin, including the continental rise. Either of these distances would give several states control over deep-water resources which they would be unable to exploit for the foreseeable future, with existing levels of technology.

The detailed descriptions of the morphology of the continental shelf provided by Shepard and other authors also reveal

M

that detached areas of the continental shelf are comparatively common.[47] This confirms the view expressed earlier that depressions in the seabed, including trenches and submarine canyons, will be discounted when states are laying claims to the continental shelves.

The characteristics of the submarine continental margin do not significantly affect the problems of drawing boundaries between the continental shelf of adjacent or opposite countries, or the constitutional competition for ownership between central and regional governments in a federation. However, there are two other political implications which should be mentioned. First, the continental shelves adjacent to different countries have unequal values. They vary significantly in extent, and in the resources which they contain. These geographical inequalities, like those which attach to the varied nature of territory, may cause political friction and disputes between states. These disputes may occur over boundaries dividing a particular shelf between countries, or over the principles which should govern the exploitation of the continental shelf. The former type of dispute reveals itself in bilateral negotiations, claims and counter claims; the second type of dispute appears at international conferences on the law of the sea. The other implication is that the ability of states to use the resources of the continental shelf will depend upon the technical skills available. Bascom wrote a very interesting article on recent important developments associated with the recovery of mineral resources from the continental shelf.[48] Amongst the most important are the ability to drill in very deep water from vessels which can remain exactly on station, the ability to navigate and locate positions at sea with extreme precision, the ability of geologists to visit the seabed in small submarines, and the ability to scan the seabed from the surface by television cameras. These are techniques which are most readily available to the developed countries of the world. It is possible that the superior ability of developed countries to exploit the continental shelves will cause problems in their relationships with developing countries.

CHAPTER SIX

Claims to Areas of the Continental Shelves

THE last chapter made a general examination of the resources of the continental shelves, and the problems of drawing boundaries to separate national claims. It is now necessary to consider specific national claims to areas of the submarine continental margin, and this will be done in three sections. First, the regional variations of the continental margin will be measured, for these give some countries a marked advantage over others. Secondly, the present methods used by countries to define their continental-shelf claims will be analysed, and thirdly, some particular international boundaries between national claims will be scrutinised.

REGIONAL VARIATIONS OF THE SUBMARINE CONTINENTAL MARGIN

Shepard has provided the best available description of the world's submarine continental margins and it is not proposed to duplicate that work here.[1] There is also a very good coloured map of the world, produced by the Geographer, which shows the areas of the submarine continental margin in three categories: areas at a depth of less than 200 metres (109 fathoms); the continental shelf and slope deeper than 200 metres and with gradients in excess of 1:40; and the continental rise with gradients between 1:40 and 1:1,000.[2] The Mercator projection distorts the areas of the submarine continental margin in polar areas, but it is still the best world map on this subject.

Economic and political geographers are interested in the *absolute* area of the submarine margin available to each coastal state, and the *comparative* extent to which the geographical situation of the coastal state has placed it at an advantage or a disadvantage. These interests can be satisfied by a publication of the Geographer listing the area of the seabed which would accrue to each state if all boundaries were drawn according to the equidistance principle, and if one of four seaward limits of claims was used.[3] The four seaward limits to claims are the 200 metre (109 fathom) isobath; the edge of the margin, which is taken to occur at the 3,000 metre (1,640 fathom) isobath; 40 nautical miles from the coast; and 200 nautical miles from the coast. Certain caveats are listed which must be kept in mind when the tables are used. The most important of these are that the effects of straight baselines were ignored; simplified, rather than precise equidistance lines were drawn; the limits of insular margins often had to be estimated; the best available marine surveys were used, but their quality is uneven throughout the world; and that the figures are most reliable when used to indicate comparative orders of magnitude amongst states.

The first investigation of these figures was concerned with the comparative advantage conferred on each coastal state by its geographical circumstances. If it is assumed that equidistant lines are drawn between opposite and adjacent submarine claims, the area of the margin available to each state will depend on four factors. These factors are the width of the submarine continental margin, the configuration of the coastline, the length of the coastline and the proximity of neighbouring claims. A useful index, which summarises the effects of these variables and allows comparison to be made of the geographical advantages and handicaps of various states, is obtained by dividing the area of the submarine margin accruing to each state, within lines of equidistance with its neighbours, by the length of the coastline: this means that the index represents the area of seabed in square nautical miles which attaches to each nautical mile of the state's coastline. In this form the indices for countries with widely divergent coastlines can be compared. This calculation was made for 121 coastal political units, of which 117 were independent states. Papua New Guinea was considered as part of Australia. The values, which ranged from 1 in the case of Fiji to 1,100 in the case of Mauritius, were then inspected and five groups were distinguished; these are recorded in Table 14. Before the groups of countries are considered it must be noted that countries will fall into common groups for different reasons: for example, a small index may result from either a very narrow shelf or a shelf-locked location due either to near neighbours or a concave coastline; while the divisions between groups have been selected at apparent breaks in the continuity of the numbers, the whole scale does represent a spectrum from the least fortunate to the most fortunate; the index gives no measure of the value of the submarine area available. While Tanzania has an index which is nine times that calculated for Bahrain, it is entirely possible that the submarine areas off the latter state will prove to be more valuable than those located off Tanzania.

The first group contains eleven countries which obtain less than 21 square nautical miles of seabed for each nautical mile of coastline, by the method of calculation described. They fall into two distinct groups. Fiji, the Maldive Islands, Western Samoa, Nauru, and the Philippines suffer the disadvantage of narrow continental shelves, which results from their geological history of volcanic activity and the growth of coral reefs. The other six countries all suffer from the close proximity of neighbouring

TABLE 14 Index values representing number of square nautical miles per nautical mile of coast. Numbers in brackets indicate rank in absolute size of available continental margin

Index values	Countries				
1–21	Bahrain (113) East Germany (109)	Fiji (114) Iraq (118)	Maldives (104) Nauru (120)	Philippines (38) Singapore (121)	Togo (116) W Samoa (111) Zaire (117)
22–52	Albania (105) Algeria (89) Bangladesh (73) Barbados (112) Belgium (115) Cameroun (103) Costa Rica (86) Cuba (36) Cyprus (92)	Dahomey (110) Denmark (76) Egypt (60) Ethiopia (71) Finland (61) Greece (30) Guatemala (98) Haiti (82) Iran (46)	Israel (101) Jordan (119) Kuwait (106) Lebanon (102) Morocco (51) Mozambique (31) North Korea (74) Oman (40) Panama (54)	Peru (45) Poland (97) Qatar (100) Saudi Arabia (43) Sri Lanka (63) Sweden (47) Syria (108) Tunisia (67) Turkey (35)	USSR (5) United Arab Emirates (80) West Germany (93) Yemen (San'a) (94) Yugoslavia (85)
53–94	Angola (37) Australia (1) Bulgaria (95) Burma (24) Chile (17) China (14) Colombia (40) Congo (99) Dominica (59)	El Salvador (90) Equatorial Guinea (87) France (32) Gambia (107) Ghana (75) Guinea (84) Indonesia (3) Italy (18)	Ivory Coast (83) Japan (9) Kenya (72) Khmer (81) Liberia (77) Libya (41) Madagascar (22) Malaysia (23) Mauritania (66)	Mexico (11) Nigeria (57) North Vietnam (70) Pakistan (39) Romania (96) Sierra Leone (88) Somalia (25) Sudan (64) Taiwan (55)	Tanzania (52) Thailand (26) Tonga (91) Trinidad (79) USA (4) Venezuela (34)
95–136	Brazil (10) Canada (2) Ecuador (44) Gabon (53) Guyana (62)	Honduras (50) India (12) Ireland (29) Netherlands (68) Nicaragua (58)	Portugal (48) Senegal (69) South Africa (16) South Korea (27)	South West Africa (33) Spain (19) Surinam (65)	United Kingdom (13) Uruguay (56) Yemen (Aden) (28)
>136	Argentina (7) Iceland (15)	Jamaica (42) Malta (78)	Mauritius (21) New Zealand (6)	Norway (8)	South Vietnam (20)

claims. Bahrain, East Germany, Iraq and Singapore have the added common feature of being located on semi-enclosed seas and gulfs.

The second group, which has limiting values of 22 and 52 square nautical miles per nautical mile of coastline, consists of forty-one countries which together exhibit all the disadvantages possible. Twenty-six of the countries are located entirely, or mainly, on the shores of semi-enclosed seas. Countries located around the Persian Gulf, and the Baltic, North and Mediterranean Seas are restricted in making claims to submarine areas by the presence of nearby states on opposite coasts. Some of these twenty-six countries, such as Belgium, Jordan, and West Germany, also have concave coasts which restrict claims based on lines of equidistance. Seven countries in this group face wide oceans, but suffer from being hemmed in by neighbours which restrict the area available. The seven are Panama, Dahomey, North Korea, Cameroun, Bangladesh, Costa Rica and Mozambique. The latter is exceptional since the restriction is imposed by the large offshore island of Madagascar. Some of these states, such as Cameroun, North Korea and Bangladesh, also possess concave coastlines. Peru, Guatemala and Oman fall into this group because of their narrow submarine margins. Of the three, only the Oman submarine margin possesses a continental rise, and that is amongst the narrowest in the world. Cuba, Haiti, Barbados and Sri Lanka are all island states which suffer restrictions from neighbour's claims. The first two island states are embedded in the middle of an archipelago and are restricted in every direction. Barbados and Sri Lanka are severely restricted along their western coasts by Saint Vincent and Saint Lucia, and India respectively. The country in this group which seems quite individual is the Soviet Union. It is impossible to describe a single dominant feature in respect of this country, which has a coastline of 23,098 nautical miles. The submarine continental margin under the Barents Sea is the widest in the world, but long stretches of the coastline occur on semi-enclosed seas, such as the Black Sea, the Baltic Sea, and the Sea of Japan. The narrowness of the Bering Strait, and the long sections of concave coast, such as that around the Sea of Okhotsk, further reduce the area available according to lines of equidistance. It is unfortunate for the Soviet Union that the most prominent length of convex coast, around Poloustrov Taymyr, coincides with the narrowest section of the margin along the Soviet polar coast.

There are forty-one countries in the group limited by indexes of 53 and 94 square nautical miles per nautical mile of coastline. This group contains a greater range of geographical situations than encountered in the previous two groups, and it is not possible to parcel them into discrete categories. It is evident, from inspection, that some of the countries in this group have similar circumstances to some of the countries already mentioned, but that the operation of these circumstances is less severe in terms of claims to the seabed. For example, Sudan, Italy, Bulgaria, Libya, and Romania are all located on the shores of semi-enclosed seas, but they are located opposite some of the widest margins in these seas, and their neighbours do not crowd as close as in the case of Syria, Ethiopia and Albania. Congo, Guinea and Gambia are hemmed in by neighbours, but not as closely as Togo or Dahomey. There are obvious similarities between the concave coasts of Pakistan and North Vietnam, which are members of this group, and those of Bangladesh and North Korea, which have already been discussed, but once again, the effects of this concave configuration are not so acute. Dominica and the Malaysian areas of Sabah and Sarawak are located in archipelagos, but because they are on the outer edges, they do not suffer the disadvantage which afflicts Cuba and Haiti. The final illustration of this point concerns Chile. Along its northern coast the submarine margin is as narrow as that off the coast of Peru, and is similarly devoid of any continental rise; but this disadvantage is partially compensated for by a wider shelf off the glaciated, southern coast and the appearance of a continental rise.

Just as this third group contains countries, such as Equatorial

Guinea, at the lower end of the scale, so it contains countries, such as Japan, Burma and Nigeria, which have almost the highest possible values for this group, and which possess characteristics similar to those in the fourth group. The fourth group, which is limited by the values of 95 and 136 square nautical miles per nautical mile of coast, consists of twenty countries, and they reveal a combination of favourable geographical circumstances. Seven of the twenty states have coasts facing at least two seas or oceans; they are Canada, South Korea, Ireland, Nicaragua, the United Kingdom, Spain and South Africa. Such a location gives mainland countries similar advantages to islands. Korea, India, Spain and South Africa have the advantage of being formed by peninsulas jutting into areas of ocean, where they provide title to considerable areas of the seabed. Three of the states, namely Canada, Yemen (Aden) and Portugal, also include distant islands which increase the area of seabed which can be claimed. Without the island of Socotra, which gives Yemen (Aden) access to the comparatively wide shelf off the Horn of Africa, the country would suffer the same disadvantage as the neighbouring state of Oman, which can only claim areas on a very narrow submarine margin. The islands of Madeira similarly extend the area available to Portugal, and Canada's northern archipelago secures a major share of the continental margin under the Arctic Ocean. Ireland and the United Kingdom share the common advantage of being islands facing a wide ocean, and, in a rather similar manner, it is the good fortune of Uruguay, Surinam and South West Africa, that no alien islands obstruct the extension of their claims into the Atlantic Ocean. The final advantage displayed by this group is the possession of a convex coast, which helps to explain why Brazil, Gabon, Honduras and the Netherlands are placed in this fourth group. The advantage in the case of the Netherlands is particularly striking since it borders a semi-enclosed sea. This is a location which has adversely affected some countries, such as Tunisia, Poland, and neighbouring Belgium.

The remaining eight countries form the fifth group, which

score values in excess of 136 square nautical miles per nautical mile of coast. New Zealand, Jamaica, Mauritius, Malta and Iceland are all islands which are comparatively remote from neighbours, and which are located on submarine continental margins which are fairly wide. Argentina, in a similar fashion to South West Africa and Uruguay, can make an unimpeded claim to large areas of the margin under the Atlantic Ocean. Argentina does suffer from the close proximity of the British Falkland Islands in the extreme south; if they ever became part of Argentina, its claims to the seabed could be very significantly increased. South Vietnam is located on a peninsula, with a long convex coastline, which allows claims to be made to large areas of the South China Sea and the Gulf of Siam, where the submarine margins are particularly wide. Finally, Norway has the twin advantage of a long convex coast which has frontages on the North, Norwegian and Barents Seas, and the remote islands of Svalbard, which provide the basis for important claims in the Arctic Ocean.

The most important lesson to be drawn from this survey is that the geographical circumstances of each country must be considered in detail in any analysis of the extent to which it is favoured in making claims to the seabed. It is not possible to generalise that an island status and a peninsular location are always an advantage, or that location on a semi-enclosed sea is a disadvantage. Apart from the absence of a peninsular state in the first category, all these conditions are represented in every group. There is another obvious lesson for governments, diplomats and lawyers, and that is that in respect of their claims to submarine continental margins, states vary widely in their geographical good fortune. This has obvious implications for the task of finding sets of principles on which claims to that margin will be established and disputes over ownership will be resolved.

When states are ranked by the size of the submarine continental shelf which they can claim, it is immediately obvious that the countries with the longest coastlines generally fare best.

Thirty-eight of the areas considered possess coastlines in excess of 1,000 nautical miles, and thirty-five of them occur in the top thirty-eight positions of the ranked list. The countries which are absent are Saudi Arabia, Sweden, Oman, Egypt and Peru, and their geographical disadvantages have already been mentioned. The other five places in the top thirty-eight positions are occupied by South Korea, Mauritius, Yemen (Aden), Ireland and South West Africa, which possess advantages that have already been noted. The importance of a long coastline is confirmed by the fact that Canada, Australia, Indonesia, the United States of America, and the Soviet Union, which possess the longest coastlines in the world, also occupy the first five places on the ranked list. Table 14 also shows the rank of each area, and the inferior locations of countries in the first two groups are evident.

The tables provided by the Geographer allow another interesting analysis. Since, for each country or dependency, the areas which could theoretically be claimed are calculated for four seaward limits, it is possible to establish the order in which these four boundaries give particular states access to diminishing submarine areas. For example, the areas which could be theoretically claimed by Brazil, with seaward boundaries of 40 nautical miles, 200 nautical miles, the 200 metre isobath, and the continental margin are respectively 189,700; 924,000; 224,100 and 435,700 square nautical miles. Thus the apparent preference for Brazil would be 200 nautical miles, the continental margin, the 200 metre isobath and 40 nautical miles. This ranking of seaward boundaries was done for the 121 territories, and those with similar apparent preferences were grouped together. Considering that the values for some boundaries can be identical, for example when the presence of neighbouring claims restricts the area before the 200 nautical mile limit or the continental edge is reached, it will be realised that the number of combinations can be very large. In fact, as Table 15 shows, there are only eight combinations present, and some of these have very close similarities. These preferences have been described as apparent rather than real, because it should not be assumed that every

TABLE 15 Classification of states according to preferred seaward boundaries of the continental shelf

Group 1	Preferred boundaries	1. Continental margin
		2. 200 nautical miles
		3. 200 metre isobath
		4. 40 nautical miles

Argentina
United Kingdom
Uruguay

Group 2	Preferred boundaries		1. 200 nautical miles
			2. Continental margin
			3. 200 metre isobath
			4. 40 nautical miles

Australia	Gambia	Malaysia	South Vietnam
Bangladesh	Guinea	Mauritania	Surinam
Brazil	Guyana	Pakistan	
Burma	Ireland	South Korea	

Group 3	Preferred boundaries		1. 200 nautical miles
			2. Continental margin
			3. 40 nautical miles
			4. 200 metre isobath

Angola	Israel	Mexico	Somalia
Canada	Italy	Morocco	South Africa
Chile	Ivory Coast	Mozambique	South West Africa
Dominica	Jamaica	New Zealand	Spain
El Salvador	Japan	Nicaragua	Sudan
France	Kenya	Nigeria	Taiwan
Gabon	Lebanon	Norway	Tanzania
Ghana	Liberia	Oman	Trinidad
Guatemala	Libya	Panama	USA
Honduras	Madagascar	Saudi Arabia	Venezuela
India	Malta	Senegal	Yemen (Aden)
Indonesia	Mauritius	Sierra Leone	

Group 4	Preferred boundaries		1. 200 nautical miles
			2. 40 nautical miles
			3. Continental margin
			4. 200 metre isobath

Algeria	Dahomey	Greece	Philippines
Barbados	Ecuador	Haiti	Portugal
Colombia	Egypt	Maldives	Sri Lanka
Costa Rica	Equatorial	Nauru	Tonga
Cuba	Guinea	North Korea	USSR
Cyprus	Fiji	Peru	W Samoa

Group 5	Preferred boundaries		1. {Continental margin / 200 nautical miles}	
			2. 200 metre isobath	
			3. 40 nautical miles	
	China	Romania	Sweden	Thailand

Group 6	Preferred boundaries		1. {Continental margin / 200 nautical miles}	
			2. 40 nautical miles	
			3. 200 metre isobath	
	Albania	Congo	Iran	Turkey
	Bulgaria	Ethiopia	Syria	Yemen (San'a)
	Cameroun	Iceland	Tunisia	Yugoslavia

Group 7	Preferred boundaries		1. {Continental margin / 200 nautical miles / 200 metre isobath}	
			2. 40 nautical miles	
	Bahrain	Khmer	North Vietnam	West Germany
	Denmark	Kuwait	Poland	
	Finland	Netherlands	Qatar	

Group 8	The four boundaries are equally preferred			
	Belgium	Iraq	Singapore	United Arab
	East Germany	Jordan	Togo	Emirates
				Zaire

government will be in favour of the boundary which allows the maximum theoretical claim.

Argentina, Uruguay and the United Kingdom form a distinct group. These are the only countries where the boundary of the margin gives them access to the largest possible area. In some directions, these three countries have unrestricted claims, based on the equidistance principle, to submarine margins wider than 200 nautical miles. It is the possession of Scotland and the Hebrides which would allow the United Kingdom to make claims to the submarine areas south of Iceland.

The second, third and fourth groups share the common characteristics that at certain points their theoretical claims can reach the edge of the submarine continental margin, and that the seaward boundary of 200 nautical miles gives access to the largest area. The countries in the second group, which contains thirteen states and Surinam, have access to margins with an average width of between 40 and 200 nautical miles. The shelf off such countries slopes more gently than in many other areas, because the 200 metre isobath lies more than 40 nautical miles from the coast, which makes this last seaward limit the least attractive. The third group, with forty-four countries, and the three dependent territories of South West Africa, Angola and Mozambique, is the largest. The only difference between this group and the preceding one, is that the 200 metre isobath lies at an average distance of less than 40 nautical miles from the coast, and therefore that isobath is probably the least attractive seaward limit to those countries. It is important to note that these two groups together form an absolute majority of the cases considered, which suggests that there might be a strong reservoir of support at some future conference for a seaward limit of either 200 nautical miles or the submarine continental margin. The fourth group is distinguished from the two that precede it by having a continental margin less than 40 nautical miles wide. For the twenty-three countries in this group the distance limits form the two most attractive seaward boundaries. This group includes those island states of the Pacific and Indian Oceans, such as the Maldive Islands, Nauru, Fiji and the Philippines, whose continental margins are narrow as a result of volcanic activity and the growth of coral reefs.

The common characteristics of the remaining four groups of countries is that their claims, based on equidistance, do not reach either the 200 nautical mile limit, or the edge of the submarine continental margin, because of the interposition of claims by neighbouring states. The fifth group consists of the People's Republic of China, Sweden, Thailand and Romania. These countries are bordered by margins wider than 40 nautical miles, and which shelve so gently that the 200 metre isobath also lies at an average distance from the coast of more than 40 nautical miles. For these states it is immaterial whether the seaward limit is fixed at 200 nautical miles or the edge of continental margin, because lines of equidistance enclose their theoretical claim before either of these limits are reached. The seaward limit of 40 nautical miles would probably be the least attractive for them.

The sixth group, of twelve states, is very similar to that just described. Once again the convergence of lines of equidistance occurs before either the edge of the margin or the limit of 200 nautical miles are reached. The only difference is that the shelf has a steeper gradient than the shelves off the four states of group five. This means that the 200 metre isobath lies at an average distance from the coast of less than 40 nautical miles, and thus that isobath is apparently the least attractive seaward line.

The ten countries which form group seven are more severely restricted by neighbours' claims than the countries of the two preceding groups. The convergence of lines of equidistance occurs before three of the suggested seaward limits are reached. The three limits are the 200 metre isobath, the continental margin and the 200 nautical mile line. It would not matter to these states, of which Khmer, Kuwait and Poland are typical, which of these three limits is adopted, because they would all produce the same theoretical claim if boundaries were based on the equidistance principle.

The eighth and final group is the most severely restricted. The eight countries in this group are so confined by neighbours' claims that their potential areas are fixed before any of the suggested seaward limits are reached. These countries, which include Iraq, Singapore and Zaire, are the worst examples of shelf-locked countries and for them the selected seaward limit is immaterial because they would be unable to reach any of them unless their neighbours allowed significant deviations from lines of equidistance. It is entirely possible that countries in these groups will support fairly narrow limits to the seaward edge of continental shelf claims, so that the maximum area of seabed remains outside the control of states, for the joint use of all countries.

NATIONAL CLAIMS TO CONTINENTAL SHELVES

The Appendix includes information about the regulations which countries have passed concerning the seaward limits of the continental shelf. Information was not available for ten countries. Seventeen countries have made no known proclamations regarding the limits of their claims to the submarine margin. Seven of these states, including the Maldive Islands and Equatorial Guinea, possess comparatively narrow margins, and a further five, including countries such as Singapore and Jordan, are severely shelf-locked. There is no obvious reason why the remaining five countries—Tunisia, Lebanon, Ethiopia, Congo and Guinea—have failed to make any proclamation, although Guinea claims a territorial sea of 130 nautical miles which would extend to the limit of the maximum claim according to the equidistance principle.

Seven countries define their claims to the continental shelf by distances measured from the coast. South Korea, El Salvador, Chile, Peru, Panama and Nicaragua simply claim the same distance for the continental shelf that they claim for territorial waters. The remaining country, Dahomey, claims 88 nautical miles beyond the outer edge of the territorial sea, which measures 12 nautical miles. Five countries define the outer limit of their submarine claims by the 200 metre isobath. The proclamations for Pakistan and Bangladesh are the same, being made in 1950 when these two states formed one country. The Ivory Coast and Yemen (San'a) both made their proclamations in 1967, and it is hard to understand why that limit was selected, since it represents the narrowest of the four possible seaward limits considered in the previous section. The depth claim by Ecuador is not very significant, since that country claims territorial waters of 200 nautical miles which extends well beyond the 200 metre isobath.

Five countries have announced general claims to 'the seabed and subsoil' or to 'the continental platform'. There is no geographical indication of why Guyana and Ireland have made such declarations, for they have fairly favourable geographical situations which provide theoretical claims to 120 square nautical miles of seabed for every nautical mile of coast. The claims of the other three countries are more understandable. Sri Lanka is one of the island states which possesses a comparatively narrow continental shelf, and Cameroun and the United Arab Emirates are both severely restricted by the claims of neighbouring states. It may be that these last two countries have avoided the descriptive formula of the convention so that they can resist any claims by their neighbours for drawing lines of equidistance between adjacent and opposite claims. Indonesia, Iceland and the Philippines—all archipelagos—have announced claims to the continental margins as far as it proves possible to exploit them. This coincidence seems fortuitous, because careful examination of the particular circumstances of each case reveals significant differences, with Iceland being the most favoured and the Philippines the most handicapped.

By the middle of 1973 the Convention on the Continental Shelf had been ratified by forty-four countries, among which were the states in control of the four dependent territories included in this survey. This heterogeneous group of states includes states revealing a wide variation in geographical circumstances, such as Fiji, an island with a very narrow shelf; Mauritius, an island situated on a very extensive submarine margin; Finland, with a restricted claim on a semi-enclosed sea; and South Africa occupying a peninsula jutting into an ocean devoid of alien islands. The remaining twenty-two countries, although they have not ratified the convention, have proclaimed their claim to the continental margin in the terms of the convention: that is to a depth of 200 metres, or beyond where exploitation is possible.

N

SPECIFIC BOUNDARY AGREEMENTS AND
BOUNDARY DISPUTES

By the middle of 1973 there were nineteen bilateral agreements governing the boundaries between national claims to submarine areas. Eleven of the agreements were between states on opposite shores of seas and gulfs; five were between states sharing an adjacent continental margin, and three combined the features of both. The last three cases involved Italy and Yugoslavia; Finland and the Soviet Union, where the boundary started in an adjacent situation and then continued between opposite shores; and Malaysia and Indonesia, which had to draw three boundary segments, two of which separated adjacent claims and one which divided the continental shelf between opposite shores. It is noticeable that these agreements concern semi-enclosed seas, such as the North Sea, the Adriatic, the Baltic Sea, the Persian Gulf and the Arafura and Timor Seas, or straits, such as the Skagerrak and the Strait of Malacca. It is predictable that attempts will be made to negotiate boundaries in similar waters, such as the Caribbean, the South and East China Seas and the Sea of Japan. Difficulties will be most acute in those areas where there are major ideological and political differences between the competing countries.

These agreements are interesting because they show the practical solutions which states have adopted to overcome the general problems outlined in the last chapter. In the following discussion, examples will be taken from these agreements to illustrate the resolution of difficulties involving deep depressions in the structure of the continental margin; offshore islands; straight baselines, and concave coasts.

The Convention on the Continental Shelf does not make it clear whether states are entitled to claim detached areas of the shelf, separated from the coastal shelf by troughs, trenches and submarine canyons, with water depths far in excess of 200 metres, and patently incapable of exploitation at the present time. This problem first became critical in discussions between Norway and the United Kingdom. The Norwegian Trench borders the Norwegian coast from the head of the Skagerrak to latitude 62° north and restricts the width of the Norwegian continental shelf at depths of 100 fathoms (180 metres) or less to a maximum of 11 nautical miles. The width of the trench varies from 30 nautical miles, in the southern reaches, to 70 nautical miles at the northern terminus, and the maximum depth of various sections vary from 130 to 355 fathoms (235 to 650 metres). At first the British government contended that the Norwegian Trench marked the proper division between the British and Norwegian continental shelves. The Norwegian authorities contended that the Norwegian Trench was only an accidental depression in the surface of the continental shelf, and that the correct boundary was a line of equidistance between the British and Norwegian coasts. Eventually the British government accepted the Norwegian view, perhaps to avoid further delays in securing firm title to potential oil and gas fields, and an agreement was signed on 10 March 1965, fixing a boundary 359 nautical miles long, by eight turning points de-fined by geographical co-ordinates.

A similar problem occurred more recently between Australia and Indonesia. The Australian government claimed the sur-rounding continental shelf in 1953, and during subsequent years began to issue mineral exploration permits relating to the seabed between Australia and Indonesia. In the Arafura Sea, east of longitude 133° 14′ east, which intersects the Australian coast close to the Goulburn Islands, the permits were granted only as far north as the line of equidistance between Australia and West Irian and Kepulauan Aru. This suggests that Australia judged the continental shelf to be common to both Australia and Indonesia. West of this longitude, permits were granted for areas as far north as the southern edge of the Timor Trough. The Timor Trough is a deep depression in the sea floor, which has an axis roughly parallel to the south coast of Timor, and between 25 and 50 nautical miles from that coast. The width of the trough is 70 nautical miles in some sections and depths of 1,300 fathoms (2,380 metres) have been recorded. Plainly it was the view of the Australian government that in this area there were two continental shelves. There was a very narrow Timor continental shelf, and there was a very wide Australian shelf. The boundaries of the areas claimed by Australia were published in 1967.[4]

Given this view of the structure of the sea floor of the Timor Sea, the Australian government was under no obligation to consult Indonesia about the limits of the Australian claims. However, Indonesia did not share this geomorphological view. In the opinion of the Indonesian government there was a single continental shelf between the two countries, and it was therefore necessary to agree on a boundary separating the areas which belonged to each. The Timor Trough was considered by Indonesia to be an accidental depression in the sea floor, not the definitive edge of two shelves.

If the Indonesian view was correct then Indonesia was entitled to a boundary which coincided with the line of equidistance between the opposite shores. It is necessary at this point to note that the island of Timor is shared between Indonesia and Portugal, and that theoretically Portugal can also object to Australia's unilateral decision about shelf boundaries. If the limit proclaimed by Australia in 1967 is compared with the line of equidistance between Australia and Timor, it is apparent that a lens-shaped area of the shelf is involved and this is shown in Figure 19. West of the theoretical Portuguese claim, the area in dispute between Australia and Indonesia was about 6,075 square nautical miles, whereas east of the Portuguese area the same two countries were contesting an area of about 9,600 square nautical miles. The theoretical claim of Portugal concerns an area of 9,100 square nautical miles.

This serious disagreement in principle between Australia and Indonesia did not prevent them from reaching an agreement about the continental shelf in the Arafura Sea on 18 May 1971. This agreement defined the boundary for 514 nautical miles by

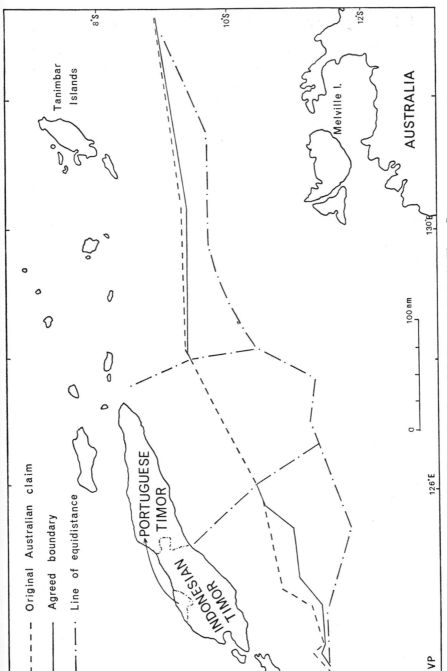

Fig 19 Continental shelf boundaries in the Timor Sea

reference to twelve turning points. The western limit of this line had the co-ordinates 8° 53′ south and 133° 23′ east. The boundary west of this terminus was reserved for further discussions. These discussions were held in October 1972, and within one week an amicable agreement had been concluded on 9 October 1972. The first article of the agreement defines the boundary, by four turning points, from the western terminus of the 1972 treaty to the theoretical line of equidistance between Portuguese and Indonesian claims in latitude 9° 28′ south. The new line lies very close to the the boundary claimed by Australia, and the concession to Indonesia amounted to about 750 square nautical miles. The second article dealt with the boundary west of the theoretical Portuguese claim. This line stretches for 195 nautical miles, by nine specified points, to the western terminus of the lens-shaped disputed area. Calculations show that Australia conceded about 1,350 square nautical miles of the continental shelf, for which exploration permits had been granted.

The eighth article of the treaty referred to those companies granted permits by Australia for exploration in areas which had been transferred to Indonesian authority. Upon application to the Indonesian government they would be able to negotiate a production-sharing contract under Indonesian law, on terms not less favourable that those production-sharing contracts already in existence.

Thus in this, unlike that involving the Norwegian Trench, the negotiators did not completely ignore the deep depression in the continental shelf. Presumably, in return for Australia's acceptance of the position that Indonesia was entitled to an area of the shelf south of the Timor Trough, the Indonesian authorities did not insist on claiming authority as far south as the line of equidistance.

It was mentioned in the last chapter that there are many cases where the problem of claims to detached areas of the submarine margin occur. One case involves a disagreement between Japan and South Korea. Two small groups of Japanese islands, called Danjo Gunto and Tori Shima, are located 95 nautical miles west of Kyushu. The largest of the islands is only 2 miles long, and one of them, called Meshima, alone serves any purpose; it is used for a lighthouse and radio signal tower. Between Kyushu and these two island groups lies the head of a submarine depression, which continues southwards between the continental shelf of the East China Sea and the Japanese Ryuku Islands. The depression, between Kyushu and the islands, is 50 nautical miles wide and 330 fathoms (600 metres) deep; however, between the islands and Fukue Island, which is the closest Japanese territory, the depression is only 20 nautical miles wide and 220 fathoms (400 metres) deep. In the view of the Japanese government, these two groups of islands entitle Japan to a share of the continental shelf of the East China Sea, and this view seems to be in accord with the convention which specifically refers to the submarine areas adjacent to the coasts of islands. This view is rejected by the government of South Korea for three reasons, which have been described by Park.[5] First, the Korean authorities argue that Danjo Gunto and Tori Shima are too insignificant to justify claims to the continental shelf. Secondly, the view is advanced that the head of the depression, between the islands and the rest of Japanese territory, constitutes special circumstances, which make an equidistant line inappropriate. Thirdly, the Korean government believes that the shelf, on which the isolated Japanese islands stand, constitutes 'a natural prolongation' of Korean territory, which is the phraseology used by the International Court of Justice in its findings on the North Sea cases. On 30 May 1970 the Korean government issued a proclamation defining mineral exploration areas on the continental shelf, one of which occupies almost all the area which might be claimed by Japan, through ownership of the two island groups. The only concession made by Korea is to exclude the seabed within 12 nautical miles of the islands.

The area in dispute forms part of the belt of seabed between Japan and Taiwan which has been identified as having the greatest likelihood of containing gas and oil fields in the northeast Asian continental margin.[6] In view of the international oil shortages which developed in 1973, it seems likely that Japan, one of the countries most severely affected, will take firm action to uphold its perceived rights to a share of the continental shelf of the East China Sea. The Japanese government has another claim to areas of the continental shelf; 465 nautical miles southwest of Danjo Gunto, the Senkaku Islands, lying 100 nautical miles northeast of Taiwan, are claimed by Japan. These islands lie at the seaward extremity of the continental shelf, extending eastwards from the coast of mainland China. Between them and the nearest Japanese islands, which are called the Sakishima Islands, there is a trough with water depths of 1,466 fathoms (2,680 metres). The Senkaku Islands are also claimed by Taiwan and by the People's Republic of China. Park has unravelled the complex history of these islands, but each contestant in this dispute can fasten on to those parts of that history which best supports their case; the matter is not free from controversy.[7]

This examination of disputes between Japan and Korea, and between Japan and China and Taiwan, introduces the vexed question of the treatment of islands in establishing continental-shelf boundaries. During the debate leading to the Convention of the Continental Shelf, many delegates referred to the problem of small islands which, unimportant in themselves, gave theoretical claims to large areas of the continental shelf. Because of the diversity of islands in size and the variation of their geographical location in terms of adjoining mainlands, it did not prove possible to establish any general rule to deal with this problem. There seems to be no other solution than for states to treat each case on its merits. There are four basic actions which states can take to solve problems which arise in drawing continental-shelf boundaries involving islands. First, it can be agreed that each island, no matter how small, forms a point on the baseline between which the line of equidistance is drawn. This decision gives full effect to the continental shelf rights of each fragment of national territory. Secondly, states can decide to ignore the existence of intervening islands and to draw the line of equidistance between mainland shores. Such a solution gives no effect to claims based on the existence of islands. Thirdly, some boundary other than a line of equidistance can be negotiated, which gives partial effect to the existence of islands. Lastly, states could select one of the preceding three lines and agree that they will share the development of any key resources which straddle the boundary. Existing agreements show examples of all four arrangements.

On 20 May 1965, the governments of Finland and the Soviet Union agreed on a boundary which separated their areas of jurisdiction in the Gulf of Finland. In 1940 the two governments had agreed on a boundary extending for 30 nautical miles into the gulf from the terminus of the land boundary. The new agreement firstly defined a median line between the territorial waters of the two countries for a further 7·4 nautical miles. The boundary then continues for a further 139·7 nautical miles, as a line of equidistance which gives all islands full effect. This solution seems appropriate in this case because neither country possesses islands which deflect the line of equidistance significantly towards the other mainland.

The North Sea boundaries negotiated between Norway and the United Kingdom; Norway and Denmark; and the Netherlands and the United Kingdom, also gave full effect to the existence of all islands.

Qatar and Iran are two countries which decided to ignore all islands when they drew a boundary between their continental shelf claims on 20 September 1969.[8] Inspection of charts of the area suggest that this decision represented a concession by Qatar, because possession of Jazirat Halul, 50 nautical miles from the coast, would have shifted the line of equidistance in Qatar's favour, if the islands had been given full effect. The main Iranian island, Sheykh Sho'eyb, is only 11 nautical miles from the coast. However, on the Iranian side of the agreed line there are several shoals, such as Shah Allum Shoal, and Cable and Stiffe Banks, and it is possible that there are tiny islands associated with these features. Whether this is the situation or not, it was probably in Qatar's interest to secure a clear title to important areas of the seabed at that stage, rather than insist on giving full effect to Jazirat Halul, which may have delayed settlement of the issue.

Continental-shelf boundaries drawn between Saudi Arabia and Iran; Saudi Arabia and Bahrain; Abu Dhabi and Qatar; and Italy and Yugoslavia provide examples of situations where partial effect has been given to the existence of islands. The arrangement and ownership of islands in the Adriatic meant that if full effect had been given to their existence Italy would have been placed at a disadvantage. If the islands had been ignored, and a line of equidistance drawn between the mainlands, then Yugoslavia would have suffered. By not insisting on the islands of Jabuka, Pelagruz and Kajola being given full effect, Yugoslavia conceded 867 square nautical miles. As a slight compensation Italy did not receive the full benefit of Pianosa Island, and thereby conceded 120 square nautical miles to Yugoslavia.[9]

One of the features which made the continental-shelf boundary between Iran and Saudi Arabia interesting was the formula used to overcome disagreements about the existence of Khark Island. This feature is located 17 nautical miles from the Iranian coast, and if it had been given full effect it would have benefited Iran. The agreement, reached on 24 October 1968, produced the following solution. Two lines were constructed, one giving full effect to Khark Island, the other ignoring its existence. The area of seabed contained between these two lines was then divided equally between the two countries. The Geographer has described this as giving 'half-effect' to an island.[10]

The agreements dividing the continental shelf between Saudi Arabia and Bahrain, Qatar and Abu Dhabi provide examples of the fourth solution. Both give some islands full effect and ignore others, and both include arrangements for sharing revenue from specific oil and gas fields. The treaty between Abu Dhabi and Qatar, concluded on 20 March 1969, gives only partial effect to Halat Dalma Island, which belongs to Qatar, and Dayyinah

Island, which belongs to Abu Dhabi. The treaty also stipulates that one of the turning points on the line will be a well on the al-Bunduq field, and that this field will be developed by Abu Dhabi, which must share the revenue from this field equally with Qatar. The shelf boundary which stretches for 98·5 nautical miles between Saudi Arabia and Bahrain gives full effect to Saudi Arabia's Kaskus Island, and Bahrain's Khor Island. However, two of the fourteen turning points are located on islands, one belonging to each country. As Figure 20 shows, the treaty signed on 22 February 1958 also designated an area of 368·4 square nautical miles, which will be developed by Saudi Arabia, which is required to share the revenue obtained with Bahrain.[11]

One possible dispute concerning the importance of islands involves Khmer and Thailand. On 1 July 1972 the government of Khmer proclaimed the boundaries of its continental shelf, and from the chart which accompanied that statement it appears to have been selective in its use of islands.[12] For example, the boundary passes straight across Kut Island, which belongs to Thailand and forms part of the straight baseline system declared by that country on 12 June 1970. In addition the line gives full effect to the Khmer islands of Wai and Panjang, while totally ignoring the Thai island of Krah and certain small islands belonging to South Vietnam. It seems unlikely that Khmer's neighbours will accept this unilateral declaration without protest.

The potential importance of islands is revealed by: Chinese claims to the Senkaku Islands north of Taiwan and to the Paracel Islands in the South China Sea; Iran's annexation of islands in the Strait of Hormuz; competition between Gabon and Equatorial Guinea over islands in Corisco Bay; through claims by Papua New Guinea to the northernmost Australian islands in Torres Strait, and by South Vietnam's claim to the alleged Khmer island of Phu Quoc.

Three international agreements define continental-shelf boundaries involving straight baselines. The treaty between

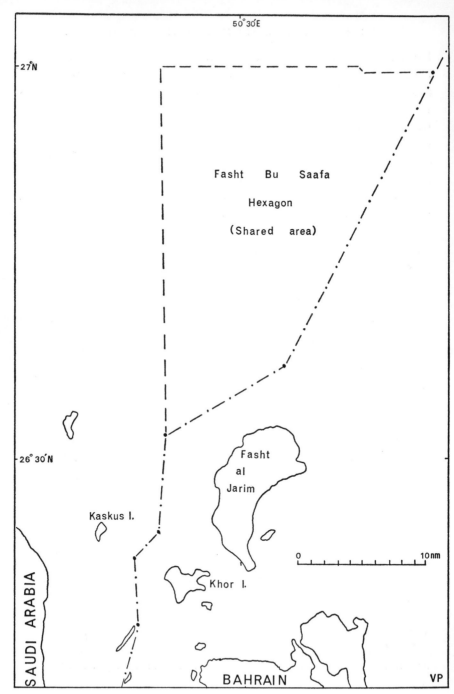

Fig 20   The continental shelf boundary between Saudi Arabia and Bahrain

Norway and the Soviet Union, signed on 15 February 1957, governs a situation where only one of the parties uses a straight baseline. The Norwegian government claims Varanger Fjord as an historic bay, and it is closed by a straight line linking the land terminus of the Norwegian–Soviet boundary with Kibergneset, which lies 30 nautical miles to the north. If Norway claimed the same territorial sea as the Soviet Union, namely 12 nautical miles, the latter country would have been placed at a disadvantage by the construction of the straight closing line. However, because Norway only claims 4 nautical miles, the intersection of the two territorial seas does not place the Soviet Union at a marked disadvantage, as Figure 21 shows. From the intersection of the territorial waters the continental-shelf boundary is drawn as a straight line to the mid-point of a line joining Kibergneset with Cape Nemetskig in the Soviet Union. It is evident that the Norwegian baseline has not been given full effect, probably because a line equidistant between that baseline and the Soviet coast would pass through areas of Soviet territorial waters.

On 27 October 1969 the governments of Indonesia and Malaysia agreed on three boundaries separating their continental shelves in the Strait of Malacca and the South China Sea. There was originally some dispute over these boundaries when only Indonesia had a system of straight baselines, and it is generally believed that Malaysia constructed a system of straight baselines to strengthen its counter claims against Indonesia. The only puzzling feature of this agreement is that the easternmost boundary, which separates Kepulaua Natuna Selatan and Sarawak, is not an equidistant line and appears to favour Malaysia.

One possible dispute concerning a continental shelf involving a straight baseline may concern Australia and Papua New Guinea. On 30 September 1969 the Australian government claimed the Coral Sea Islands Territory, which is bounded by the Australian coast, parallels 12° south and 24° south, and the meridian 157° 10′ east. This area contains numerous islands,

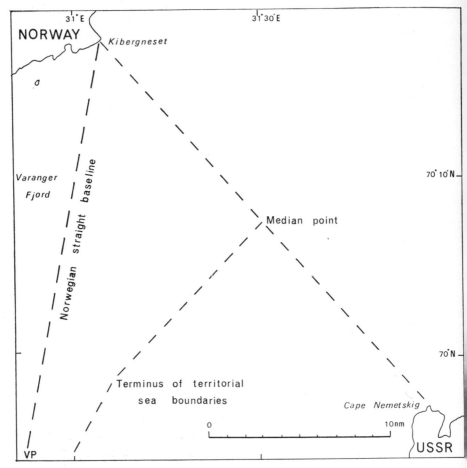

Fig 21   The continental shelf boundary between the Soviet Union and Norway

cays and reefs. The northern boundary runs within 20 nautical miles of Tagula Island, which belongs to Papua New Guinea. Since the water in this region is over 2,000 fathoms (3,660 metres) deep, it is probable that questions regarding fishing grounds will arise much sooner than a dispute over the continental shelf.

The final special circumstance which has to be considered

concerns concave coasts. In the last chapter it was noted that West Germany sought to redress its disadvantage, in respect of claims by Denmark and the Netherlands, before the International Court of Justice. As a result of the judgement in that case, West Germany was able to negotiate with Denmark and the Netherlands boundaries which were more favourable than those based on lines of equidistance.[13] The new boundaries also extend the area under German authority to the middle of the North Sea, where it is generally believed that there is greater likelihood of finding commercial fields.

Three final points should be made about agreements dealing with continental-shelf boundaries. First, provision should be made to reduce the possibility of conflict over resources which lie athwart the boundary. Some agreements, such as those between Australia and Indonesia, Saudi Arabia and Iran, and Iran and Qatar, stipulate that drilling may not be conducted within a certain distance of the boundary; the distance is 125 metres (410 feet) in the case of the treaty between Iran and Qatar and 500 metres (1,640 feet) in the case of Iran's treaty with Saudia Arabia. Several treaties, including those between Sweden and Norway, and Malaysia and Indonesia, include articles stating that the parties will consult on the best means of developing any trans-boundary resource. Secondly, it is probably assumed that once the boundary is fixed it cannot be changed either by coastal changes, or the proclamation of new straight baselines, or more accurate surveys. None of the treaties specifically mention these points, but they are probably self-evident. In some areas of the world coastal changes can occur fairly quickly, and it is not unknown for new islands to appear in certain coastal waters. An analysis of the continental-shelf boundary between Venezuela and Trinidad and Tobago notes that the Venezuelan coast has been built out since the treaty was concluded in 1942. Mud flats near the Western Channel and the Serpent's Mouth are areas of very heavy deposition.[14] The present alignment of the coast makes it appear that Venezuela secured less than its due share of the continental shelf. Plainly it would be intolerable if boundaries were subject to revision because of the kind of changes mentioned. Such a practice would mean that states had no guarantees that their long-term plans for the development of the continental shelf could be fulfilled without fresh claims from neighbouring countries.

The third point is that many of the agreements carry the boundaries through, or into, waters that are deeper than 200 metres, or the approximate equivalent of 100 fathoms. The agreements made by Norway with the Soviet Union, Sweden and the United Kingdom all involve waters in excess of these depths, as do the agreements between Italy and Yugoslavia, and Australia and Indonesia. Other countries, such as South Korea and the United States, have issued exploration permits in waters deeper than 200 metres. One of the few cases of a boundary stopping at the 100 fathom isobath occurs in the easternmost boundary between the continental shelves of Malaysia and Indonesia.

The High Seas

IT was noted in the first chapter that the attention of political geographers interested in the oceans had been focused on the waters near land. This emphasis was explained by the precise, and sometimes conflicting, claims made by states in such waters, by their use to obtain valuable resources of food and minerals, and by the concentration of commercial shipping routes near coasts. However, a general survey of the political geography of the oceans must take account of the high seas, lying beyond the limits of national sovereignty, which still occupy a larger area of the earth's surface than the total area of national territory and territorial waters. This chapter considers the high seas in three sections. The first examines the nature of the high seas and the second explores the important differences between the high seas and other maritime zones from the viewpoint of the political and economic geographer. The third section reviews the uses made of the high seas, and assesses the attitudes of different groups of countries to the major contemporary issues concerning the high seas.

THE NATURE OF THE HIGH SEAS

Modern technology now demands that two distinct areas of the high seas are recognised. First there are the waters of the high seas, and second there is the seabed which underlies those waters. The 1970s will witness the first commercial extraction of mineral resources from the deep seabed, made possible by improved exploration techniques and dredging devices. It is no longer possible to leave consideration of the deep seabed only to geophysicists and geomorphologists interested in plate tectonics. As the final section of this chapter will show, a serious political debate is now being conducted by the countries of the world to determine the rules for the exploitation of the deep seabed.

There are a number of important differences between these two components of the high seas. First, users of the high seas are aware of the precise limits of the waters. The unqualified freedoms to sail on and fly over the high seas apply outside the limits of territorial waters; the freedom of fishing in the high seas also lies outside territorial waters or exclusive fishing zones, if they have been proclaimed. The last two chapters demonstrated that there is no precise outer limit of national claims to the continental shelf. There would be no doubt about the freedom of states to lay submarine cables or pipelines on the seabed in the middle of the Indian or Pacific Oceans, but there could be no such certainty in areas closer to shore, yet still outside territorial waters. The Convention on the Continental Shelf gives the coastal state the right to impede the laying of submarine cables and pipelines, while taking reasonable measures to explore and exploit the continental shelf. This distinction means that along most coasts of the world the marginal areas of the high seas will consist only of the waters, for the underlying seabed will be subject to national claims and control. The third article of the Continental Shelf Convention specifically notes that the rights of the coastal state over the continental shelf do not affect the legal status of the waters or air space above as high seas.

The second difference between the waters and seabed of the high seas concerns the use which has been made of them, throughout history. There is a long tradition, whose beginnings are unknown, of man sailing on the oceans and catching fish there, whereas the first submarine cable was laid across the Atlantic in 1866 and the commercial exploitation of the mineral resources of the deep seabed is only just beginning. Several other distinctions arise from this important difference. Over several centuries, a comprehensive code of rules and international law have been developed to govern navigation, safety standards and the control of illegal activities on the high seas. This point is illustrated by the debate on the Convention on the High Seas in 1958, which was less acrimonious than the debates on the other subjects and that this convention, in 1973, had been ratified by more countries than any of the other three conventions. There are no such clear rules to govern the use of the seabed, and attempts to produce a body of laws to cover this situation during the period 1970–3 simply served to demonstrate the sharp divisions which exist on this question. It also follows that the waters of the high seas have been fairly thoroughly charted, and that the important variations in salinity, fish stocks, and the climatic elements, such as fog and gales, which affect navigation, have been detected. This means that reasonably accurate assessments of the potential wealth of the waters have been made and such assessments have already resulted in conservation measures, such as those to avoid the destruction of certain species of whales. By contrast, knowledge of the configuration and structure of the seabed is still fragmentary, and estimates of the mineral wealth lying on and under the seabed are only crude guesses.

It is predictable that when an accurate survey of the resources of the seabed is eventually made, it will reveal significant regional variations. Thus commercial use of the seabed in the future will exhibit the same regional concentrations already evident in respect of the waters of the high seas. Maps showing the arterial shipping lanes indicate that they occupy only comparatively small proportions of the oceans. The high densities of marine traffic in the north Atlantic and around the Cape of Good Hope are in direct contrast with the very low densities in the south Atlantic and Cape Horn. Some of the remarkable accounts of South Sea islanders, who have drifted thousands of miles without sighting any ships, confirm that this is also an area with a low density of commercial traffic. It seems likely that the deep troughs, such as those in the western Pacific, and the seabed underlying seasonally stormy waters in high latitudes, and zones with fast-flowing ocean currents will be amongst the last exploited for their mineral resources, because of the technical problems these conditions present. For example, at the end of the 1970s there were renewed reports that oil would be found off the Falkland Islands. Some authorities in the oil industry believe that seasonal storms and strong ocean currents would make extraction of petroleum in this region very difficult. Since transport costs of minerals derived from the sea will play as important a role in determining total costs and profit margins as they do in respect of minerals mined on land, it follows that resources closest to potential markets will be developed first. Those markets will probably continue to be located mainly in North America and West Europe. It is also reasonable to expect that the greatest emphasis in the early exploration and exploitation of the deep seabed will be on those minerals which command the highest prices, or which have a special strategic importance. Natural gas and crude petroleum will be obvious targets for deep-sea exploration, and it is fortunate that drilling and extraction techniques for these fuels are amongst the best developed.

DIFFERENCES BETWEEN THE HIGH SEAS AND OTHER MARITIME ZONES

The economic and political geographer must recognise that the high seas possess qualities which set them apart from internal waters, territorial waters, fishing zones and the continental shelf. The most obvious difference is noted by the second article of the Convention on the High Seas, which states that 'no state may validly purport to subject any part of them to its sovereignty'.[1] In all the other maritime zones, states exercise varying degrees of authority and sovereignty, either over the total zone or over the activities which may be conducted there. This means that throughout the main body of the high seas there are no disputes over areas between states; it has been shown earlier that such disputes are amongst the most common and serious between states in other maritime zones. Disputes between states in the high seas are comparatively infrequent and are more likely to be concerned with questions of insurance and liability in the case of accidents involving ships sailing under different national flags, or with the origin and destination of anadromous fish. Around the margins of the high seas, disputes between states may be more common. They would generally involve disputes over the status of the waters. The coastal state may claim territorial waters or exclusive fishing zones, which are disputed by another state whose nationals wish to use those areas as part of the high seas. This type of dispute occurred over the activities of American fishermen off the western littoral of South America where some states claim territorial waters of 200 nautical miles. Disputes of this type could arise over the insistence of some countries on the right to overfly those areas of the high seas which have only recently been incorporated into the territorial waters of another state.

Since World War II it is apparent that the area of the high seas has been reduced as the area of other maritime zones has increased. This can be attributed to a number of causes. First, several old states, and the majority of states created since 1955, claim territorial seas wider than 3 nautical miles, and sixteen states now claim more than 12 nautical miles. Secondly, many states have constructed extensive systems of straight baselines which have pushed the outer edge of the territorial seas further from the low-water mark. The straight baselines proclaimed by Burma and the archipelago states of Indonesia and the Philippines provide good examples of this process. Thirdly, a number of states have claimed special zones beyond their territorial seas in which they claim the right to regulate particular activities. The most obvious of these are the exclusive fishing zones, but others allow the state to make regulations to avoid pollution of the sea. Canada has given a lead in this activity by declaring a zone, 100 nautical miles wide, where it can act to control all activities which could pollute Canadian Arctic waters.[2] The United Kingdom, Portugal, Singapore and Uruguay are other countries which have followed suit. Fourthly, some erosion of the high seas has been caused by the construction of drilling platforms on the continental shelves outside territorial waters. Such structures are most numerous in the Gulf of Mexico, the North Sea and the Persian Gulf, and off the west coast of the United States of America. States are permitted to declare safety zones 1 kilometre (0·6 miles) wide around these constructions. Finally, the temporary erosion of the high seas occurred in the Pacific around Muroroa Atoll, in 1973, when the French government was conducting nuclear tests and declared wide safety areas from which alien ships and planes were prohibited.

The third difference, which was noted at the beginning of this chapter, is that the high seas are used less intensively for commercial and recreational navigation, fishing, and mineral exploration and exploitation, than the other maritime zones closer to shore. An important difference from the viewpoint of landlocked states is that on the high seas they possess the same rights and opportunities as coastal states, a situation which does not obtain in the case of other maritime zones. This explains the existence of merchant marine sailing under the flags of Switzerland and Bolivia. This equality will be more prized by landlocked states, if the present dream of extracting large quantities of mineral wealth from the deep seabed becomes a reality.

The final difference is that the high seas provide one of the most important theatres where international co-operation on a large scale can be fostered. If the present difficulties over the regime to govern the exploitation of the seabed can be overcome, it will mean that genuine international co-operation has already been achieved and that the way is opened for co-operation on an increased scale.

NATIONAL INTERESTS IN THE HIGH SEAS

States or their citizens use the high seas for nine purposes. Easily the most important at the present time is the transport of cargo and people, either by ship or plane. The freedoms of surface navigation and overflight are important bases for the interconnected, international economy. Without these freedoms the interchange of commodities would possibly be restricted, and would certainly be made more costly, with serious repercussions for levels of development in most countries of the world. The second, most important, use of the high seas is for commercial fishing, and it was noted in the fourth chapter that the most productive areas of the high seas occur over the continental shelves.

The remaining uses of the high seas are not as important as commercial transport and fishing, although predictably some will increase in importance while others will decline. Britain and France, which formerly possessed empires, and the Soviet Union and the United States of America, which today play a major role in international politics, use the high seas for security and political purposes. This use involves the maintenance of a navy and the establishment of detecting devices either on the seabed or in space. During the last century imperial navies were the instrument which helped in the acquisition and control of colonies. During the first half of the twentieth century navies played vital roles in two world wars. But since then their role has been much less apparent. The United States of America has used its navy effectively off Lebanon, Cuba and South Vietnam, but otherwise naval actions have been rare by comparison with the spate of land conflicts. Cohen has written a very interesting article forecasting reduced reliance by the major navies on surface vessels, and a much greater reliance on submarines and missiles.[3] This development, together with the increasing use of nuclear fuels, is releasing navies from the need for foreign bases. Had this book been written twenty-five years ago an analysis of naval bases would have formed an important section.

Communication between continents by submarine cables and the transport of suitable commodities through pipelines are two other uses made of the deep seabed. It is unlikely that either will significantly increase in importance for communication via satellites is becoming increasingly common and will probably become less expensive. Transport via submarine pipelines is only appropriate for narrow seas, and fears about pollution may discourage the further construction of such pipelines. Some countries and organisations conduct research in connection with the high seas. Some of this research is of a strictly academic nature, connected with the formation of continents or the biology of plants and fish. Other research is aimed to improve the commercial exploitation of the high seas, generally by locating fish and mineral resources, and by understanding the processes which operate to create or change them.

The extraction of minerals from the deep seabed is only just beginning; current production takes place on the continental shelf subject to the authority of coastal states. There is plenty of evidence that this use of the high seas will become increasingly important. Later discussion will show that there are deep disagreements between states on the structure of an international regime to control this activity. The high seas are also used for recreational purposes such as cruising and fishing. This would rank as one of the least important uses, apparently devoid of any risk of international conflict. However, Christy has noted that the effective operations of Japanese long-line fishermen off the coast of the United States, in catching large numbers of marlin and swordfish, has stimulated sportsmen to seek legislation to preserve a sufficient number of these fish for recreational purposes.[4]

The final use which is made of the high seas is for waste disposal. Waste products enter the high seas from four sources. First there is the deliberate and accidental discharge of waste during man's activities on the high seas. These activities include the dumping of explosives, radioactive waste and other harmful products which governments wish to remove from their territory and arsenals. They also include discharge from vessels of rubbish and ballast. Oil rigs on the continental shelf may also yield waste products which are dumped in the high seas. Secondly, there is the discharge from outfalls constructed into the oceans from the shore near large cities. Thirdly, waste material is often released into rivers which carry it to the sea. Finally, waste gases poured into the atmosphere may be carried over the oceans and may take part in the exchanges between the oceans and the atmosphere. Schachter and Serwer have published an excellent account of problems of marine pollution, treating the subject by investigation of the nature of the waste products rather than by their source.[5]

If these various uses are contrasted according to the number of states involved in them, four groups of uses emerge. Most states in the world would use the high seas for commercial transport, fishing, the disposal of waste, recreation, and communication via submarine cables. Plainly these states vary widely in the intensity of different uses, but the important point is that they all would be affected, to some extent, by international regulations governing these activities. A much smaller group of states would add research and the transport of material by submarine pipelines to the five uses in the first group. Academic research is a luxury which many developing countries cannot afford, and commercial research is most likely to be undertaken by the developed countries which use the high seas most intensively. Countries which deal extensively in petroleum products and those located on narrow seas make the greatest use of submarine pipelines. The third group contains only the extraction of minerals from the deep seabed, which appears to be the prerogative of major developed countries, such as the Soviet Union, the United States of America, Britain, France, West Germany and Japan. Finally, the operation of navies in distant areas of the high seas is undertaken only by the former major colonial powers, France and Britain, and by the Soviet Union and the United States of America.

This review indicates a division between the developing states of the world, which conduct fewer activities on the high seas, and the developed states which make a much wider range of uses of the same area. This impression is confirmed when the scales of particular activities are examined. It is the developed countries which operate the largest merchant marines and commercial airlines; it is the well-equipped fleets of developed countries which catch the largest volume of fish in the high seas; more use is made of submarine cables by developed countries; and they probably contribute a larger proportion of industrial waste to the high seas. The transport of cargo and people across the high seas is a lucrative industry which yields most profit to the developed countries. Governments, such as those of Norway and Britain, derive revenue from the taxes paid by shipping lines and airlines; these operations generate invisible exports in the form of insurance premiums; they also provide employment for nationals and a measure of security in time of war. It is therefore not surprising that many developing countries set as an early target the creation of a national shipping line. Panama, Liberia, and Honduras are three developing countries which have sought access to this commercial activity by encouraging the registration of vessels under their flag. Since each state is able to determine the conditions by which it will register ships under its flag, some states have been able to solicit custom by fixing less demanding conditions than other countries. The developed European countries generally oppose this development of flags of convenience, not because of inferior safety standards or lower wage rates on ships registered in this way, but because such vessels have lower operating costs and are therefore more competitive with national lines. The Convention on the High Seas insists that there must be 'a genuine link between the State and the ship', but this has proved an ambiguous condition with little effectiveness.[6]

It is also true that the developed countries of the world are better placed than the developing countries to take advantage of major new opportunities now becoming available in the field of mineral extraction. This means that the developing countries are generally unconcerned with the erosion of the high seas by national claims, since they are less equipped to use the present and potential resources of those regions. Earlier chapters have made it clear that the main erosion of the area of the high seas is being caused by the unilateral claims of developing countries to straight baselines, to historic bays, to wide territorial seas and to exclusive fishing zones. Most developing countries, especially in Africa and South America, have no fears concerning the disappearance of areas of high seas in international straits, because their exports and imports do not pass through such straits, and they have no naval vessels which might be barred from passage. Indeed the knowledge that the erosion of the extent of the high seas operates against the freedom of action of major powers may be a positive recommendation for some countries of the Third World. The government of China has persistently warned these countries to be on their guard against the efforts of the United States of America and the Soviet Union to establish hegemony over the world's oceans. In an effort to reduce the naval operations of major powers the General Assembly of the United Nations declared, in December 1971, that the Indian Ocean was a zone of peace in which warships should not be used to threaten the littoral states. However, the declaration has not prevented the continued presence of foreign fleets in those waters.

The prime difference between developed and developing countries in connection with the high seas concerns their attitude to the international authority that the United Nations recommended be established to control exploitation of the seabed outside the limits of national jurisdiction. It was noted in Chapter Five that in 1970 the General Assembly of the United Nations passed a resolution which contained the following two statements.

Affirming that there is an area of the seabed and the ocean floor, and the subsoil thereof, beyond the limits of national jurisdiction, the precise limits of which are yet to be determined . . .

Solemnly declares that: . . . All activities regarding the exploration and exploitation of the area and other related activities shall be governed by the international regime to be established.[7]

A number of states and groups of states subsequently published drafts of the regime which they favour, and there are some significant areas of disagreement. However, before these contentious matters which are of interest to economic and political geographers are considered, the areas of agreement should be stated. All the drafts concur that the area shall not be subject to appropriation by any state; that the area must be used exclusively for peaceful purposes; that the area is open to use by all states, including those which are landlocked; that operations should be conducted in a manner which will neither harm the marine environment, nor unjustifiably interfere with other uses of the high seas.

By the middle of 1973 the United States of America, the Soviet Union, Tanzania, and three groups of states had published drafts which defined the composition, powers and area of operation of the proposed international regime.[8] One of the groups of states consisted of the Organisation of African Unity, another contained thirteen South American countries, and the third group contained the landlocked states of Afghanistan, Austria, Hungary and Nepal, the severely shelf-locked countries of Belgium and Singapore, and the Netherlands, which is less severely shelf-locked. Comparison of these six drafts revealed five main areas of disagreement.

The first discrepancy concerns the limits of the area within which the international regime operates. The South American states, which do not include the landlocked countries of Paraguay and Bolivia, make no reference to the definition of the outer boundary of national jurisdiction. However, reference in the text to the need to respect the rights and legitimate interests of coastal states suggests that such states would be free to establish areas of national jurisdiction which fulfilled those rights and interests. The Tanzanian draft allows states to define their area of national jurisdiction either by an isobath measured in metres, or a distance in miles measured from the baseline used to fix the territorial sea. No maximum depth or distance is suggested. This arrangement coincides with the declaration by the Organisation of African Unity, which does not fix an outer limit to national sovereignty. According to this African draft, the international area lies outside the economic zones which states are entitled to define in accordance with 'regional considerations'. The Soviet Union fixes the limit of the international area at the edge of the continental shelf. Unfortunately this definition is imprecise, and there is no indication of whether the continental slopes and rises are considered as parts of the shelf. The Soviet draft leaves open the question of the limits of the international area where there is no continental shelf. In fact, there is always a continental shelf, although it may be extremely narrow, and presumably this article is included in order to allow some compensation to countries which have only narrow shelves. The American text defines the edge of the international area as the 200 metre isobath, and it makes careful provision for extending national boundaries where troughs, at greater depths than 200 metres, intersect the continental shelf. However, unlike the versions already considered, the American draft also proposes a zone known as the International Trusteeship Area. This zone lies between the 200 metre isobath and a line on the seabed, beyond the continental slope, where the gradient declines at a specific value. The actual value is not nominated, and would be settled by negotiation. The coastal state acts on behalf of the international regime within the Trusteeship Area. Oxman has noted that the coastal state does have a considerable measure of authority and control in this marginal zone.[9] The American proposal would require the negotiation of boundaries between adjoining Trusteeship Areas, and obviously only states which can reach the edge of the shelf will be able to avail themselves of the advantage of this provision. The group of land-locked and shelf-locked states proposes a similar arrangement. They would allow coastal states to fix their continental-shelf claims either by the 200 metre isobath or a line 40 miles distant from the baseline of the territorial sea. Belgium and Singapore are unable to reach either of these limits before meeting the claims of neighbouring and opposite states, and the Netherlands, while its submarine claims extend more than 40 miles from the coast, does not reach water deeper than 92 metres (50 fathoms). As an inducement to states to accept these narrow limits, the proposal then allows the construction of a 'coastal state priority zone' which is 40 miles wide. In this special zone the International Authority can neither conduct any exploration and exploitation, nor license such activities, without the consent of the coastal state. It is plainly in the interests of landlocked and shelf-locked states that the area of the seabed administered by the International Authority should be as large as possible. The Canadian authorities have indicated that the American definition of the outer edge of national jurisdiction as the 200 metre isobath is considered as being too restrictive, because Canada would thereby forfeit some of its continental shelf.[10] The Australian government favours acceptance of a patri-monial sea of 200 miles for three reasons.[11] First, this would probably moderate claims to wide territorial seas, and therefore reduce possible interference with the freedom of navigation. Secondly, in certain places the Australian continental shelf is narrower than 200 miles, and therefore Australia would acquire rights to a wider area than at present. Thirdly, Australia would also acquire control over the fishing rights in the patrimonial sea. However, since sections of the Australian shelf stretch for 350 miles from the coast, Australia will emphasise existing rights to control the total shelf, beyond the edge of the patri-monial sea. Only four other states are in this favoured position, thus it may be hard to attract support for this attitude.

The American draft differs from the other five in not speci-fically allowing the International Authority to undertake exploration and exploitation on its own behalf. The South American suggestion is that the Authority should undertake all exploitation itself or in partnership with private companies or states, and the remaining texts allow the Authority to undertake the project itself, or simply to license the area to a member state. Luard has criticised the idea of licensing states, which will in turn license companies.

> In fact, such a system has every possible disadvantage. It maximises the disputes which will occur concerning criteria and the allocation of blocks, since these become conflicts between states. It establishes a hotch-potch of differing regulations and jurisdictions across the entire seabed, of a confusing and totally unnecessary kind. It perpetuates the nation-state system in earth's last frontier, and parcels out hundreds of little colonies in an area which until now has been one of the few international zones of the world. Above all it maximises the bargaining power of a small number of technically qualified companies, for whose services 130 odd administering governments would be obliged desperately to compete.[12]

All the drafts follow the lead of the General Assembly resolution and stipulate that the exploration and exploitation must be carried out for the benefit of mankind as a whole, 'and taking into particular consideration the interests and needs of the developing countries'. However, the various drafts give different emphasis to this aim. The South American proposal is quite specific about this point. It requires the Authority to give technical assistance to developing countries, to employ qualified persons from developing countries, to locate processing plants for the resources extracted from the sea in developing countries, and to reserve zones for the preferential exploitation of developing states. The other drafts made only general statements about the importance of taking the special needs of developing countries into account, with the American and Soviet proposals apparently giving less emphasis than the others.

There was sharp disagreement amongst the drafts over the composition of the executive council of the International

Authority. The draft from the landlocked and shelf-locked states called for equal representation between coastal and non-coastal states. Only the South American and African drafts did not call for some representation of landlocked states, although the American proposal, that two of the twenty-four members should represent either landlocked or shelf-locked countries, meant that it would be possible for landlocked countries not to be represented. The other suggestions stipulated a number varying from three to five. In view of the fact that there are fourteen landlocked states in Africa, it will be surprising if the Organisation of African Unity does not support moves for representation of that group.

The Tanzanian, American, Soviet and South American proposals call for a balance in the geographical representation of the members of the council, but the American draft also distinguishes two main groups of states on economic grounds. The first group consists of the six most industrially advanced members, determined by gross national product. The second group consists of all other states. The council, according to the American proposal, would consist of the six members of the first group and eighteen members of the second group, of whom at least twelve must be classified as representing developing countries. Voting decisions under this system require a simple majority of both groups of states. This device gives an effective veto to the major industrial countries of the North Atlantic, if they have an identity of interest. This claim for a special position for the most developed countries presumably stems from the belief that they are conceding the most by agreeing to the creation of an international authority.

The final area of contention results from the fears of some developing countries that exploitation of minerals on the deep seabed will upset commodity prices. Developing countries such as Chile and Zambia, which depend so heavily on mineral exports, would not welcome exploitation of new resources on the seabed which would reduce world prices. For this reason the South American proposal calls for the Authority to have the power to take any necessary measures to prevent production from the seabed from having adverse economic effects on developing countries. The Tanzanian recommendation is that a price stabilisation board should be created which will keep world mineral commodity process under review and make adjustments in prices to ensure that there are no severe fluctuations. The other proposals make no recommendation on this point. It will probably be asking too much of the developed states, after foregoing their technical advantage for submarine mining, to insist that they subsidise mineral production in developing countries. This will be particularly true where petroleum is discovered in view of the recent increases in the price of crude petroleum by the Organisation of Petroleum Exporting Countries.

There seems to be scope for a real compromise on this issue. The developed maritime countries wish to avoid further erosion of the area of the high seas, and this lies within the gift of the developing countries. The developing countries wish to establish an international authority to control exploitation of the deep seabed, to prevent the states with advanced techniques from winning most of the potential mineral wealth. This can only be achieved if the developed states with the technical skills are prepared to forego their evident advantage in this area.

P

The Law of the Sea Conference, Caracas 1974

THIS conference, which was attended by the representatives of 148 countries, began on 20 June and lasted ten weeks. The only effective decision of the conference was that it should be reconvened in Geneva from 17 March to 3 May 1975. The first week of the conference was spent on procedural debates connected with the voting system to be adopted, and these gave an early indication of the division of opinion between a number of developed states, including the United States and the Soviet Union, and a larger number of developing states including the People's Republic of China, which occurred regularly during the remainder of the meeting. The group of developed countries were in favour of substantive decisions requiring the support of two-thirds of the states attending the conference; that would be ninety-nine votes. A much larger group of countries, including some developed states, favoured the decision being based on the support of two-thirds of the delegates present and voting, providing that number was a majority of the countries attending the session. This formula was selected and should mean that the developing countries will find it easier to control the result of votes on substantive resolutions in Geneva.

The next three weeks were occupied by a general debate, during which the leaders of national delegations outlined the attitudes of their governments to the various questions to be settled. This did not seem to be a very fruitful period, because governments were simply repeating views and arguments that had been rehearsed at preparatory meetings for the conference. Two points about this general debate are important. First, the group of forty-one African states emerged as the regional bloc which showed the greatest consistency in attitudes to various questions. Second, China confirmed its intention to use the conference to berate, and if possible isolate, the United States and the Soviet Union. The theme which the Chinese delegation stressed was one which had been repeated frequently in broadcasts from Peking and in Chinese publications. It is that the two super-powers are seeking to establish a selfish control over the oceans at the expense of the Third World countries, including China. If China detects a political advantage in prolonging the confrontation on these questions between developed and developing countries, then the chances of a final settlement will become more remote.

For five weeks after the end of the general debate, three committees, each consisting of all interested representatives, examined proposals on three major questions. The first committee considered areas of the ocean beyond national jurisdiction. The second committee investigated issues connected with ocean areas under the national jurisdiction of coastal states, and the third dealt with the control of pollution and scientific research in the oceans.

The first committee was primarily concerned with the nature of an international authority to control mining on the deep-sea bed. A very large number of developing countries wanted all rights to deep-sea mineral deposits to be vested in an international authority with the right to exploit them itself, and to regulate the activities of other parties in terms of areas used and tonnage produced. This concept of the role of the international authority is based on the twin fears that otherwise the developed countries will exploit the best deposits before the developing countries have acquired the essential technology, and that the new source of minerals will depress prices, which will adversely affect some developing exporting countries.

Most of the developed countries wanted the authority to be concerned primarily with licensing the activities of companies and states, and supervising standards of safety and environment protection. The authority would also be responsible for collecting and disbursing a proportion of the revenue for developing states, and arranging facilities whereby such states could acquire the technology necessary for deep-sea mining. Spokesmen for this group discounted the probability that deep-sea mining would depress the export revenues of developing countries. They believe that the future demand for copper and nickel will offset this new source of supply, and that in any case nickel is primarily the product of developed countries, including Canada, France and the Soviet Union. Cobalt is the one mineral which most authorities agree will be affected adversely; at present Zaire produces two-thirds of the world's supply, and in such a case the developed countries would not oppose some form of assistance to the country concerned.

In the second committee there was fairly general agreement that coastal states should be able to claim territorial waters 12 nautical miles wide and an exclusive economic zone not wider than 200 nautical miles measured from the baseline. However, it was not possible to secure agreement about the rights of ships to pass through international straits which would be entirely occupied by territorial seas 12 nautical miles wide, or about the degree of sovereignty of the coastal state in the exclusive economic zone. For the United States, the Soviet Union and some developed countries, including the United Kingdom, the right of unimpeded transit through such straits was not considered to be negotiable. This right was stated to be essential for commercial and naval vessels, including submerged nuclear submarines, and civil and military aircraft. Many developed countries insisted with equal force that commercial vessels would have to rely on the traditional right of innocent passage, and that naval craft would have to seek permission before using the strait. This latter rule would also apply to military planes, while commercial aircraft would have to make bilateral agreements.

The rights claimed by developing coastal states over the exclusive economic zone would have the effect of making such waters indistinguishable from territorial waters. The developed countries required that navigation was free outside the territorial waters, and that coastal states which were incapable of fully exploiting fishing grounds within the exclusive zone should permit foreign nationals, who have traditionally fished there, to have continued access. The degree of sovereignty in the exclusive zone also occupied the third committee when it discussed research. The developed countries sought the right to conduct open research, with safeguards for the coastal state within the exclusive zone, but the developing countries insisted that no research could be conducted in such areas without specific permission. On the question of pollution controls, which was the second matter examined by the third committee, the developing countries wanted a double standard, which would be more severe in respect of vessels belonging to developed countries. This proposal was urged on the grounds that the developed countries had already been responsible for a major proportion of ocean pollution, and that they were capable of expending the funds necessary to modify vessels and marine procedures.

Unless there is a major change in the attitudes of one or both of the broad groups of states the prospects for a successful outcome in Geneva remain poor. In any case, before the conference reconvenes, some coastal states will have made new unilateral claims to areas of the marginal sea, and pressure from interested groups in developed countries will have increased to allow the exploitation of the deep-sea bed by means of existing techniques. Both these developments will make ultimate agreement more difficult.

National Maritime Claims

THE following table shows national claims to territorial seas, the continental shelf and exclusive fishing zones. The information is represented in that order, separated by semi-colons, according to the following code.

1 All unqualified numbers refer to nautical miles.
2 Other numbers are qualified by the following symbols: f (fathoms), m (metres) and km (kilometres).
3 The letters sb indicate that part of the territorial sea is measured from straight baselines.
4 Five different symbols are used to indicate claims to the continental shelf as follows. csc (signatory to the Convention on the Continental Shelf); cd (state uses the same definition as the Convention on the Continental Shelf); cp (continental platform); ss (surface and subsoil of the continental shelf); e (limit defined as the limits of exploitability).
5 The symbols ? and – are used respectively when the nature of the claim is not known and when no claim has been made.

Albania 12, sb; csc; 12
Algeria 12; –; –
Argentina 200, sb; cd; 200
Australia 3: csc; 12

Bahrain 3; –; –
Bangladesh 12; 100f; 12
Barbados 3; –; –
Belgium 3; ?; 12

Brazil 200; cd; 200
Bulgaria 12; csc; 12
Burma 12, sb; cd; 12
Cameroun 18; cp; ?
Canada 12, sb; csc; 12
Chile 200; 200; 200
China 12, sb; ?; 12
Colombia 12; csc; 12
Congo 12; –; 15
Costa Rica 12; csc; 200
Cuba 3, sb; ?; 3
Cyprus 12; –; 12
Dahomey 12; 100; 12
Denmark 3, sb; csc; 12
Dominican Republic 6, sb; csc; 12
Ecuador 200, sb; 200m; 200
Egypt 12, sb; cd; 12
El Salvador 200; 200; 200
Equatorial Guinea 12; –; –
Ethiopia 12, sb; –; 12
Fiji 3; csc; –
Finland 4, sb; csc; 4
France 12, sb; csc; 12
Gabon 100, sb; ?; 30
Gambia 50; ?; 18
Germany, East 3, sb; ss; 3
Germany, Federal Republic of 3, sb; cd; 3
Ghana 30; cd; 12
Greece 6; csc; –
Guatemala 12, sb; csc; –
Guinea 130, sb; –; 12
Guyana 3; ss; –
Haiti 12, sb; cd; 15
Honduras 12; cd; ?

Iceland 4, sb; e; 50
India 12; cd; 6
Indonesia 12, sb; e; 12
Iran 12; cd; 50
Iraq 12; ss; –
Ireland 3, sb; ?; 12
Israel 6; csc; 6
Italy 6; cd; 12
Ivory Coast 6; 200m; 12
Jamaica 12; csc; 12
Japan 3; ?; 3
Jordan 3; –; 3
Kenya 12, sb; csc; –
Khmer 12, sb; csc; 12
Korea, North 12; –; –
Korea, South 20–200; 20–200; 20–200
Kuwait 12; ?; 12
Lebanon ?; –; 6
Liberia 12; cd; –
Libya 12; cd; –
Madagascar 50, sb; 150; 12
Malaysia 12, sb; csc; 12
Maldives 3 – 55, sb; –; 100
Malta 6; csc; 12
Mauritania 30, sb; cd; 12
Mauritius 12, sb; csc; –
Mexico 12, sb; cp; 12
Monaco 3; –; 12
Morocco 70; cd; 70
Nauru 12; –; 12
Netherlands 3; csc; 12
New Zealand 3; csc; 12
Nicaragua ?; 200m; 200
Nigeria 30; csc; 30
Norway 4, sb; csc; 12

Oman 12; cd; 50
Pakistan 12; 100f; 50
Panama 200, sb; 200; 200
Peru 200; 200; 200
Philippines ?, sb; ss; ?
Poland 6, sb; csc; 12
Portugal 12, sb; cd; 12
Qatar 3; ss; –
Romania 12; csc; 12
Saudi Arabia 12; ?; –
Senegal 12, sb; 200m; 110
Sierra Leone 200; csc; –
Singapore 3; –; 3
Somalia 200; ?; 12
South Africa 6; csc; 12
Soviet Union 12, sb; csc; 12
Spain 6; csc; 12
Sri Lanka 12, sb; ss; ?
Sudan 12, sb; cd; –
Sweden 4, sb; csc; 12
Syria 12, sb; cd; 12
Taiwan 3; csc; 12
Tanzania 50, sb; ?; 12

Thailand 12, sb; csc; 12
Togo 12; –; 12
Tonga 12; csc; –
Trinidad and Tobago 12; csc; 12
Tunisia 12; –; 12
Turkey 6/12, sb; cd; 12
United Arab Emirates 3; ss; ?
United Kingdom 3, sb; csc; 6
United States 3; csc; 12
Uruguay 200, sb; cd; 12
Venezuela 12, sb; csc; 12
Vietnam, North 12; –; 20km
Vietnam, South 3; cd; 50
Western Samoa 3; –; –
Yemen (Aden) 12, sb; 300 m+e; 12
Yemen (San'a) 12, 200m; 12
Yugoslavia 10, sb; cd; 12
Zaire 12; –; 12

References

CHAPTER ONE

1 Semple, E. C. *Influences of Geography and Environment* (New York, 1911), 282
2 Fairgrieve, J. *Geography and World Power* (1941, 8th ed), 51
3 Mahan, A. T. *The Influence of Sea Power Upon History 1660–1783* (Boston, 1890)
4 Mackinder, H. J. 'The geographical pivot of history', *Geo Jour*, 23 (1904), 421–37
——. *Democratic Ideals and Reality* (1919, reprinted New York, 1950)
5 Mackinder, H. J. 'The geographical pivot of history', 431
6 Mackinder, H. J. *Democratic Ideals*, 80
7 Spykman, N. J. *American Strategy in World Politics* (New York, 1942)
——. *The Geography of the Peace*, ed H. R. Nicholl (New York, 1944)
For a detailed criticism of Spykman's writings in political geography see J. R. V. Prescott, *The Geography of State Policies* (1968), chapter 2
8 Cohen, S. B. *Geography and Politics in a Divided World* (New York, 1964)
9 Cohen, 138
10 Cohen, 66
11 Fairgrieve, *Geography and World Power*
Whittlesey, D. *The Earth and the State* (New York, 1944)
Fischer, E. in *Principles of Political Geography*, ed H. W. Weigert (New York, 1957), 190–202

12 Bowman, I. *The New World* (1923), 336–41, 574
    Whittlesey. *The Earth and the State*
13 Fischer. *Principles of Political Geography*, 182–7
    Pounds, N. J. G. 'Access to the sea', *Annals of the Association of American Geographers*, 49 (1959), 256–68
    East, W. G. 'The geography of landlocked states', *Transactions of the Institute of British Geographers*, 28 (1960), 1–22
14 Pounds. *Political Geography*, chapters 9 and 11
15 Fischer. *Principles of Political Geography*, 177
16 Dale, E. H. 'Some geographical aspects of African landlocked states', *Annals of the Association of American Geographers*, 58 (1968), 485–505
17 See letters by R. N. Schnidt and L. L. Johnson together with Dale's reply, for a partial list of the paper's faults, in *Annals of the Association of American Geographers*, 59 (1969), 820–2
18 Glassner, M. I. *Access to the Sea for Developing Landlocked States* (The Hague, 1970)
19 Marshall-Cornwall, J. 'Review', *Geographical Journal*, 139 (1973), 144–5
20 Minghi, J. 'Review', *The Canadian Geographer*, 17 (1973), 87–8
21 Glassner, 10
22 Glassner, 49
23 Whittington, G. 'The Swaziland railway', *Tidjschrift voor Economische en Sociale Geographie*, 57 (1966), 68–73
    Grüll, J. 'Sambia-Tansania: eine ostafrikanische Transitbahn', *Mitteilungen der Osterreichischen Geographische Gesellschaft*, 108 (1966), 199–201
    Doganis, R. S. 'Zambia's outlet to the sea', *Journal of Transport Economics and Policy*, 1 (1967), 46–51
    Perry, J. W. B. 'Malawi's new outlet to the sea', *Geography*, 56 (1971), 138–40
24 Hilling, D. 'The problem of West African landlocked states' in *Essays in Political Geography*, ed C. A. Fisher (1968), chapter 14
25 'Report of the Second Committee on the territorial sea', *American Journal of International Law*, 24 supplement (1930), 247–8
26 Boggs, S. W. 'Delimitation of the territorial sea', *American Journal of International Law*, 24 (1930), 541–55
    ——. 'Problems of water boundary definitions', *Geographical Review*, 27 (1937), 451–6
    ——. 'National claims in adjacent seas', *Geographical Review*, 41 (1951), 185–209

——. 'Delimitation of seaward areas under national jurisdiction', *American Journal of International Law*, 48 (1961), 240–66

27 Jones, S. B. *Boundary Making: a Handbook for Statesmen, Treaty Editors and Boundary Commissioners* (Washington, 1945)
Moodie, A. E. 'Maritime boundaries' in *The Changing World*, eds W. G. East and A. E. Moodie (1956), 942–59

28 Pearcy, G. E. 'Geographical aspects of the law of the sea', *Annals of the Association of American Geographers*, 49 (1959), 1–24

29 The Geographer. 'Limits in the sea', *International Boundary Study*, Bureau of Intelligence and Research, State Department (Washington, since January 1970)

30 Black, W. A. 'The Labrador codfishery', *Annals of the Association of American Geographers*, 50 (1960), 267–96
Helin, R. A. 'Soviet fishing in the Barents Sea and the North Atlantic', *Geographical Review*, 54 (1964), 386–409
Villanow, J. 'The Soviet fishing fleet', *Geographical Review*, 53 (1963), 310–12
Minghi, J. 'The conflict of salmon fishing policies in the North Pacific', *Pacific Viewpoint*, 2 (1961), 59–86
Alexander, L. M. 'Offshore claims and fisheries in northwest Europe', *Yearbook of World Affairs*, 14 (1960), 236–60
Logan, R. M. 'Geography and salmon', *Journals of the West*, 8 (1969), 438–46

31 Emery, K. O. 'Geological aspects of sea-floor sovereignty' in *The Law of the Sea*, ed L. M. Alexander (Ohio, 1967), 139–59

32 Mero, J. L. *The Mineral Resources of the Sea* (1965)

33 Melamid, A. 'The political geography of the Gulf of Aqaba', *Annals of the Association of American Geographers*, 37 (1947), 231–40
——. 'Legal status of the Gulf of Aqaba', *American Journal of International Law*, 53 (1959), 412–14

34 Bruel, E. *International Straits* (1947)
Bouchez, L. J. *The Regime of Bays in International Law* (Leyden, 1964)
Strohl, M. P. *The International Law of Bays* (The Hague, 1963)
Sorensen, M. 'The territorial seas of archipelagos', in *Questions of International Law Presented to J. P. A. Francois on the Occasion of His Seventieth Birthday* (Leyden, 1964)

35 Shalowitz, A. L. *Shore and Sea Boundaries* (Washington, vol I, 1962, vol II, 1964)

36 Alexander, L. M. *The Law of the Sea* (Ohio, 1967)

——. 'Geography and the law of the sea', *Annals of the Association of American Geographers*, 58 (1968), 177–97

CHAPTER TWO

1 Bowett, B. W. *The Law of the Sea* (Manchester, 1967), 64
2 Fenn, P. T. 'Origins of the theory of territorial waters', *American Journal of International Law*, 20 (1926), 465–82
3 Walker, W. L. 'Territorial waters: the cannon shot rule', *The British Yearbook of International Law*, 22 (1945), 210–31
4 Jessup, P. C. *The law of territorial waters and maritime jurisdiction* (1927, repr 1970, New York), xxxiv
5 Fenn, 465–82
6 Whittlesey, D. *The Earth and the State* (New York, 1944), 565
7 Fenn, 478
8 Grotius, H. *De Jure Belli ac Pacis*, II (Paris, 1625), chapter III, section 13
9 Fenn, 481
10 Moore, S. A. *History and Law of the Foreshore* (1888), 224
11 Bodin, I. *Les Six Livres de la République* (Paris, 1576), 215
12 Baty, T. 'The three mile limit', *American Journal of International Law*, 22 (1928), 503–37
   Kent, H. S. K. 'The historical origins of the three mile limit', *American Journal of International Law*, 48 (1954), 537–53
   Walker, 210–31
13 Kent, 539
14 Laursen, L. *Danmark-Norges Traktater, 1523–1750, med dertil horende Aktstykker* (Copenhagen, 1933), 189–91
15 Raested, A. *La Mer Territoriale* (Paris, 1913), 111
16 Walker, 215
17 Meijer, C. B. V. *The Extent of Jurisdiction in Coastal Waters* (Leiden, 1937), 500
18 Kent, 545
19 *State Papers, Foreign, Denmark*, vol 112, Titley to Holderness, 6 January 1761
20 Fulton, T. W. *The Sovereignty of the Sea* (Edinburgh, 1911), p 156
21 Walker, 211–18
22 Quoted in T. W. Balch. 'Is Hudson Bay a closed or an open sea?' *American Journal of International Law*, 6 (1912), 414
23 Galiani, F. *De' Daveri de' Principi Neutrali Verso i Principi Guerregianti, e di Questi Verso Neutrali* (Naples, 1782)

24 Hall, A. R. *Ballistics in the Seventeenth Century* (Cambridge, 1952), 169
25 Crocker, H. G. *The Extent of the Marginal Sea* (Washington, 1919), 636
26 Baty, 517–32
27 Crocker, 659–60
28 Reeves, J. S. 'The codification of the law of territorial waters', *American Journal of International Law*, 24 (1930), 486–99
29 Fulton, 663–4
    Hall, W. E. *Treatise on International Law* (Oxford, 1917), 157
    Westlake, J. *International Law* (Cambridge, 1907), 184
30 Fulton, 569
31 United Nations. *Official Records of the Second United Nations Conference on the Law of the Sea*, vol 3 (New York, 1962), 190
32 Fulton, 119
33 Crocker, 641
34 Bouchez, L. J. *The Regime of Bays in International Law* (Leyden, 1964), 28
35 Moor, J. B. 'Letter to the editor', *Annuaire de l'Institut de Droit International*, 13 (1894–5), 146
36 Martens, G. F. de. *Nouveau Recueil Général des Traités*, vol I, third series (Leipzig, 1908), 864–6
37 Translated by Kent, 545
38 Fouchille, P. *Traité de Droit International Public*, vol 1 (Paris, 1925), 200
39 Jessup, 28
40 'Report of the Second Committee on the Territorial Sea', *American Journal of International Law*, 24 supplement (1930), 247–8
41 Pritchard, D. W. 'What is an estuary: a physical viewpoint', in *Estuaries*, ed G. H. Lauff, American Association for the Advancement of Science (Washington, 1967), 3
42 The Geographer. 'Straight baselines of Argentina', *International Boundary Studies, Series A, Limits in the Seas*, 44 (Washington, 1972), 1
43 Adami, V. *National Frontiers in Relation to International Law*, translated by T. T. Behrens (1927), 50
    Lapradelle, P. de. *La Frontière: Etude de Droit International* (Paris, 1928), 215–16
44 Report of the Second Committee, 249–50
45 Boggs, S. W. 'Delimitation of the Territorial Sea', *American Journal of International Law*, 24 (1930), 541–55

46 Boggs, S. W. 'Problems of water boundary definitions', *Geographic Review*, 27 (1937), 451–6
——. 'Delimitation of the territorial sea', 552–3
47 Lapradelle, 215–16
48 United Nations. *Conference on the Law of the Sea*, vol 3 (New York, 1958)
49 *Conference on the Law of the Sea*, vol 3 (1958), 161–2
50 *Conference on the Law of the Sea*, vol 3 (1958), 228, 242
51 *Conference on the Law of the Sea*, vol 3 (1958), 148, 240
52 *Conference on the Law of the Sea*, vol 3 (1958), 14, 145
53 *Conference on the Law of the Sea*, vol 3 (1958), 241

CHAPTER THREE

1 United Nations. *Conference on the Law of the Sea*, Vol 3 (New York, 1958), 35
2 Africa Research Bulletin (Exeter, 1972), political series, 2597, 2625, 2658
3 *Conference on the Law of the Sea*, vol 3 (1958), 10
4 *Conference on the Law of the Sea*, vol 3 (1958), 67
5 *New China News* (Melbourne, 4 April 1973), 15
6 *Conference on the Law of the Sea*, vol 3 (1958), 104; see also 29 for the Japanese view
7 *Conference on the Law of the Sea*, vol 3 (1958), 26; and, United Nations. *Second Conference on the Law of the Sea*, vol 1 (New York, 1962), 45
8 *Conference on the Law of the Sea*, vol 3 (1958), 26, 104
9 Keenan, P. B., Lester, A., Martin, P. *Shawcross and Beaumont on Air Law*, vol 1 (1966), 194–5
Cooper, J. C. *Explorations in Aerospace Law*, ed I. A. Vlasic (Montreal, 1968), 200–2
10 International Civil Aviation Organisation. *Convention on International Civil Aviation* (Montreal, 1965, 3rd ed)
11 International Civil Aviation Organisation. *International Air Services Transit Agreement* (Montreal, 1954)
12 Denaro, J. M. 'States' jurisdiction in aerospace under international law', *Journal of Air Law and Commerce*, 36 (1970), 697
13 International Civil Aviation Organisation. *Annual Report of the Council 1971* (Montreal, 1972), 101–3
14 Bowett, D. W. *The Law of the Sea* (1967), 7–9
15 *Conference on the Law of the Sea*, vol 3 (1958), 50, 65

16 *Second Conference on the Law of the Sea*, 190, 226, 285–6, 309–10
17 *Conference on the Law of the Sea*, vol 3 (1958), 50
18 *Conference on the Law of the Sea*, vol 3 (1958), 6, 7, 11, 12, 22
19 *Conference on the Law of the Sea*, vol 3 (1958), 7
20 *Conference on the Law of the Sea*, vol 3 (1958), 41
21 Department of External Affairs. *Current Notes on International Affairs*, 29 (Canberra, 1958), 355
22 International Court of Justice. 'Fisheries case – judgement of 18 December 1951', *Reports of Judgements, Advisory Opinions and Orders* (Leyden, 1951), 129, 133, 140–2
23 International Court of Justice, 141–2
24 McGill, J. T. 'Coastal landforms of the world', *Geographical Review*, 48 (1958), end paper
25 The Geographer. 'Ireland', *Limits in the Sea*, no 3 (1970)
26 The Geographer. 'Finland', *Limits in the Sea*, no 48 (1972)
27 Naval Intelligence Division. *Denmark* (1944), 29
28 Naval Intelligence Division. *Yugoslavia*, vol 1 (1944), 123–4
29 The Geographer. 'Denmark', *Limits in the Sea*, no 19 (1970), 8
30 The Geographer. 'Mauritania', *Limits in the Sea*, no 8 (1970), 1
31 *Conference on the Law of the Sea*, vol 1 (1958), 8
32 Strohl, M. P. *The International Laws of Bays* (The Hague, 1963), 269
33 Bouchez, L. J. *The Regime of Bays in International Law* (Leyden, 1964), 199–302
34 This is still a matter for debate amongst international lawyers, but the majority of eminent jurists favour the view that there is no right of innocent passage through historic bays. See *Conference on the Law of the Sea*, vol 1 (1958), 21–7 and Bouchez, 281
35 *Conference on the Law of the Sea*, vol 1 (1958), 3–8
    Bouchez, 215–37
    Strohl, 253–68
    The Geographer. 'Claims to national jurisdiction', *Limits in the Sea*, no 36 (1973)
36 Hyde, C. C. *International Law, Chiefly as Interpreted and Applied by the United States* (New York, 1947, 2nd ed), 469, 482
37 The Geographer. 'The People's Republic of China', *Limits in the Sea*, no 43 (1972), 2
38 The Geographer. 'Finland', 1–2
39 The Geographer. 'The maritime boundary between the United States and Mexico', *Limits in the Sea*, no 45 (1972)

40 *Conference on the Law of the Sea*, vol 1 (1958), 292–4, and vol 3, 162–3
41 *Conference on the Law of the Sea*, vol 1 (1958), 114–64
42 *Petroleum Press Service* (April 1973), 131–2
43 Couper, A. D. *The Geography of Sea Transport* (1972), 62–3
44 Couper, 67
45 Couper, 63
46 Couper, 63
47 Levine, I. O. 'Les projets de percement de l'isthme de Kra et leur histoire', *Affaires Etrangères*, 2 (1937), 83–97

CHAPTER FOUR

1 The Geographer. *Map of World Phytoplankton Production* (Washington, 1972)
2 Coull, J. R. *The Fisheries of Europe: an Economic Geography* (1972), 39–40
3 Coull, 42–3
4 Coull, 48–53
5 Ranke, W. 'Die Agglomerationsraume der atlantischen Fern-fishereien', *Petermann's Geographische Mitteilungen* (1969), 269–73
6 Food and Agricultural Organisation. *Yearbook of Fishing Statistics, 1971*, vols 32 and 33 (Rome, 1972)
7 Nguyen-Van-Chi-Bonnardel, R. 'Les problèmes de la pêche maritime au Senegal', *Annales de Géographie*, 78 (1969), 25–56
8 Nguyen-Van-Chi-Bonnardel, 30
9 Strohl, P. *The International Law of Bays* (The Hague, 1963), chapter 8
10 Bowett, D. W. *The Law of the Sea* (1967), 19
11 United Nations. *Conference on the Law of the Sea*, vol 1 (New York, 1958), 246
12 Nguyen-Van-Chi-Bonnardel, 36
13 Coull, 125
14 *The Times* (London), 28 August 1970
15 Coull, 121
16 Helin, R. A. 'Soviet fishing in the Barents Sea and the north Atlantic', *Geographical Review*, 54 (1964), 400–1
17 Johnston, D. M. *The International Law of Fisheries* (New York, 1965), chapters 5–7
18 Strohl, 332

19 Morgan, R. *World Sea Fisheries* (1955), 164–5
20 Johnston, 177
21 Fulton, T. W. *The Sovereignty of the Sea* (Edinburgh, 1911), 638
22 The text of the convention is reproduced by Bowett, 92–101
23 Bowett, 102–8
24 Thompson, W. F., and Freeman, N. L. 'History of the Pacific halibut industry', *International Fisheries Commission Report No 5* (New York, 1930)
    Gregory, H. E., and Barnes, K. *The North Pacific Fisheries* (New York, 1939), 225–42
25 Minghi, J. V. 'The conflict of salmon fishing policies in the North Pacific', *Pacific Viewpoint*, 2 (1961), 59–86
26 Logan, R. M. 'Geography and salmon', *Journal of the West*, 8 (1969), 438–46
27 Prescott, J. R. V. *The Geography of Frontiers and Boundaries* (1967), 132–3
28 For a useful discussion of this concept see W. L. Chapman, 'Fishery resources in off-shore waters' in *The Law of the Sea*, ed L. M. Alexander (Ohio, 1967), 87–105; and Coull, 13–14
29 Statement by Australian representative. *Current Notes on International Affairs*, August 1971 (Canberra), 420–3
30 Franklin, C. M. *The Law of the Sea* (Washington, 1961), 110–13

CHAPTER FIVE

1 Jessup, P. C. *The Law of Territorial Waters and Maritime Jurisdiction* (1927, reprinted 1970, New York), 15
    Hurst, C. J. B. 'Whose is the bed of the sea?', *British Yearbook of International Law* (1953–4), 34–43
2 Franklin, C. M. *The Law of the Sea* (Washington, 1961), 30
3 House of Commons. *Parliamentary Debates*, fifth series, no 163, fourth volume of session 1923, columns 993 and 1417
4 Fulton, T. W. *The Sovereignty of the Sea* (Edinburgh, 1911), 612
5 Auguste, B. B. L. *The Continental Shelf* (Paris, 1960), 53
6 O'Connell, D. P. 'Sedentary fisheries and the Australian continental shelf', *American Journal of International Law*, 49 (1955), 185–209
7 Mouton, M. W. *The Continental Shelf* (The Hague, 1952), 142
8 Wenk, E. 'The physical resources of the ocean', *Scientific American*, September 1969, 167–76

Q

Gidel, G. *Le Droit International Public de la Mer* (Chateauroux, 1932), 510

9 Mouton, 143

10 *American Journal of International Law*, 40 (1946), official documents, 46

11 Whiteman, M. M. 'Conference on the law of the sea: Convention on the Continental Shelf', *American Journal of International Law*, 52 (1958), 629–59

12 The copy of the convention used in preparing this section was reproduced in D. W. Bowett. *The Law of the Sea* (1967), 88–91

13 Whiteman, 639

14 Mero, J. L. *The Mineral Resources of the Sea* (New York, 1964), 16–18, 55–7

15 Emery, K. O. *The Sea off Southern California* (New York, 1960)
Chesterman, C. W. 'Descriptive petrography of rocks dredged off the coast of central California', *Proceedings of the Californian Academy of Sciences*, 27 (1952), 359–74
Hanna, G. D. 'Geology of the continental slope off central California', *Proceedings of the California Academy of Science*, 27 (1952), 325–58
Dietz, R. S., Emery, K. O., and Shepard, F. P. 'Phosphorite deposits on the sea floor off southern California', *Bulletin of the Geological Society of America*, 53 (1942), 815–48

16 Mero, 69

17 Mero, 75–6

18 This section on surface mineral deposits of the continental shelf, is largely based on an excellent report by E. C. F. Bird. *Preliminary Report on the Possible Existence of Heavy Mineral Deposits on the Sea Floor Around the Australian Coast* (Presented to the Planet Mining Company Pty Ltd in May 1966, mimeographed). See also P. Chen. 'Heavy mineral deposits of western Taiwan', *Bulletin of the Geological Society of Taiwan*, 4 (1963), 13–21

19 Bird, 4

20 Guilcher, A. 'Quaternary events of the continental shelves of the world', in *The Geology of the East Atlantic Continental Margin*, ed F. M. Delany (1970), 31–46
Shepard, F. P. 'Thirty-five thousand years of sea-level', in *Essays in Marine Geology in honor of K. O. Emery* (Los Angeles, 1963), 1–10

21 Cruikshank, M. J. *The Exploration and Exploitation of Off-shore Mineral Deposits*, MSc thesis (University of Colorado, 1962)

22 Emery, K. O. 'The continental shelf', *Scientific American*, September 1969, 121
23 Mero, 96–7
24 Mero, 93–5
25 *Petroleum Engineer*, March 1973
26 Franklin, 65–83
27 Bowett, 88
28 Auguste, chapter 1
    Brown, E. D. *The Regal Regime of Hydrospace* (1971)
    Finley, L. W. 'The outer limit of the continental shelf: a rejoinder to Professor L. Henkin', *American Journal of International Law*, 64 (1970), 42–61
    Henkin, L. 'A reply to Mr. Finley', *American Journal of International Law*, 64 (1970), 62–72
29 Brown, 9
30 Brown, 30. See also D. A. Kamat. 'Recent developments in the law relating to the seabed', *Indian Journal of International Law*, 11 (1971), 9–19
31 Chase, T. E., Menard, H. W., and Mammenicks, J. *Bathymetry of the North Pacific* (Los Angeles, 1970), a map in 10 sheets
32 Barry, F. J. 'The administration of the Outer Continental Lands Act', *Natural Resources Lawyer*, 1 (1968), 38–48
33 Brown, 7
34 Bowett, 89–90
35 Shalowitz, A. L. *Shore and Sea Boundaries*, vol 1 (Washington, 1962), 231
36 Brown, chapter 2
37 Quoted in Brown, 56
38 International Court of Justice. *North Sea Continental Shelf Cases*, vol 1 (The Hague, 1968), 58
39 International Court of Justice, 30, 68–9
40 International Court of Justice. 'The North sea continental shelf cases', *Reports of Judgements, Advisory Opinions and Orders* (The Hague, 1969), 53–4
41 Brown, 43–71
    Friedmann, W. 'The North Sea continental shelf cases: a critique', *American Journal of International Law*, 64 (1970), 229–40
42 Friedmann, 237, 239
43 Brown, 71
44 International Court of Justice, vol 2 (1968), 21; and International Court of Justice (1969), 37

45 O'Connell, D. P. 'The Australian maritime domain', *Australian Law Journal*, 44 (1970), 192–208
——. 'Problems of Australian coastal jurisdiction', *Australian Law Journal*, 42 (1968), 39–51
46 Shepard, F. P. *Submarine Geology* (New York, 1963), chapters 8 and 10
Cotter, C. *The Physical Geography of the Ocean* (1965), chapter 5
King, C. A. M. *An Introduction to Oceanography* (1963), chapter 2
Heezen, B. C., and Tharp, M. 'The floors of the ocean. 1. North Atlantic', *Geological Society of America*, Special paper 65 (1969)
47 Shepard, *Submarine Geology*, chapter 8
48 Bascom, W. 'Technology and the ocean', *Scientific American*, September 1969, 199–217

CHAPTER SIX

1 Shepard, F. P. *Submarine Geology* (New York, 1963), chapters 8 and 10
2 The Geographer. *Map Showing Theoretical Division of the Continental Shelf and Seabed* (Washington, 1971)
3 The Geographer. 'Theoretical areal allocation of the seabed to coastal states', *Limits in the Sea*, no 46 (1972)
4 Petroleum (Submerged Lands), Second Schedule, Areas Adjacent to States and Territories, No 118. *Government Gazette* (Canberra, 1967), 958–63
5 Park, C. 'Oil under troubled waters', *Harvard International Law Journal*, 14 (1973), 212–60
6 Committee for coordination of joint prospecting for mineral resources in Asian off-shore areas. *Technical Bulletin*, 17 (1969)
7 Park, 248–52
8 The Geographer. 'Iran–Qatar', *Limits in the Sea*, no 25 (1970)
9 The Geographer. 'Italy–Yugoslavia', *Limits in the Sea*, no 9 (1970)
10 The Geographer. 'Iran–Saudi Arabia', *Limits in the Sea*, no 24 (1970)
11 The Geographer. 'Bahrain–Saudi Arabia', *Limits in the Sea*, no 12 (1970)
12 Service National des Mines de la Géologie et du Petrole, Ré-

publique Khmer, *Decret Portant Delimitation du Plateau Continental Khmer* (Phnom Penh, 1972)

13 'Official documents', *American Journal of International Law*, 65 (1971), 901–14

14 The Geographer. 'Venezuela–Trinidad and Tobago', *Limits in the Sea*, no 11 (1970)

CHAPTER SEVEN

1 The copy of the Convention on the High Seas used in the preparation of this chapter is reproduced in D. W. Bowett, *The Law of the Sea* (1967), 72–80

2 *International Legal Materials*, 9 (1970), 543–54

3 Cohen, P. 'The erosion of surface naval power', *Foreign Affairs*, 49 (1971), 330–41

4 Christy, F. T. 'Maritime wealth: how much? for how long?', *Economic Impact*, 4 (1973), 43–4

5 Schachter, O., and Serwer, D. 'Marine pollution problems and remedies', *American Journal of International Law*, 65 (1971), 84–111

6 Bowett, 56

7 *International Legal Materials*, 10 (1971), 220–1

8 *International Legal Materials*, 9 (1970), 1046–80; 10 (1971), 982–1012; and 12 (1973), 210–13

9 Oxman, B. 'Conflicting approaches to the control and exploitation of the oceans', *American Journal of International Law*, 65 (1971), 121–2

10 'Conflicting approaches', 120

11 'Preventing a scramble for the sea', *Australian Foreign Policy Record*, October 1973, 652–4

12 Luard, E. 'Dividing the spoils of the sea into national parcels', *The Times* (London), 19 July 1972, 8

Index

References to figures are shown in italic

Adami, V., 51, 235
Adams, J. Q., 18
Adriatic Sea, 35, 146, 190
Afar and Issa, 98, 109
Afghanistan, 19
Air navigation, 76–7, 107
Albania, 71, 79–80, 90, 92, 178, 180, 185, 226
Alexander, L. M., 11, 22, 23, 233, 234, 239
Algeria, 178, 184, 226
Amazon river, 50
Angola, 154, 155, 178, 184, 186
Arafura Sea, 190
Aral Sea, 28
Archipelagos, 23, 50, 60, 64, 104–6
Arctic Ocean, 181, 182
Argentina, 50, 62, 72, 80, 92, 93, 120, 134, 144, 178, 182, 184, 185, 226
Atlantic Ocean, 16, 37, 119, 121, 122, 123, 124, 125, 135, 181, 182, 207, 220
Auguste, B. B. L., 239, 241
Australia, 98, 218, 226; continental shelf, 143, 144, 148, 154, 155, 159, 163, 170, 177, 178, 183, 184, 191–4, 201–2, 203, 204; fishing, 127, 133; territorial sea, 67, 71
Austria, 42, 216
Azo, P., 35

Bab al Mandab Strait, 109
Bahamas, 105
Bahrain, 146, 177, 178, 179, 185, 198, 199, 200, 227
Balch, T. W., 234
Baltic Sea, 28, 104, 120, 179, 190

Bangladesh, 178, 179, 180, 184, 188, 227
Barbados, 69, 178, 179, 184, 227
Barents Sea, 173, 179, 182
Barnes, K., 239
Barry, F. J., 159, 241
Bartolus, S. de, 35, 36
Bascom, W., 174, 242
Baselines for territorial seas, 44, 48–9, 59, 62, 63, 73
Baty, T., 37, 234, 235
Bays, 23, 45–7, 51–4, 52, 60–1, 62, 63, 64, 94, 124, 129–30, 131
Belgium, 46, 133, 135, 178, 179, 181, 185, 216, 218, 227
Bird, E. C. F., 11–12, 150, 240
Black, W. A., 22, 233
Black Sea, 28, 67, 109, 111, 121, 179
Bodin, I., 36, 234
Boggs, S. W., 11, 21, 53, 54, 55, 56, 64, 100, 232–3, 235, 236
Bolivia, 19, 210, 216
Bosporus, 109
Botswana, 20
Bouchez, L. J., 23, 97, 233, 235, 237
Bowett, D. W., 234, 236, 238, 239, 240, 241, 243
Bowman, I., 18, 232
Brazil, 72, 77, 134, 138, 155, 159, 178, 181, 183, 184, 227
Brown, E. D., 157, 168, 169, 241
Bruel, E., 23, 233
Brunei, 155
Bulgaria, 61, 98, 178, 180, 185, 227
Burma, 59, 80, 81, 93, 94–5, 100, 178, 181, 184, 209, 227

Bynkershoek, C. van, 36, 40

Cambodia, *see* Khmer
Cameroun, 69, 72, 130, 178, 179, 185, 189, 227
Canada, 27, 44, 49, 98, 99, 210, 218, 224, 227; continental shelf, 144, 160, *162*, 170, 171, 178, 181, 183, 184; fishing, 121, 125, 134, 136, 137–8
Canary Isles, 105, 119, 132, 134
Cape of Good Hope, 28, 111, 112–13, 114, 207
Caspian Sea, 28
Chapman, W. L., 239
Chase, T. E., 241
Chen, P., 240
Chesterman, C. W., 240
Chile, 72, 77, 103, 143, 178, 180, 184, 188, 220, 227
China, 34, 227; continental shelf, 178, 185, 186, 196, 199; political attitudes, 25–6, 43, 74, 222, 223; territorial sea, 70, 98, 99
Christy, F. T., 212, 243
Coastal features, their economic and political significance, 17–18, 24–5
Cohen, P., 211, 243
Cohen, S. B., 14, 16–17, 231
Colombia, 114, 144, 178, 184, 227
Congo, 98, 133, 155, 178, 180, 185, 188, 227
Continental shelf, 22–3, 143; claims to detached areas, 158–60; definition of the outer edge, 156–8; division between states, 160–71; division within federal states, 170–1; physical characteristics, 171–4; regional variation, 172–3, 175–83; resources, 29–30, 143–5, 147–56; specific boundary agreements, 190–204
Cooper, J. C., 236
Corinth Canal, 110, 111
Costa Rica, 114, 123, 133, 178, 179, 184, 227
Cotter, C., 242
Coull, J. R., 119, 120, 238
Couper, A. D., 112, 113, 114, 238
Crocker, H. G., 235
Cruikshank, M. J., 240
Cuba, 69, 72, 105, 161, *164*, 178, 179, 180, 184, 211, 227
Cyprus, 101, *102*, 178, 184, 227

Dahomey, 178, 179, 180, 184, 188, 227
Dale, E. H., 19, 232
Dardanelles, 109
Denaro, J. M., 236
Denmark, 105, 227; continental shelf,

166–9, 178, 185, 197, 203; fishing, 116, 127, 133, 135; straight baseline, 80, 81, 85, 87, *88*; territorial sea, 37–8, 45, 46, 47, 69, 72, 100, 104
Dietz, R. S., 240
Distant fishing fleets, 120–2
Doganis, R. S., 21, 232
Dominica, 71, 80, 92, 98, 100, 133, 178, 180, 184, 227

East, W. G., 11, 19, 232, 233
East Germany, 178, 179, 185, 227
Ecuador, 72, 77, 80, 81, 82, 95–7, 100, 103, 105, 178, 184, 188, 227
Egypt, 69, 109, 111, 112, 155, 178, 183, 184, 227
El Salvador, 178, 184, 188, 227
Emery, K. O., 23, 142–3, 233, 240, 241
Equatorial Guinea, 69, 70, 71, 178, 180–1, 184, 188, 199, 227
Estuaries, 49–50, 62, 64, 93–4
Ethiopia, 105, 178, 180, 185, 188, 227

Fairgrieve, J., 14, 17, 231
Fenn, P. T., 34–5, 36, 234
Fiji, 105, 177, 178, 184, 186, 189, 227
Finland, 60, 67, 69, 80, 81, 83, 100, 104, 178, 185, 189, 190, 197, 227
Finley, L. W., 241
Fischer, E., 17, 18, 19, 231, 232
Fishing, 22, 25–6, 27, 117
Fishing grounds, 117–20, 121
Fishing zones, 26–7, 37, 209, 225; causes of disputes, 117–28; solution of disputes, 128–41
Fouchille, P., 235
France, 16, 33, 46, 98, 109, 111, 210, 224, 227; continental shelf, 143, 145, 162, 163, 178, 184; fishing, 46, 135, 138; high seas, 211, 213, 214; straight baselines, 80, 83, 100; territorial sea, 38, 39, 40, 41, 42, 49, 70
Franklin, C. M., 155, 239, 241
Freeman, N. L., 239
Friedmann, W., 168, 169, 241
Fu Chu, 99
Fulton, T. W., 42, 135, 234, 235, 239

Gabon, 69, 71, 72, 98, 119, 130, 132, 155, 178, 181, 184, 199, 227
Galiani, F., 41, 42, 234
Gambia, 60, 72, 132, 178, 180, 184, 227
Gentilis, A., 35, 36
Geographer, the, 11, 22, 97, 118, 176, 233, 235, 237, 238, 242, 243
Germany, 42, 46, 100, 135, 162; *see also* East *and* West Germany
Ghana, 72, 178, 184, 227

Gidel, G., 144, 240
Glassner, M. I., 19–20, 232
Grant, President U.S., 18
Greece, 45, 59, 163, 178, 184, 227
Greenland, 37, 73, 105, 121
Gregory, H. E., 239
Grotius, H., 35–6, 234
Grüll, J., 21, 232
Guam, 15
Guatemala, 61, 98, 178, 179, 184, 227
Guilcher, A., 240
Guinea, 70, 72, 80, 82, 93, 103, 132, 178, 180, 184, 188, 227
Gulf of Aqaba, 23, 69
Gulf of Siam, 182
Guyana, 103, 178, 184, 189, 227

Hague Conference on the Law of the Sea (1930), 42, 45, 48–54, 61, 64, 144
Haiti, 80, 82, 92–3, 133, 161, 164, 178, 179, 180, 184, 228
Hall, A. R., 235
Hall, W. E., 42, 235
Hanna, G. D., 240
Hawaii, 15
Heezen, B. C., 242
Helin, R. A., 22, 127, 233, 238
Henkin, L., 241
High seas, 205–10; international authority controlling high seas' bed, 215–21, 223–4; national interest in, 211–21
Hilling, D., 21, 232
Historic bays, 51, 54, 61, 62, 64, 73, 92, 94, 97–100, 101
Hodgson, R., 11, 22
Honduras, 72, 178, 181, 184, 214, 228
Hong Kong, 60
Hudson Bay, 98, 99
Hurst, C. J. B., 239
Hyde, C. C., 99, 237

Iceland, 228; continental shelf, 149, 178, 182, 185, 189; fishing, 27, 116, 117, 120, 122, 123, 126, 127, 129, 133; straight baselines, 80, 83, 85, 86; territorial sea, 37, 67, 69
India, 43–4, 61, 70, 145, 178, 179, 181, 184, 228
Indian Ocean, 111, 122, 123, 124, 125, 150, 186, 215
Indonesia, 27, 60, 77, 105, 106, 228; continental shelf, 152, 155, 159, 163, 166, 178, 183, 184, 189, 190, 191–4, 201, 203, 204; territorial sea, 70, 103–4, 207
Innocent passage, 30, 33, 75, 107
Internal waters, 48

International canals, 110–15
International straits, 23, 27, 50–1, 103–4, 106–10, 224–5
Iran, 69, 109–10, 145, 154, 155, 178, 185, 197–8, 199, 203, 228
Iraq, 109–10, 166, 178, 179, 185, 187, 228
Ireland, 80, 83–5, 89, 126, 133, 135, 143, 178, 181, 183, 184, 189, 228
Islands, 44, 47–8, 50, 57, 62, 63, 83, 85–9, 196–7
Israel, 69, 111, 178, 184, 228
Italy, 42, 43, 59, 133, 146, 155, 178, 180, 184, 190, 198, 204, 228
Ivory Coast, 69, 119, 133, 178, 184, 188, 228

Jamaica, 178, 182, 184, 228
Japan, 27, 107, 113, 114, 115, 213, 228; continental shelf, 144, 155, 178, 181, 184, 194–6; fishing, 25–6, 120, 122, 124, 125, 126, 129–30, 131, 136, 137, 141; territorial sea, 42, 43, 59, 61, 69, 71, 75, 105
Jefferson, President T., 28–9, 41, 46
Jessup, P. C., 234, 235, 239
Johnson, L. L., 232
Johnston, D. M., 128, 238, 239
Jones, S. B., 21, 233
Jordan, 69, 166, 178, 179, 185, 188, 228

Kamat, D. A., 241
Kattegat, 39
Keenan, P. B., 236
Kent, H. S. K., 37, 40, 234
Kenya, 98, 178, 184, 228
Khmer, 64, 166, 178, 185, 187, 199, 228
Kiel Canal, 110, 111
King, C. A. M., 242
Kra Canal, 114–15
Kuwait, 69, 112, 178, 185, 187, 228

Landlocked states, 18–21, 216, 220
Lapradelle, P. de, 51, 235, 236
Laursen, L., 234
Lebanon, 66, 67, 145, 178, 184, 188, 211, 228
Lesotho, 20
Lester, A., 236
Levine, I. O., 114, 238
Liberia, 178, 184, 214, 228
Libya, 70, 178, 180, 184, 228
Logan, R. A., 22, 137, 233, 239
Low-tide elevations, 44, 50, 62, 63
Low-water mark, 44, 48, 49, 59, 82
Luard, E., 243

Macau, 60

Mackinder, H. J., 14, 15–16, 17, 231
Madagascar, 80, 89, 105, 178, 179, 184, 228
Mahan, A. T., 14–15, 231
Malacca Strait, 27, 103–4, 108, 190
Malaysia, 27, 45, 103–4, 155, 166, 170, 178, 180, 184, 190, 201, 203, 204, 228
Maldives, 67, 105, 117, 178, 184, 186, 188, 228
Malta, 133, 178, 182, 184, 228
Mammenicks, J., 241
Marshall-Cornwall, J., 19, 232
Martens, G. F. de, 235
Martin, P., 236
Mauritania, 69, 72, 80, 93, 178, 184, 228
Mauritius, 105, 177, 178, 182, 183, 184, 189, 228
McGill, J. T., 237
Mediterranean Sea, 37, 67, 111, 121, 179
Meijer, C. B. V., 234
Melamid, A., 23, 233
Menard, H. W., 241
Mero, J. L., 23, 148–9, 150, 152, 153, 154, 233, 240, 241
Mexico, 80, 81, 95, 101–3, 155, 178, 184, 228
Minghi, J., 11, 19–20, 22, 137, 232, 233, 239
Monaco, 60, 69, 71, 133, 166, 228
Moodie, A. E., 21, 233
Moor, J. B., 47, 235
Moore, S. A., 234
Morgan, R., 239
Morocco, 41–2, 123, 132, 133, 134, 178, 184, 228
Mouton, M. W., 239, 240
Mozambique, 80, 85, 90, 178, 179, 184, 186

Naples, 36–7
Nauru, 70, 133, 177, 178, 184, 186, 228
Nepal, 19, 216
Netherlands, 26, 33, 98, 216, 218, 228; continental shelf, 163, 166–9, 178, 181, 185, 197, 203; fishing, 46, 116, 129, 133, 135; territorial sea, 38, 39, 40, 46
New Zealand, 71, 133, 155, 178, 182, 184, 228
Nguyen-Van-Chi-Bonnardel, R., 123, 238
Nicaragua, 66, 67, 114, 178, 181, 184, 188, 228
Nigeria, 72, 155, 178, 181, 184, 228
Nixon, President R. M., 28

North Korea, 166, 178, 179, 180, 184, 228
North Sea, 26, 37, 45, 46, 120, 166, 167, 169, 179, 182, 190, 197, 203, 210
North Vietnam, 166, 178, 180, 185, 229
Norway, 39, 105, 214, 229; continental shelf, 155, 159, 178, 182, 184, 191, 197, 201, 202, 203, 204; fishing, 126, 133, 135; territorial sea, 67, 69, 79, 83, 101, 104

O'Connell, D. P., 239, 242
Oman, 123, 133, 178, 179, 181, 183, 184, 229
Oxman, B., 217, 243

Pacific Ocean, 16, 119, 121, 122, 123, 125, 136, 159, 186, 210
Pakistan, 178, 180, 184, 188, 229
Panama, 15, 61, 72, 77, 98, 99, 113, 178, 179, 184, 188, 214, 229
Panama Canal, 110, 111, 113–14
Papua New Guinea, 45, 105, 148, 177, 199, 201–2
Park, C., 195, 242
Pearcy, G. E., 22, 233
Perry, J. W. B., 21, 232
Persian Gulf, 16, 28, 68, 109–10, 123, 147, 166, 179, 190, 210
Peru, 27, 229; continental shelf, 154, 155, 178, 179, 180, 183, 184, 188; fishing, 122, 126, 127, 130; territorial sea, 70, 72, 77, 78, 103
Philippines, 15, 60, 67, 105, 106, 177, 178, 184, 186, 189, 209, 229
Plowden, E., 36
Poland, 61, 133, 178, 181, 185, 187, 229
Pollution, 26, 27, 33, 75, 209–10, 212–13, 225
Portugal, 133, 210, 229; continental shelf, 178, 181, 184; straight baselines, 80, 82, 93, 94, 98, 100; territorial sea, 43, 46–7, 60, 70
Portuguese Guinea, 79–80, 81, 82, 85, 87, 103, 159
Portuguese Timor, 60, 121, 163, 192–4
Pounds, N. J. G., 11, 15, 18–19, 232
Prescott, J. R. V., 231, 239
Pritchard, D. W., 49, 235
Puerto Rico, 15, 105

Qatar, 69, 146, 154, 155, 178, 185, 197–8, 203, 229

Raested, A., 234
Ranke, W., 120–1, 238
Ratzel, F., 13, 14
Red Sea, 16, 123

Reeves, J. S., 235
Rio de la Plata, 50, 62, 93–4
River mouths, 49, 61–2, *63*, 64, 93–4
Romania, 178, 180, 185, 186, 229

Saudi Arabia, 70, 112, 146, 154, 155, 178, 183, 184, 198, 199, *200*, 203, 229
Schacter, O., 213, 243
Schnidt, R. H., 232
Sea-land contrasts, 28–30
Seal hunting, 43
Sea of Marmara, 109
Sea of Japan, 180, 190
Seas, influence on national characteristics, 13–14; influence on national policies, 14–17
Selden, J., 35–6
Semple, E. C., 14, 25, 231
Senegal, 69, 122–3, 126, 127, 133, 178, 184, 229
Serwer, D., 213, 243
Shalowitz, A. L., 23, 233, 241
Shelf-locked state, 163, 166–9, 177, 216, 220
Shepard, F. P., 173, 175, 240, 242
Sierra Leone, 67, 72, 77, 103, 132, 178, 184, 229
Singapore, 60, 111, 114, 166, 178, 179, 185, 187, 188, 210, 216, 218, 229
Skagerrak, 37, 190
Solomon Isles, 105
Somali Republic, 69, 178, 229
Sorensen, M., 23, 233
South Africa, 27–8, 133, 178, 181, 184, 189, 229
South China Sea, 159, 182, 190, 199
South Korea, 67, 68, 120, 124–5, 136, 178, 181, 183, 184, 188, 194–5, 196, 204, 228
South Vietnam, 68, 69, 123, 133, 166, 178, 182, 184, 199, 211, 230
South West Africa, 119, 120, 121, 122, 152, 178, 181, 182, 183, 184, 186
Soviet Union, 16, 28, 34, 77, 111, 222, 223, 224, 229; continental shelf, 155, 159, 160, 178, 179–80, 183, 184, 190, 197, 201, *202*, 204; fishing, 25–6, 120, 122, 124, 125, 127, 129–30, *131*, 141; high seas, 211, 214, 215, 216, 217, 219, 220; territorial seas, 38–9, 42, 43, 47, 48, 61, 70, 73, 74, 98, 100, 101
Spain, 43, 121, 126, 132, 133, 134, 178, 181, 184, 229
Spanish Sahara, 69
Spykman, N. J., 14, 16, 17, 231
Sri Lanka, 105, 132, 133, 143, 147, 178, 179, 184, 189, 229
Straight baselines, 59–60, 64, 73, 78–97,

104–6, 116, 124, 129, 130, *131*, 161–2, *165*, 199–201, 209
Strait of Hormuz, 109–10
Strohl, M. P., 23, 97, 233, 237, 238
Sudan, 178, 179, 184, 229
Suez Canal, 109, 110, 111–13
Surinam, 178, 181, 184, 185
Sweden, 229; continental shelf, 178, 183, 185, 186, 203, 204; fishing, 133, 135; straight baselines, 80, 83, 100; territorial seas, 37, 41, 45, 48, 59, 68, 69, 71, 73–4, 98, 104
Syria, 178, 180, 185, 229

Taiwan, 69, 105, 133, 178, 184, 195–6, 229
Tanzania, 177, 178, 184, 216, 217, 220, 221, 229
Territorial sea, 33–4, 35, 36–8; cannon shot rule, 39–42; changes in claims, 70–2; concept, 32–3, 34–6; Convention (1958), 32, 57–64; definition, 44–65; division between states, 44–5, 55, 56, 57, *58*, 62, 64, 100–4; Mediterranean rules, 39–41; recent debate, 73–8, 224–5; Scandinavian rules, 37–9; widths, 36–44, 67–70, 224–5
Thailand, 59, 114–15, 229; continental shelf, 152, 166, 178, 185, 186, 199; straight baselines, 80, 81, 82, 85, 87, 89–90, *91*, 99
Tharp, M., 242
Thompson, W. F., 239
Timor Sea, 190
Togo, 166, 178, 180, 185, 229
Tonga, 70, 105, 178, 184, 229
Trinidad and Tobago, 105, 144, 154, 155, 178, 184, 203, 229
Trucial States, *see* United Arab Emirates
Truman, President H. S., 144
Tunisia, 98, 133, 143, 178, 181, 185, 188, 229
Turkey, 45, 67, 78, 80, 83, 109, 163, 178, 185, 229

Uganda, 19
United Arab Emirates, 68, 155, 178, 185, 189, 198, 199, 229
United Kingdom, 16, 33, 104, 111, 210, 224, 229; continental shelf, 143, 144, 154, 159, 178, 181, 184, 185, 190, 197, 204; fishing, 25, 27, 46, 116, 126, 127, 129, 132, 133, 135; high seas, 211, 213, 214; straight baselines, 80, 81, 83, 105; territorial seas,

36, 38, 39, 40, 41, 43, 46, 59, 60, 75, 76, 77, 79, 98, 101
United Nations Conference on the Law of the Sea (1958), 42, 45, 57–64, 78, 132, 138, 144–7, 162, 207
United Nations Conference on the Law of the Sea (1960), 42, 78, 132
United Nations Conference on the Law of the Sea (1974), 78, 222–5
United Nations Convention on the Continental Shelf, 144–7, 156 160–1, 189, 190–1, 196, 206
United Nations Convention on Fishing and Conservation, 129, 138, 140
United Nations Convention on the High Seas, 207, 208, 214
United Nations Convention on the Territorial Sea, 32, 57–64, 78
United States of America, 15, 16, 17, 27, 28, 69, 104, 110, 113, 114, 210, 222, 223, 224, 229; continental shelf, 22, 144, 149, 152, 154, 155, 159, 160, 162, 170, 178, 183, 184, 204; fishing, 25–6, 27, 125, 126, 136, 137–8; high seas, 211, 213, 214, 215, 216, 217, 218–19, 220; territorial seas, 41–2, 43, 44, 46, 47, 59, 71, 75, 76, 77, 98, 101–3, 105
Uruguay, 43, 50, 62, 72, 134, 178, 181, 182, 184, 185, 210, 229

USSR, *see* Soviet Union

Vatican, 19
Venezuela, 80, 82, 93, 94, 103, 144, 155, 160, 163, 178, 184, 203–4, 229
Venice, 35, 45
Villanow, J., 22, 233

Walker, W. L., 37, 40, 234
Walvis Bay, 60
Washington, President G., 41
Weigert, H. W., 231
Wenk, E., 143, 239
Western Samoa, 177, 178, 184, 230
West Germany, 59, 80, 82, 85, 126, 166–9, 170, 178, 185, 203, 213, 227
Westlake, J., 43, 235
Whiteman, M. M., 240
Whittington, G., 21, 232
Whittlesey, D., 14, 17, 18, 35, 231, 232, 234

Yemen (Aden), 178, 181, 183, 184, 230
Yemen (San'a), 70, 178, 185, 188, 230
Yugoslavia, 80, 81, 85, 87, 90, 133, 145, 178, 185, 190, 198, 204, 230

Zaire, 178, 185, 187, 224, 230